Fretboard Logic SE

Special Edition - Vols. I & II

Bill Edwards Publishing
17329 Emerald Chase Dr
Tampa FL 33647

Dedication

To my many teachers, for contributing to my understanding of the instrument and music, and especially my students, for making me constantly reexamine what I thought I already knew.
and
For the people who read Fretboard Logic and encouraged me to continue on.

Teachers who wish to use this method may purchase it at a special discount by contacting us directly. We maintain an online database for the purpose of referring both teachers and students who are using Fretboard Logic in their area. For a listing in our registry please contact us at:

Bill Edwards Publishing
17329 Emerald Chase Dr
Tampa FL 33647
(813) 985-2689 Phone
(813) 971-9222 Fax
mail@billedwards.com Email
billedwards.com Website

Printed in the United States of America

Note Box

This book is a hands-on learning tool. It contains graphic illustrations of patterns that are to be played after the text has been read, left column then right, top to bottom. They are generally presented in order of difficulty in each section. **For the material to be learned and retained, it is essential that the diagrams be played repeatedly until familiar**. Sometimes ideas are best presented by explanation and sometimes by illustration. Both are used whenever possible.

Contents

Quote Box

I am a little world made cunningly.

John Donne

Preface

The idea for this book originated in the 1970's when the author was a guitar instructor at a music store. During that period, he stumbled upon something that demonstrated that despite years of lessons and countless books and courses, his teaching methods were still pretty disorganized. While mapping out a student's scale forms for the zillionth time, he finally recognized that although there were seven fundamental tonal orientations (modes), there were actually only five relevant guitar patterns, which corresponded to certain recurring chord forms as well. When the scale forms were rearranged to be played lengthwise along the neck, everything finally fit together for the first time in years of playing and teaching. He became aware that there was a guitar-specific pattern organization that was completely separate from the various musical considerations such as theory, technique and style. He eventually came to the conclusion that the issues of this pattern organization should take first priority over the issues of music or style, if a truly structured learning experience was to occur.

Fretboard Logic evolved from the discovery that as a result of the guitar's tuning, number of strings, and string to string intervals (4th, 4th, 4th, 3rd, 4th), exactly three separate and specific pattern types occur on the fretboard: Chord Forms, Scale Forms and Lead Patterns. For learning purposes, each of these three pattern types will be examined in the same four contexts: First, as Basic Forms; second, as Forms in Positions; third, as forms in CAGED Sequence along the fretboard; and fourth, Naming them musically, from their form and position. There are five basic Chord Forms, five basic Scale Forms, and two basic Lead Patterns, and they are integral to one another as patterns.

A word about the format of the book. Given what is known about learning and the function of the two hemispheres of the brain, commonly known as left and right brain, the pages of the book have been divided into half text and half graphics whenever practical. The pattern nature of the fretboard also lends itself to this approach. Important concepts and points of interest are captioned in shadow boxes. Relevant terms are italicized or boldfaced. When boldfaced, terms are defined in context and included in a glossary at the end of the third and last volume of the series.

Man's mind, once stretched by a new idea,
never regains its original dimensions.

Oliver Wendell Holmes Jr.

Introduction

The guitar has changed in many ways since it evolved away from its ancestors but the tuning system of six strings tuned EADGBE, which is fundamentally different from any other instrument, has reigned as the standard for hundreds of years. The reason for this is that no one has yet been able to improve on it, nor, as you will see, are they ever likely to. In fact, many players have taken this aspect of the instrument for granted without ever questioning it. When you consider that virtually everything that is played on the instrument gets "filtered" through this tuning system, it is ironic that of the millions of people who play, very few fully understand the reasoning behind the pitch selection of the strings. Yet, what could be more essential than a working knowledge of the instrument itself? Most guitar methods tackle bits and pieces of many subjects and present them collectively in the equivalent of baby steps. Fretboard Logic SE Part I will teach you a great deal about just one thing: how the tuning works out on the fretboard in terms of patterns.

First a little background is in order. In this introduction, we'll look at the different classes of tunings for stringed instruments, and then discuss monophonic versus polyphonic capabilities. Next we'll examine instruments that increment in one or two dimensions and some of the problems associated with interpreting music given the different designs. Finally we'll make some observations on ergonomics and the human interface, and conclude with a comparison of methods and a discussion of objectives.

There are two primary classes of tunings for stringed instruments. They are either symmetrical, meaning equal string to string intervals, or chordal, meaning tuned to a specific chord. For example, most of the string family, violins, violas, etc., are tuned symmetrically in 5ths. The electric bass is likewise tuned in straight 4ths. On the other hand, traditional five-string banjo tuning is GDGBD, making an open stringed G Major chord, and a pedal steel is tuned to either an E9th or a C6th chord. The guitar's tuning system is neither symmetrical nor chordal. It is literally in a class by itself. The notes EADGBE from bass to treble, result in the intervals of 4th, 4th, 4th, 3rd, and 4th. The tuning produces the intervals which create the pattern organization on the fretboard.

A **monophone** is an instrument which can only produce one tone at a time. If an instrument is **polyphonic,** it is designed to produce multiple tones simultaneously, making harmonic material such as chords and their voicings possible. Instruments of the brass, woodwind and string families are generally monophonic. Keyboard instruments such as pianos, organs, etc., are polyphonic. Normally, monophones are played in groups such as brass bands, string quartets, and symphony orchestras. The members of the string family, including violins, violas, cellos, etc., given multiple strings, can produce more than one or two notes at a time, but the curvature of the bridge makes playing more than two simultaneous notes impractical in continuous usage. Even with a relatively flat bridge, the guitar would have a similar problem given the limitation of four fretting fingers, if not for the difference in tuning systems. The pattern organization produces an optimization of four fretting fingers, and therefore a practical polyphony.

Another difference in overall instrument design concerns whether the notes increment in only one or two dimensions. On a keyboard, the notes get higher or lower in only one dimension (right to left). On a violin, the notes increment in two dimensions creating a matrix of the playing area. In a matrix, there can be several duplicates of the exact same pitch, whereas on a keyboard, there is one and only one of each.When reading for a matrix instrument, a designation or a choice must be made to determine which of the available duplicates is to be played. However, the symmetry of the tuning means that the musical patterns, such as whole step, whole step, half step, etc., will continue to apply from position to position and string to string, making certain note choices more logical than others. Put another way, the shape of, say, a minor scale will be the same on any string and in any position. The odd interval on the guitar prevents this. With piano, there are several one-to-one correspondences which simplify things for the person reading music. One finger plays one key, producing one pitch, represented by one dot on the staff in standard notation. On guitar, a separate designation is often necessary to specify the string upon which a note should be played. It would appear that since the guitar increments in two dimensions, producing multiples of most notes, combined with the irregular intervals which eliminate musical symmetry, that we are provided with the worst of all possible worlds in terms of design. That would be true only if you attempt to understand the guitar in terms of the matrix of the violin, or the polyphony of the keyboard. The guitar cannot be truly understood in terms of either the violin or the piano except by contrast and comparison (although I am convinced that many teachers and guitar method authors have attempted both).

A major premise of this method is that the issues of the guitar should be understood separate from the issues of music for learning purposes. They are always at work together while playing, but while learning, they are best kept apart in one's mind. The guitar is imbued with a pattern organization which can be considered an ergonomic *interface* between the player and the music he or she plays. On the instrument side, the patterns are the interface for the four fretting fingers as output devices. On the music side, the tone groups and rhythms combine to produce a vibratory interface for our ears as input devices, which we perceive as music of differing quality and character. Those qualities and characters in turn become perceived as styles and physiological messages to which we respond as human beings given our own background and development. The fretboard, to repurpose the old tire ad, is where the rubber meets the road. If you're familiar with computers, think of a piano keyboard as a hardware interface. By contrast, the guitar's should be considered a software interface, and not so obvious. The concept of interface can also be related to the typewriter keyboard in an interesting, if somewhat bizarre, way. Most people never question why each key is placed where it is on a typewriter or computer keyboard. If asked, they usually think what is termed the "QWERTY" organization, was developed for speed and ease of typing. In fact, the reverse is true. The mechanical linkages of the old style typewriters were easily overrun and jammed by an average typist. The designers were unable to come up with a speedier design, so some "Dilbertian" engineer hit upon the idea of slowing people down. The typewriter interface was designed to actually slow down the user to prevent key jams. Fortunately, the guitar's interface was designed to improve output, unlike the typewriter keyboard.

Fretboard Logic was developed to help guitarists achieve their musical goals regardless of whatever style of music or type of guitar is preferred. By becoming acquainted with the guitar's interface, you'll be able to apply other areas of study in a more organized manner. A large percentage of guitarists are self taught and rely on gathering random nuggets of information from here and there without much in the way of a game plan. Unfortunately, a thorough grasp of the fretboard layout is not really the kind of thing that you can pick up off a recording, or learn from a friend. It tends to get lost in the sauce, as the cook said.

Most guitar books fall into three categories: Popular arrangements, methods and what can only be termed reference books. Many books that are advertised as teaching methods are actually only useful for occasional reference material, since the material is not presented with any semblance of organization or structure. The attitude of the authors seems to be, "You figure it out." Fretboard Logic is not just another mindless "chord encyclopedia" or redundant "scale and mode" book. How chords and scales work out on the guitar is actually explained in terms of the fretboard pattern organization. On the other hand, a lot of guitar methods overwhelm even dedicated students by trying to cover reading, theory, technique, repertoire, style, etc., all at one time but on a simplified level. Many teach songs that are of no interest except perhaps, to small children. Books that are style oriented such as rock, heavy metal, blues, jazz, country, and classical methods, often do much the same thing, limiting the focus to certain kinds of music, guitars, techniques and/or artists. The problem with this is they often try to do too much at one time without proper foundations, and frequently students just drift away, perhaps blaming themselves for lack of talent. And another thing. Educational publishers prefer to use public domain material since they don't have to pay out composer royalties. Maybe you don't want to play songs that were a hit 75 years ago. The classic one for this is the kid who went into his first guitar lesson dreaming of "Eruption" and came out playing "Go Tell Aunt Rhody."

With all that said, I want to conclude with some observations that may surprise you. As a practicing guitarist, I am of the firm belief that no one else can make you a better player. It is up to each of us as individuals to stand out among the others. There is no method, gimmick, book or video which has the ability to make you play better or worse. Being a quality player means continually practicing and playing with the intent of improving, never giving up and often sacrificing much in the process. You can't substitute a few weeks or months of intense effort for years of sustained effort. That's not even the worst of it. It is all too easy to lose the hard won ground gained by sustained practice, to a few weeks or even days off from the grind. Ok, so you're thinking, "Well, what about those self-taught guys who never read a book or took a lesson and play better than a lot of guys who have taken lessons for years?" As far as I'm concerned, any guitarist can reasonably claim that he or she is self-taught even if they've taken years of lessons and read countless books. The reason is that only we as individuals can make that all important leap from theory to practice, and practice to perfection. Also, it comes easier for some than others.

I see Fretboard Logic as a kind of rosetta stone for guitar players. In other words, it is merely a learning tool. On the other hand, it won't make anyone a better player until they find a way to use it to produce music that other people want to listen to. Each of us has to find our own way to make that happen.

The Five Basic Chord Forms

Although musically, **chords** are groups of three or more different notes played at the same time, on the guitar they are realized through Five Basic Chord Forms, or shapes. (Not three as shown in the little chord computers and certainly not dozens, as suggested in the chord encyclopedias.) There are exactly five fundamentally different ways to play chords as fretboard forms provided for by the tuning. These forms are the **C, A, G, E and D Forms.** They are presented first as open, or unbarred forms, using the first three fingers of the left hand. They can be considered the cornerstone of the fretboard's pattern organization.

For beginners, the circles show where you place each fretting finger, just behind the frets without touching them. The numbers in the circles represent which finger of the left hand to fret with so that the Index = 1, Middle = 2, Ring = 3, and Pinky = 4. The lines going up and down represent the six strings, and the lines going across are the frets. The dark bar at the top is the nut, indicating open position. An "X" over a string means don't play it with the right hand, and an "0" means play it unfretted or open. **Open** can mean unfretted or unbarred.

If you're a just starting out you can gauge how well you know a chord form by being able to do these three things:

1) Play all the chord tones (fretted and open) clearly with no buzzing or muted strings.

2) Memorize the form.

3) Make the changes from chord to chord quickly and accurately.

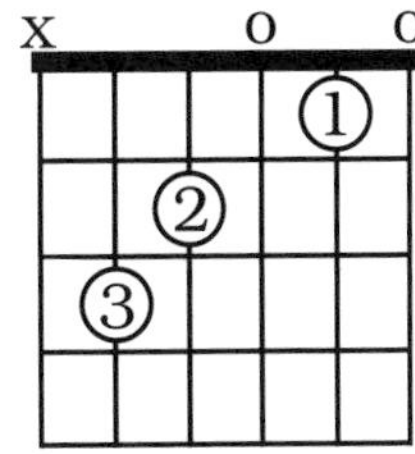

C Form
Open Position
(This is the Fretboard Description.)
C Chord
(This is the Chord Name.)

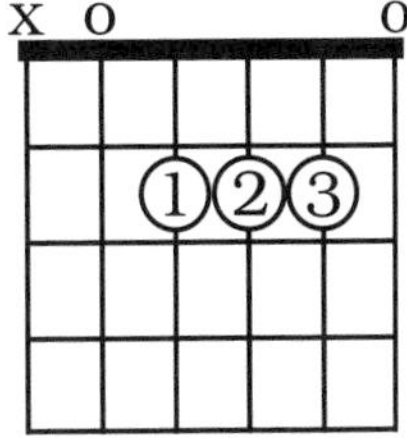

A Form
Open Position
(Guitar Description)
A Chord
(Chord Name)

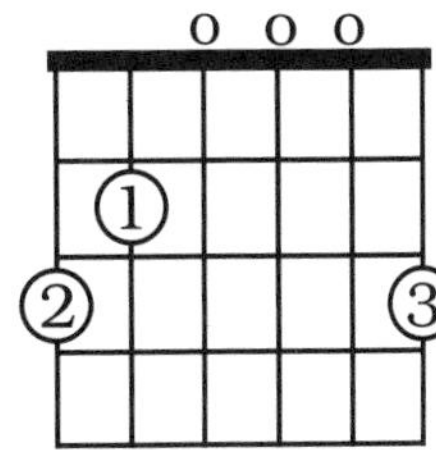

G Form
Open Position
(Description)
G Chord
(Name)

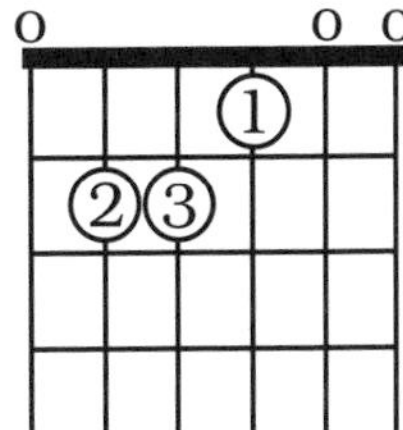

E Form
Open Position

E Chord

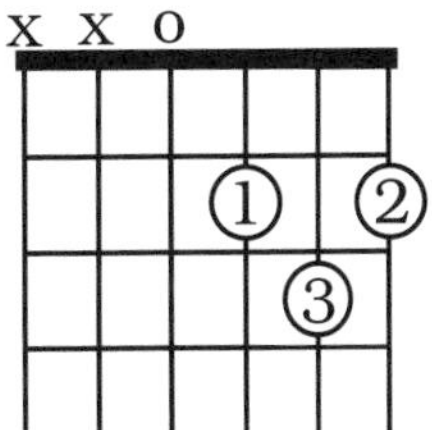

D Form
Open Position

D Chord

Forms and Positions - Chords

The next stage is to treat the open chord forms as moveable, so they can be described as Forms in other Positions. This involves using the index finger to **bar,** (aka barre) or cover simultaneously, some or all of the strings while fretting the Chord Form with the three remaining fingers. This will require more strength and accuracy than the open chords, and is usually easier on the electric guitar than the classic or steel string acoustic.

For now, the **position** is simply the number of the fret your index finger is barring. For example 7th position is barring the 7th fret using any form. The point is to recognize and identify chords by their Form and Position. Almost any chord that can be played as an open form can be used in other positions. To notate a position other than open, a number is placed next to the fret marker. If you are new to bar chords, start out by making the open forms using the 2nd, 3rd, and 4th fingers of the left hand as illustrated in the left hand column. Next make just the bar alone in various positions. Then combine. **The first two or three positions are the hardest, so don't waste too much time trying to fret them there at first.**

Three exercises for becoming familiar with forms and positions and making your hand stronger for bar chords are as follows:

1) Start with the open forms using just the last three fingers and, releasing pressure, slide up the frets, fingers on strings, playing each as you go.

2) Bar any position and then change just the forms.

3) Combine the two previous exercises by playing up the neck from the open position and changing the form each time you move to a new position.

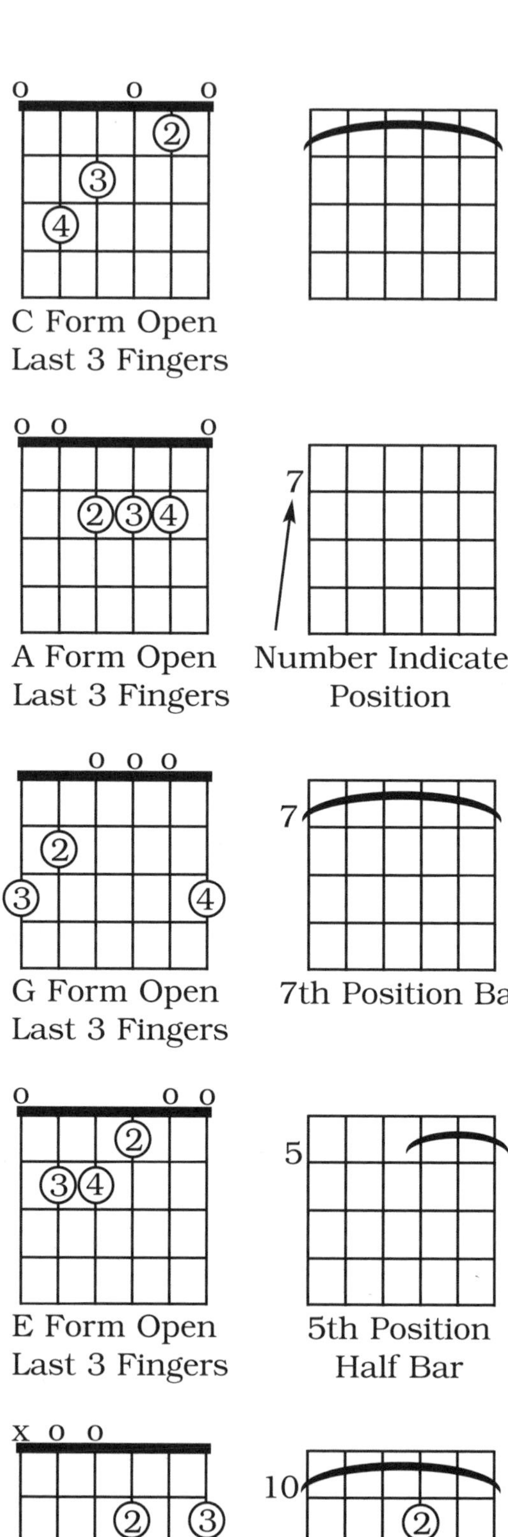

Forms and Positions - Chords

The left column illustrates the Five Basic Chord Forms in the 5th position.

You will soon realize that there are two easy bar chords, two hard ones, and one in the middle. The E form and the A form are the easiest, the G and D are the hardest (because of the reach) and the C form is somewhere in between.

In order to make them more accessible for beginners, the forms have been illustrated in the right hand column with alternate fingerings and partial forms. It's easier to *recognize* them as full forms but it's usually easier to *play* them using partial forms. In each case, how you actually use them will depend on the circumstances.

Since the E and the A forms are the easiest to play, they tend to get used the most, and the rhythm part in many popular guitar songs consists of one or another of these forms moved around in various positions. Regardless of the style of music your prefer, you'll soon find you need facility with more than just the most common ones. Practice each form equally in various positions and don't limit yourself to just the easy ones.

The barred chords are more difficult than the open chords especially on acoustic guitars. If you are having trouble, have your guitar restrung with the lightest possible strings, and ask your repairman to set your **action** or relative string height, as low as possible. If they still seem too hard to play, you can even loosen the string's tension to a lower pitch until you build strength. **Don't let yourself get stuck on any one thing. Come back to it later as you get stronger.**

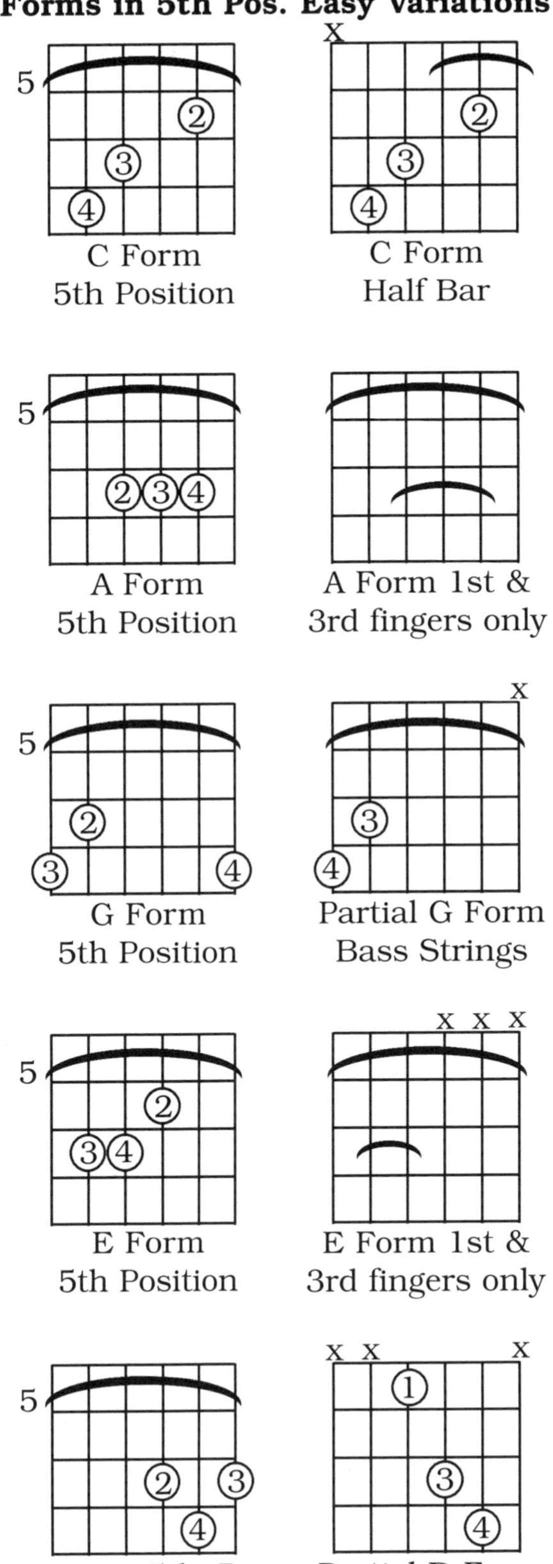

Forms and Positions - Chords

Play through the following assorted forms and positions saying the description out loud as you go. Now is the time to get into the habit of using the fretboard descriptions. **Say "C Form, 4th Position"** not "C in the 4th position" or "C chord, 4th position." **Verbally distinguish the guitar forms from the chord names from now on. Each time.**

For now it is important to identify them by describing what your eyes are seeing and your fingers are playing. The *form* is what you play, the *chord* is what you hear. Note that the C and E forms are directly adjacent to the bar, whereas the A, G and D forms require a space of one fret between the bar and the form.

In the beginning, hand fatigue may be a problem. In fact, the strain can show up in your shoulders and back as well. Fortunately the more you play, the stronger you get. I'll bet any orthopedist would advise you to get up and do some stretching exercises if your hands get tired but you want to keep at it. Also don't forget about the numerous partial forms. If you can visualize the partial G and D forms with no trouble, don't hesitate to substitute them for the full forms for ease of playing.

The important thing is to keep in mind that there are 5 forms to choose from - not just two or three. There is no doubt that many readers have bought huge chord books and then wondered how in the world you were supposed to remember all the different chords graphed out in them. If you try to memorize them you'll probably only remember a few of the more common ones. The way to learn them easily and permanently is to be able to build them from one or another of the five basic forms. This chord "building" is taken up in detail in Part II, and it is based on what is being presented here.

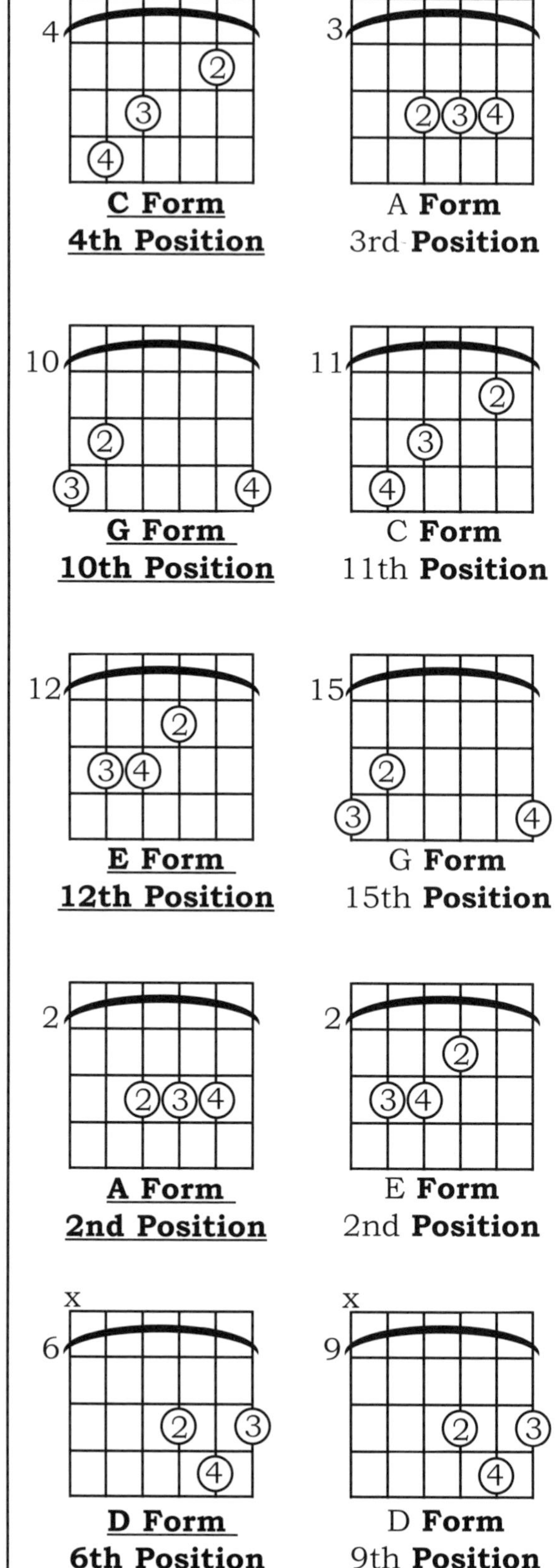

The CAGED Sequence - Chords

If you've never seen this before, by the time you finish the section, you'll understand why the author considers the inventor(s) of the guitar's tuning system among the unsung heros in music history. I don't know who gets the credit, but I've always wondered if he or she thought it out, tried a zillion combinations, or just stumbled onto it because their guitar was always out of tune. When the five basic chord forms are arranged in order along the length of the fretboard, they produce a contiguous **C-A-G-E-D Sequence** that provides the player with a failsafe method for finding their way around the neck, form by form. No matter which form or position you are using, the CAGED Sequence is all around you. It repeats at the twelfth fret and continues until you run out of real estate. Each form in the sequence is the exact same chord *musically*, played five different ways, *guitaristically*. The end of one form is the beginning of the next.

In order to convey the structure of the CAGED Sequence, we have jumped somewhat out of order by **naming,** or identifying musically, some chords without having laid the proper groundwork for this. Naming chords is taken up in the following section. While you play each form of the CAGED Sequence, visualize the forms that are adjacent to it. Keep in mind that you are traversing the fretboard form by form, as opposed to position by position. If your hand gets tired from the constant pressure, just lay your fingers on the strings with little or no pressure applied and proceed through the sequences.

The essence of this procedure is that you are playing the same music chord using different guitar forms in a sequence.

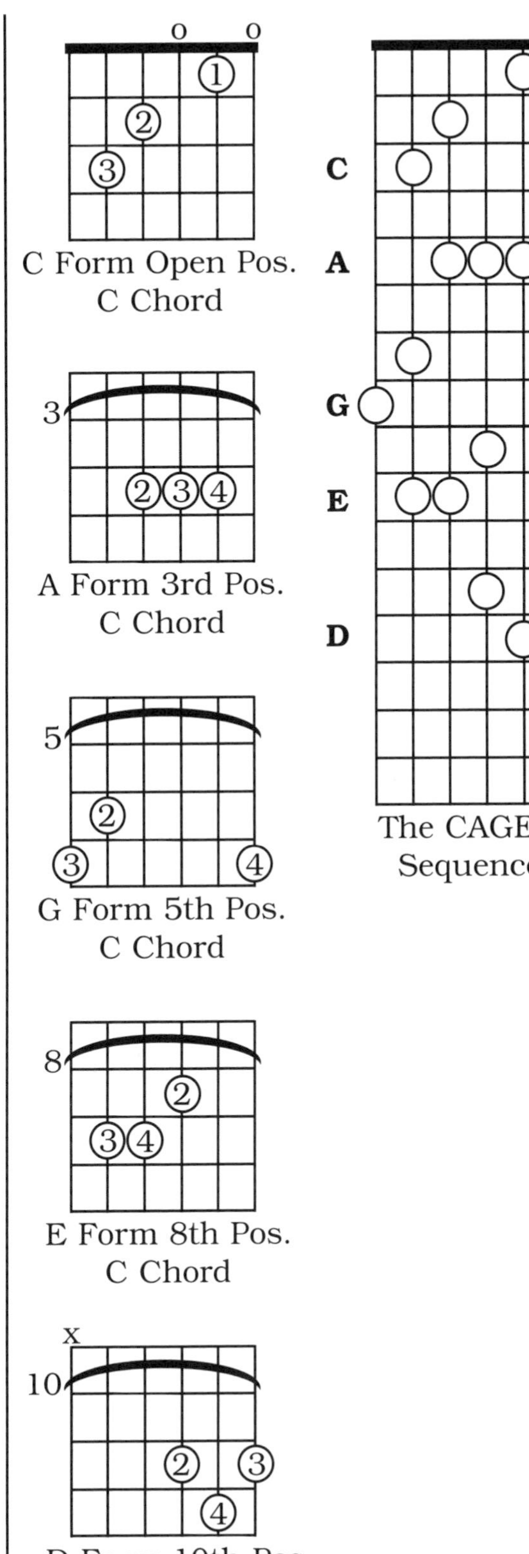

The CAGED Sequence - Chords

The end of each form is the beginning of the next. The sequence never changes relative to itself. In other words, it can start in any position, with any of the basic forms, and the others will always be in the same location relative to it. Once you have established any form in any position, you should be able to recognize the sequence starting with the next form directly above and below the one you are playing.

Only the CAGED Sequences starting with the open C Form and G Form have been diagrammed but you should be familiar with the concept as a whole. The next exercise (not illustrated) is to play through the CAGED Sequence for chords starting with the A, E, and D forms in the open position. Then start with forms in the middle positions and do the sequence in both directions. If you don't understand the sequence well enough to do them without the graphs, go back to the beginning of the section and keep playing the diagrams until "it clicks." Each time through gets easier and more familiar. You have to picture the forms that are adjacent to the ones you are actually playing. The trick seems to be to hold the form in place until you've visualized the next one. Remember that the approach to the Scale Forms and Lead Patterns will be based upon what is shown for the Chord Forms.

The column on the right shows an extended version of the CAGED Sequence to illustrate that it continues on for as far as you can play. Electric guitars generally have a more accessible fretboard than their classical and acoustic counterparts, so a larger percentage of the playing area is going to be usable. **All of the chord forms in the sequence are completely separate from each other except for the C and D forms, which share a note on the second string.**

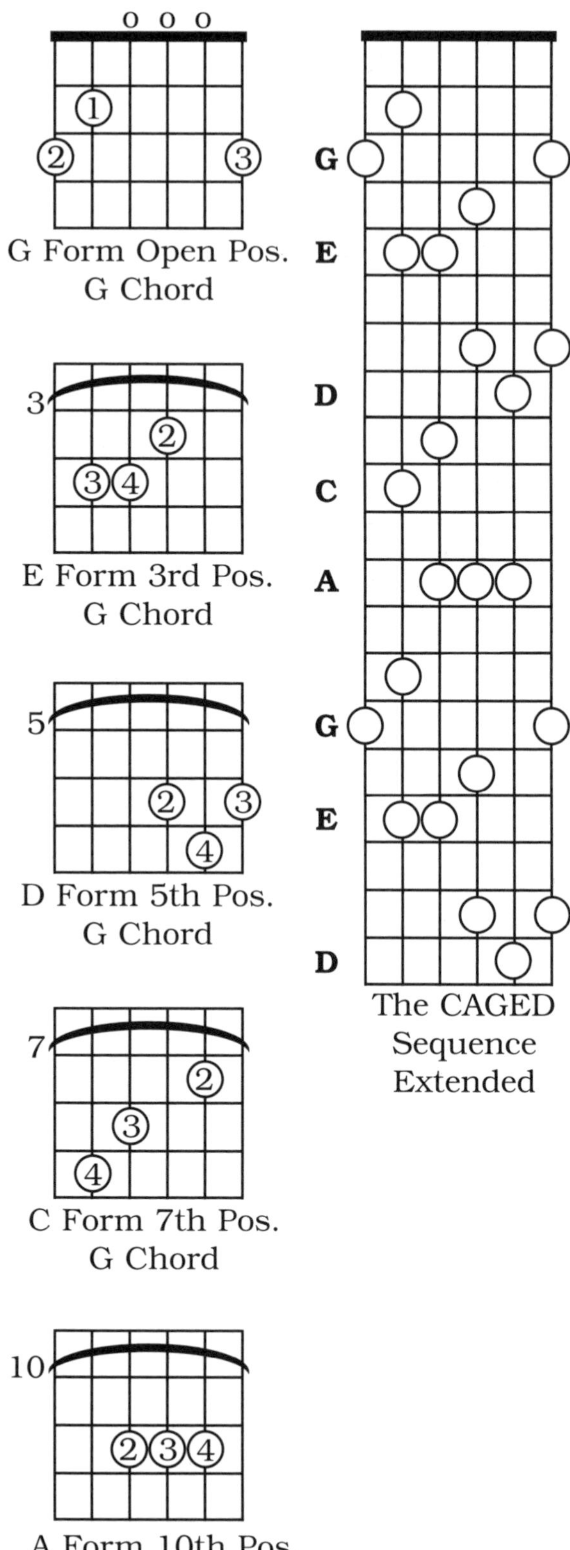

Naming Chords by Form and Position

This section will require somewhat more mental effort on the part of the reader than previously. Up to this point, the majority of what has been presented has been relatively easy to visualize on the fretboard. Some ideas are not easily illustrated and have to be grasped in a more abstract manner. Naming chords by counting letters and accidentals is an example.

So far we have used only descriptive terminology. Forms, Positions, and Sequences only describe what is happening on the fretboard in a guitar orientation. The next step is to name the chords in a musical orientation. Again, the form is what you feel and see on the fretboard whereas the chord is what you hear played. In the last section we used different forms to play the same chord. Here we'll use the same form to play different chords. Some examples of chord *names* are E, Ab, B, and F#. Examples of chord *types* would be major, minor, suspended, and augmented seventh. A complete chord identification including both name and type would be something like C min., Ab diminished, and C# maj. 7th. Abbreviations and symbols are generally used rather than the complete written name and type. This section of Part I will discuss naming the chords only. The different chord types are another subject altogether, and are taken up in Part II.

A minimum of three things are necessary to identify chords by their correct musical name. You need to know: 1) The music alphabet, 2) How accidentals (sharps and flats) work, and 3) How to count fret by fret using letters and accidentals. It sounds ridiculously simple but it winds up being harder than it seems. Counting on your fingers can be a transitional help but only if you do it right. Spread your fingers out wide and hold them still. Use a finger of the other hand for counting, not the thumb. This probably looks suspiciously like I'm teaching people their "ABCs" and how to count on their fingers but, oh well, there's no denying it. Call it better guitaring through Pre-K basics. Here goes:

1) The music alphabet uses only the first 7 letters, ABCDEF and G. (No H, I, etc.) You need to know it forward and backwards from any letter. It is also important to think of it as a circle so that the letter after G is A, and the letter before A is G.

2) A sharp (♯) is when you *raise* any note or chord (move it one fret toward the body). The term "raised" indicates the pitch is higher by what is known as a 1/2 step. A flat (♭) is when you *lower* a note or chord or (move it one fret toward the headstock). The note above A is A♯; the note below E is E♭ (for now).

3) To count fret by fret, you combine the letters with either the sharps or flats, but not both. For now, we'll put a sharp in between each letter and count forward. The counting rule is: letter, then same letter sharped; next letter then same letter sharped, and so on. There are two exceptions to this. **The exceptions are the pairs B and C, and E and F.** There is no ♯ or ♭ in between B and C or E and F. Starting with the letter A, and counting one fret at a time, the order of notes and chords is: A, A#, B, C, C#, D, D#, E, F, F#, G, G# and back to A. Regardless what letter, form or position you start from, they count the same. If counting on your fingers gets in the way, don't use it.

Naming Chords by Form and Position

This system of counting letters works the same for notes and chords. The graph on the left shows the notes starting with the 5th string open A. The graph on the right shows the fret-by-fret counting of the A Chord Form. **Column 2 is continued on the next page.** All five forms work the same way. The order of the fret-by-fret counting stays the same. It just depends on which letter, note or form you start from. If you start with an open C Form, start your counting from the letter C. If you start from the E Form, start counting with E, and so on.

Don't forget the B-C and E-F rule. There is no sharp or flat between these pairs. On a piano keyboard we naturally tend to see groups of three black keys and then pairs of two. If you look from the point of view of the white keys, you'll notice that there are two pairs of notes that don't have a black key between them. Those notes are B & C and E & F. The B-C and E-F pairs are easy to see on the piano, but on the guitar you just have to remember them.

As you are playing the forms from the open position, start by using the last three fingers, and as you move up, count the bar finger to mark your place. After all, the bar designates the position. This way the counting procedure is the same for every form. Otherwise you'll have to count something different on each form, and it will take longer and be harder for no good reason.

> You name chords by counting fret by fret from the open position, or nut, **starting with the letter of the form you are using.**

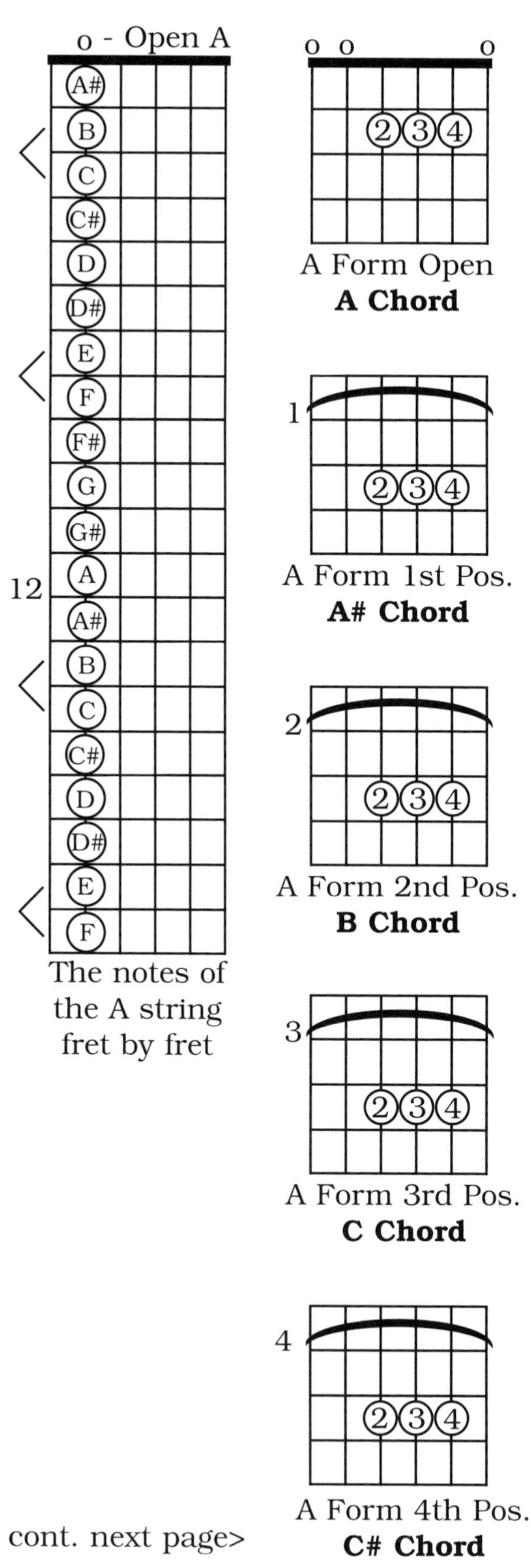

The notes of the A string fret by fret

A Form Open
A Chord

A Form 1st Pos.
A# Chord

A Form 2nd Pos.
B Chord

A Form 3rd Pos.
C Chord

A Form 4th Pos.
C# Chord

cont. next page>

Naming Chords by Form and Position

The graphs on both sides continue the fret-by-fret counting of the A form from the previous page up to the fourteenth fret.

Don't spend too much time or effort trying to play chords in the first few barred positions perfectly. That's where the string tension is highest. Just concentrate instead on keeping the form intact during the initial transition from the open form to the barred. That seems to be where things are most likely to go to pieces formwise. It is natural to want to play the open forms the easy way at first, but it only makes it harder for the transition to the barred forms and so harder to name the chords. After you get used to the idea of naming by counting the letters, it won't matter so much which fingers you use. If you have previously learned to identify chords by naming the "root" on the fifth or sixth string, please try to avoid this. It is old fashioned and not well thought out. It requires the use of several different means to accomplish one thing. It also tends to cause players to think they can base everything on the two easiest forms. Again, get into the habit of verbally distinguishing between the form you are using and the actual chord name. It is important that the terms and concepts be differentiated and applied. The key to being able to count the forms fret by fret is to practice saying the music alphabet (A A# B C C# D D# E F F# G G# A...) over and over until you know it without mistakes from any letter. Then, when you add the forms on the fretboard, you can better divide your attention between the mental and physical requirements. Counting the flats is harder simply because we aren't used to saying the alphabet backwards especially with the added confusion of the the B-C, E-F exceptions.

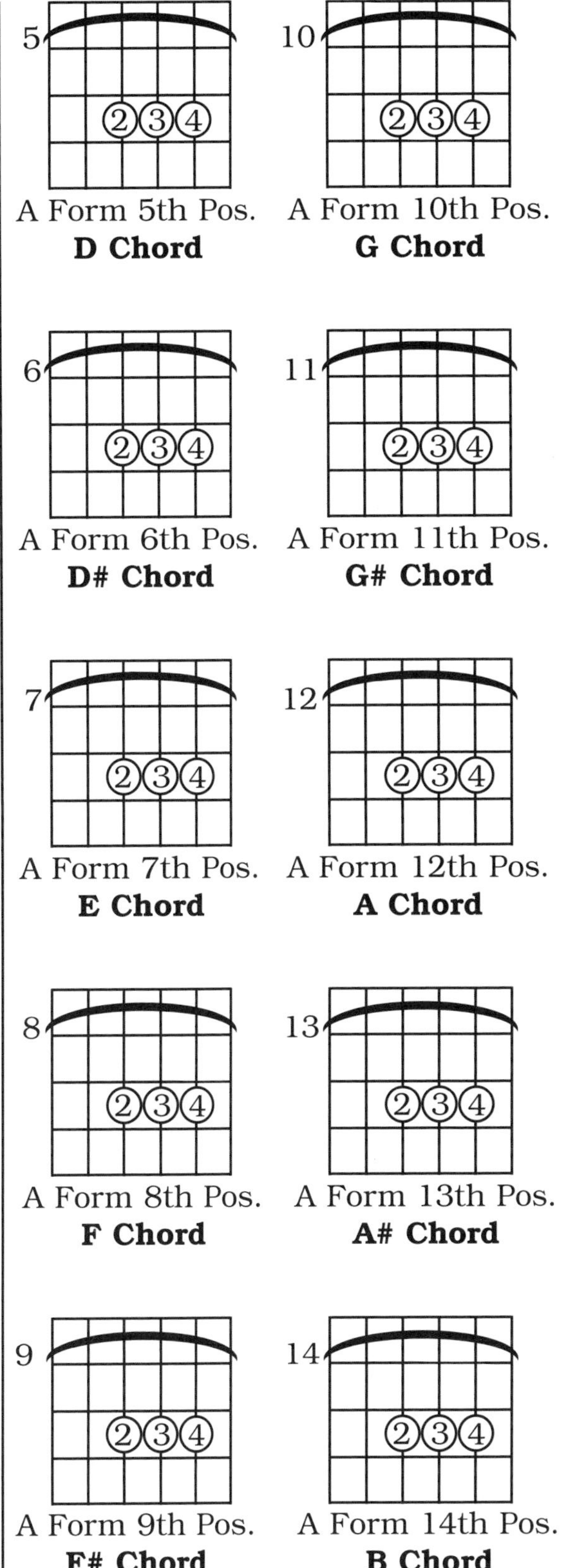

Naming Chords by Form and Position - Sharps

The left column graph counts and names the first five positions using the E Form.

The right hand column counts and names the first five positions using the C Form.

Don't forget that the position is the number of the fret you are barring with your index finger. It is the same for all the forms.

When you've completed these exercises, count up the remaining forms that aren't illustrated to at least the 12th position. If you do them right, when you get there you will be on the same chord that you started with.

If you're starting out, a good way to practice counting up the frets for naming is to put a form, any form, in any position and hold it in place. Don't let it move. Then, with the index finger of the right (or non-fretting) hand, count up to the bar by starting right on the nut and laying your index finger across the strings just like it is a bar. Count and move this "bar" as you go until it is on top of the bar of the fretting hand. It is a simple method but also visually oriented, and has often made the difference between whether a student learns to name chords correctly in one sitting or not.

The key, I believe, is to remember to start counting with the letter name of the form you are using.

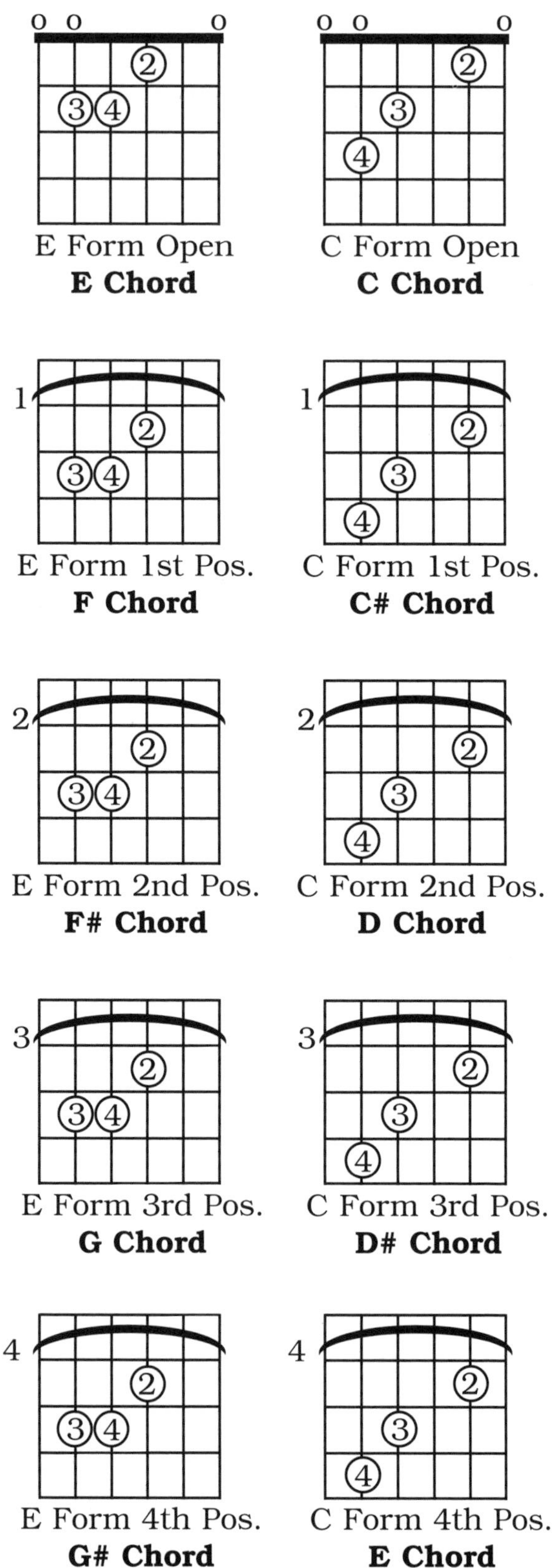

Naming Chords by Form and Position - Flats

Having done it with sharps, and gone up the fretboard successfully will make the next part, going down using flats, easier. Play the chords starting in the left column saying both the form and position and the chord name, then do the right column and continue onto the next page.

Working with flats, everything is reversed, and so a little more difficult. The key to doing this is to say the music alphabet using flats backwards a few times for practice before starting. The idea is to get the order straight in your mind so that looking at the different forms and positions and thinking new names won't throw you off. Also, you probably identify certain forms and positions as sharped, and this can also throw you off. As with the sharps, once you see it for a couple of forms, the process becomes automatic. Again, it is more important to know how the system works than to memorize chord names with no real understanding.

You will quickly realize that the chords in between the letters have two possible names. For example, Bb when counting down the fretboard, is the same as A# when counting up. For now either name is correct. Later on, which one is to be used will be determined by a music concept known as key.

> Music's meant to be fun, not like some crass music machine... that's not what we care about at all. We care a damn lot about music but like, so what if you mess up a couple of chords? Big deal. The point is you tried, and that's what counts.
>
> Johnny Rotten 

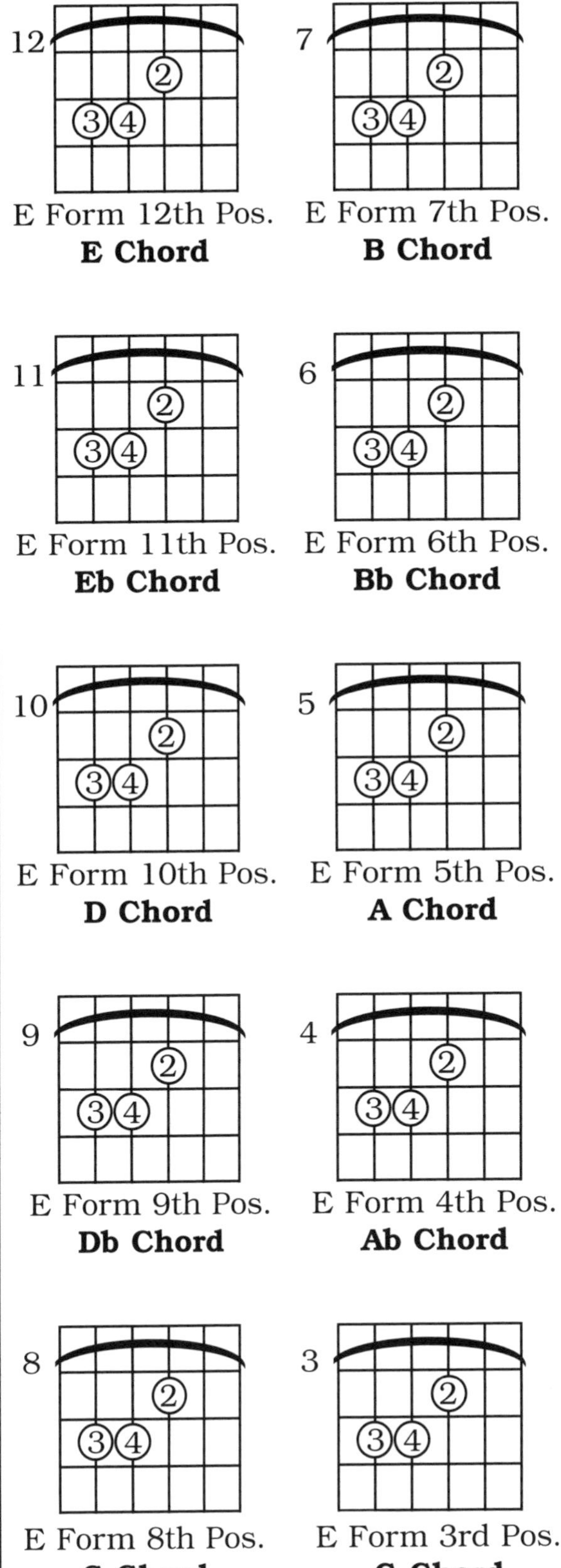

Naming Chords by Form and Position - Flats

The column on the left completes the E forms counted down a fret at a time from the 12th position from the preceding page, ending with the open E Form.

On the right, the G Forms have been diagrammed for five positions starting at the 12th using flats. These are not continued on the next page, but count down the fretboard until you reach the open G Form anyway. If you have done it right you will wind up at the open G chord. Next count down the other three undiagrammed forms from the 12th position. You should end up at the familiar open chord each time. Don't forget to try using the index finger of the right hand as a movable counter. While holding a form in position for naming, lay the index across the nut and count up or down to the fretting hand bar, one fret at a time.

> Distinguish between Naming chords by counting a fret at a time, and connecting the forms by the CAGED Sequence. Counting fret by fret will give you the correct name for any chord, and the CAGED Sequence gives you the overall layout of the fretboard plus a shortcut to naming.

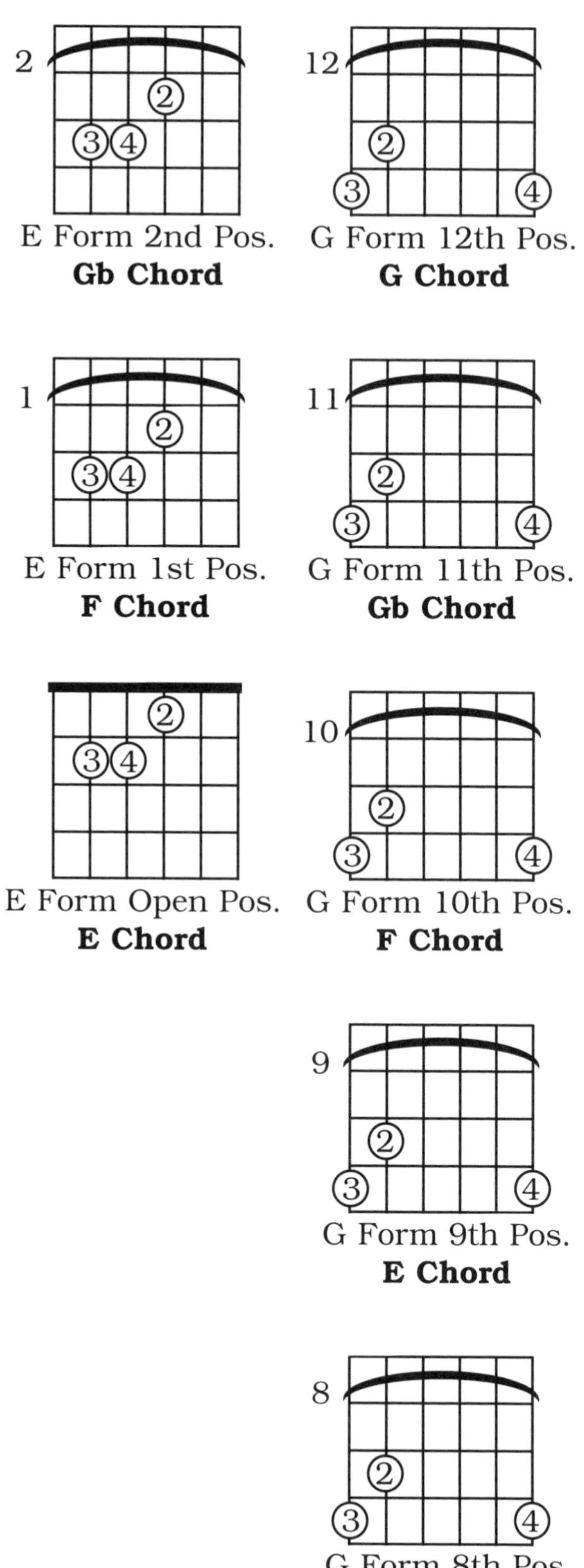

Recap

By now you should be able to recognize all five Basic Chord Forms in any position, connect them in CAGED Sequence from any position, and name the chord from any form and position.

Now would be a good time to go back and review everything from the beginning. It always makes more sense the second time, and you may discover something you missed.

Scales and Scale Forms

Whereas chords are notes played simultaneously, **scales** are groups of notes played in succession. As with the Chord Forms, the guitar's tuning provides five specific patterns for these as well, and they correspond in a precise manner. Although the Chord Forms are held in place and fairly easy to see and remember, Scale Forms must be visualized as a continuous pattern when being learned, since only one note at a time is played.

Over the years I've encountered various labeling and coinage for the Five Basic Scale Forms. I believe they have been more or less pasted on by well-meaning but ill-informed guitar teachers. Among them are the Greek modes (Ionian, Dorian, Phrygian, etc.), Roman numerals and alphanumerics (Form I, Form IA, Form II, Form IIA, etc.), primary/secondary terms like "transitional patterns," descriptors like "boxes," and stylistic names like "blues scale" and "rock pattern." I imagine few things to be more confusing to a guitar student than the variety of arbitrary naming conventions given to the Basic Scale Forms. The problem stems at least partially from the music vs. instrument overlap. Also, terms used in one field of endeavor are often misused, varied or corrupted when applied in another. Tremolo and vibrato are a good example of this type of confusion. Tremolo, by definition, is a steady change in volume whereas vibrato is a change in pitch. So naturally the guitar companies call their pitch changing bars, "tremolos."

Similarly, the Greek names for modes pertain to a music concept and have no function on a fretboard unless you choose to limit yourself to playing to and from the E strings starting with a certain finger. (Any teacher who still uses the Greek modes to identify Scale Forms to a beginning guitar student should be flogged.) It is easy to see how the mode and Scale Form confusion began, however. The association between the two seems convenient with respect to the aforementioned E strings on either end of the fretboard. It is similar to the limitation that occurs when players use the fifth or sixth string to identify chords with. On a guitar, the only naming convention that is sufficiently comprehensive is to identify the Scale Forms by their corresponding Chord Form. You will see that the Scale Forms can be visualized as a natural continuation of the Chord Forms, instead of a separate and unrelated entity.

We tend to take the paths of least resistance when learning, and you will find it easier to learn the Scale Forms by developing them as pattern extensions to the chord forms you already recognize than the arbitrary IIA form or the arcane Mixolydian mode. Trust me. And another thing. The dot scheme on guitar fretboards should go down in history as one of the worst design implementations ever, right along side color coded keyboards on those old electronic organs. How the current fretboard dot placement scheme has lasted, I'll never understand. With the exception of the ones at the 12th and the 5th frets, they just seem to get in the way.

The most basic scales consist of five notes and are called **pentatonic**, or five-toned. There's nothing complicated about that particular Greek term.

The Five Basic Scale Forms

Just as there are Chord Forms that are easily recognized in any position, there are also Scale Forms that make patterns which can be easily learned and used. There is a C Scale Form that corresponds to the C Chord Form, an A Scale Form that is related to the A Chord Form, and so on.

Since the Scale Forms are not held in place like the Chord Forms, the general idea behind which finger to use for which note is four fingers to four frets, as illustrated in the top left diagram. For example, if you are playing a Scale Form in the second position, the index finger frets the necessary strings at the 2nd fret, the middle finger frets the strings at the 3rd fret, the ring frets them at the 4th, and the pinky takes the 5th.

However, you will soon encounter Scale Forms that span more than four frets. This requires what is termed a finger **extension,** meaning a note that is played either above or below the usual four fret area. The position does not actually change though, and for all practical purposes, only the index and pinky fingers make extensions.

Not all Scale Forms will begin with the index finger, and not all Scale Form positions will be designated by the first finger. The index is sometimes treated as an extension so the Scale Form can better correspond to the Chord Form.

The graphs in the left hand column illustrate basic finger position for Scale Forms and extensions. Play through each of them one string at a time, ascending and then descending. The right column illustrates the Five Basic Scale Forms. The D Scale Form is the only one of the five basics to require an extension. The fingerings shown are optional, and as with chords, the correct fingers to use for scales will depend on the particular circumstances.

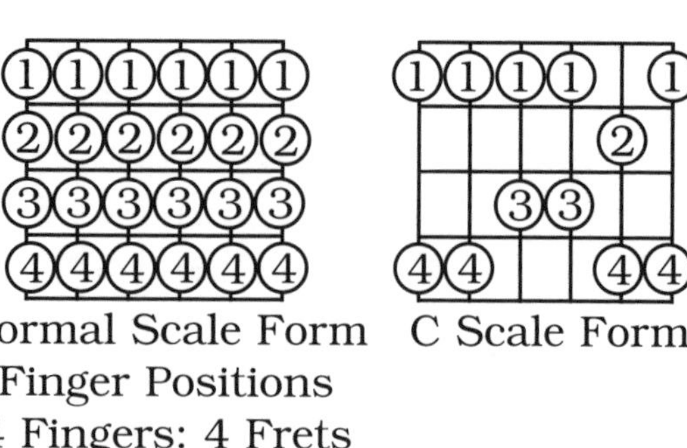

Normal Scale Form Finger Positions 4 Fingers: 4 Frets

C Scale Form

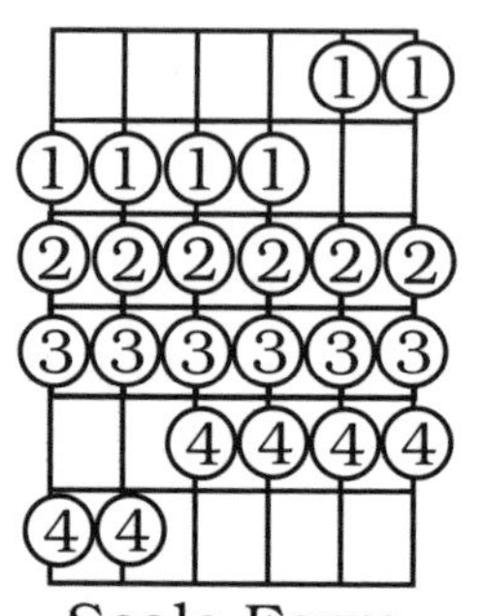

Scale Form Finger Positions with Extensions

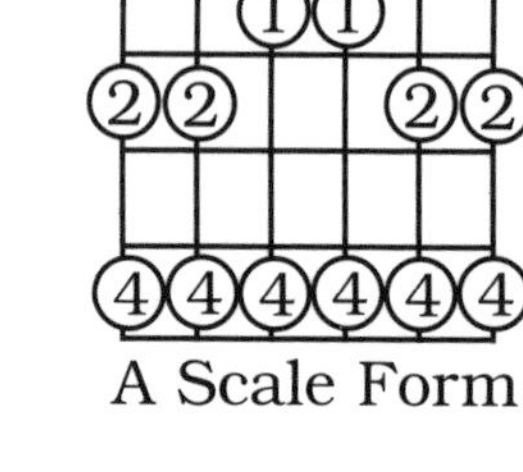

A Scale Form

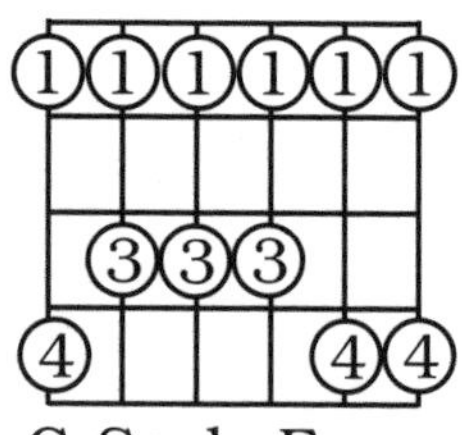

G Scale Form

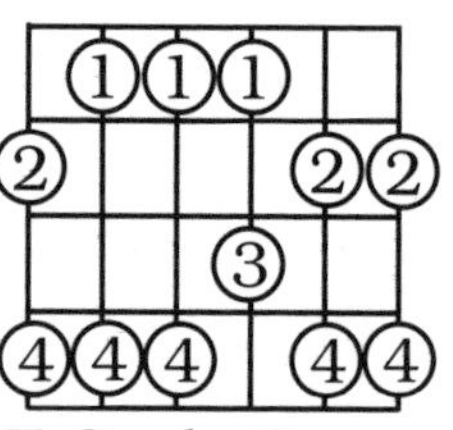

E Scale Form

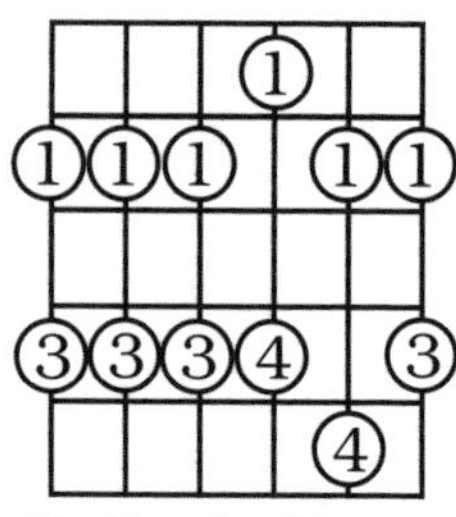

D Scale Form

The Five Basic Scale Forms

The left hand column illustrates that the Chord Forms are actually an integral part of the Scale Forms. This also shows why calling the Scale Forms anything else puts the subject into another area of discussion. The term "C Scale Form" (or C Form Scale) is a purely guitar oriented designation, and doesn't apply to any other instrument. As with the different types of chords, learning different types of scales will be a matter of developing them from the basic forms.

Practice playing the Basic Scale Forms in various positions. Learn them forward and backward from memory. When playing with a pick, it is a good idea to start with a down stroke and alternate directions for each note. It will be hard at first especially when changing from string to string, but discipline yourself now and you will benefit many times over later especially in terms of speed and accuracy. If you are using your fingers to pluck the strings, alternate them as well, using thumb and index or middle and index.

The forms in the right column have been contrasted to show that the end of one is the beginning of another. The "bottom" of the C Form is the "top" of the A Form. The bottom of the A is the top of the G, the top of the D form is the bottom of the E, and so on.

> When learning scales, try to play as slowly as possible for accuracy the first few times. If the first few tries are correct, it will be much easier than trying to unlearn a rush job. The best way is to play dead slow until you are familiar with the form.

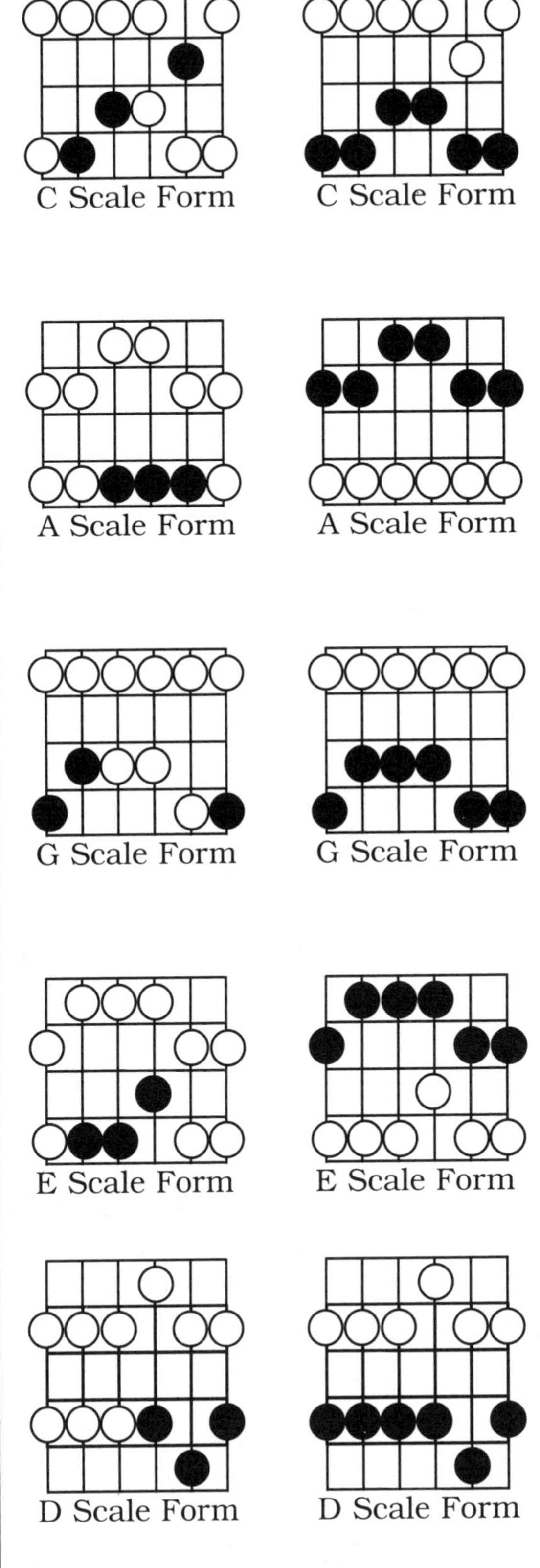

Forms and Positions - Scales

Describing scales by form and position is similar to the method for chords. The pattern stays the same, but is moveable and can be played in various locations on the fretboard. The main difference stems from the fact that the position of the Scale Forms is not always referenced by the index finger as were each of the Chord Forms. The C and G Scale Forms are located by the index like the chord forms. For example, if you were to play a G form scale in the 4th position, your index would fret the strings at the 4th fret. As drawn, the D Form is also positioned by the index but contains an index extension that moves it temporarily out of place.

The A and E Scale Forms (*) are not referenced by the index finger for position. The index notes in these two scale forms are treated like extensions in order for the Scale Forms to better follow the Chord Forms as patterns.

The graphs in the left hand column illustrate the reference point of the Basic Scale Forms in various positions. The graphs on the right show the relative positions of the corresponding Chord Forms.

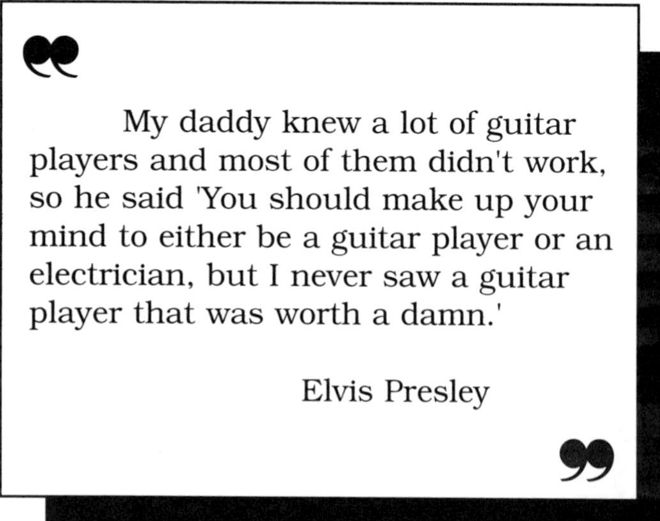

My daddy knew a lot of guitar players and most of them didn't work, so he said 'You should make up your mind to either be a guitar player or an electrician, but I never saw a guitar player that was worth a damn.'

Elvis Presley

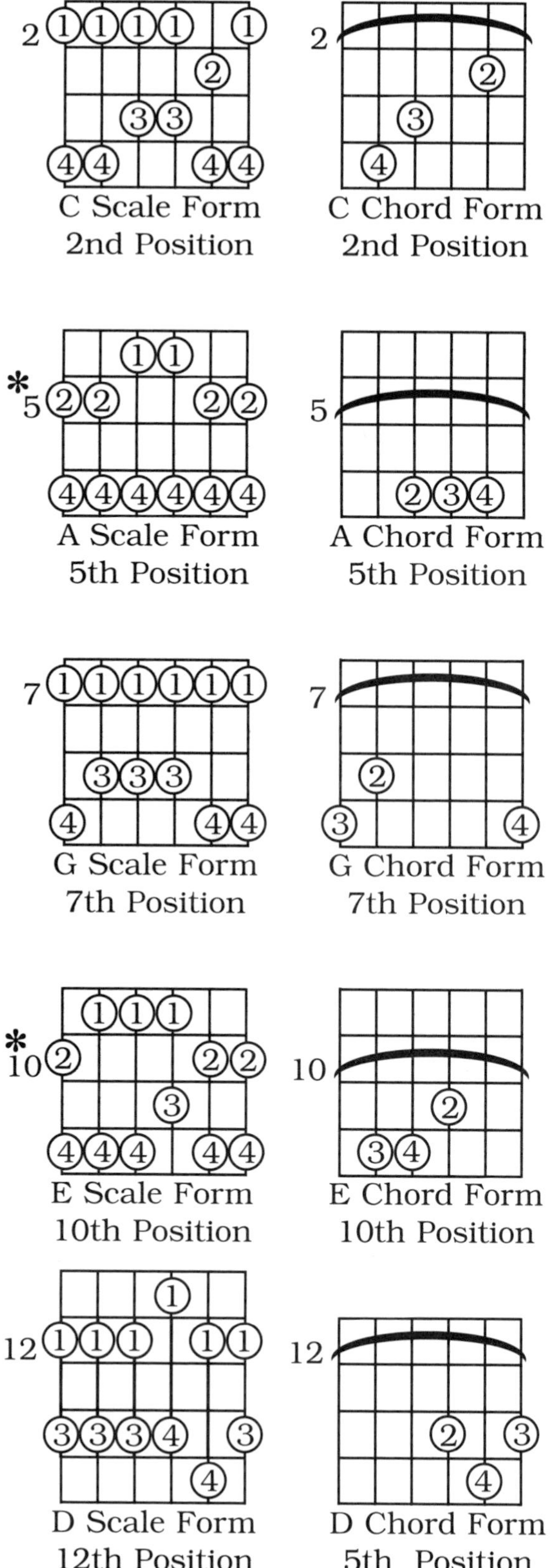

The CAGED Sequence - Scales

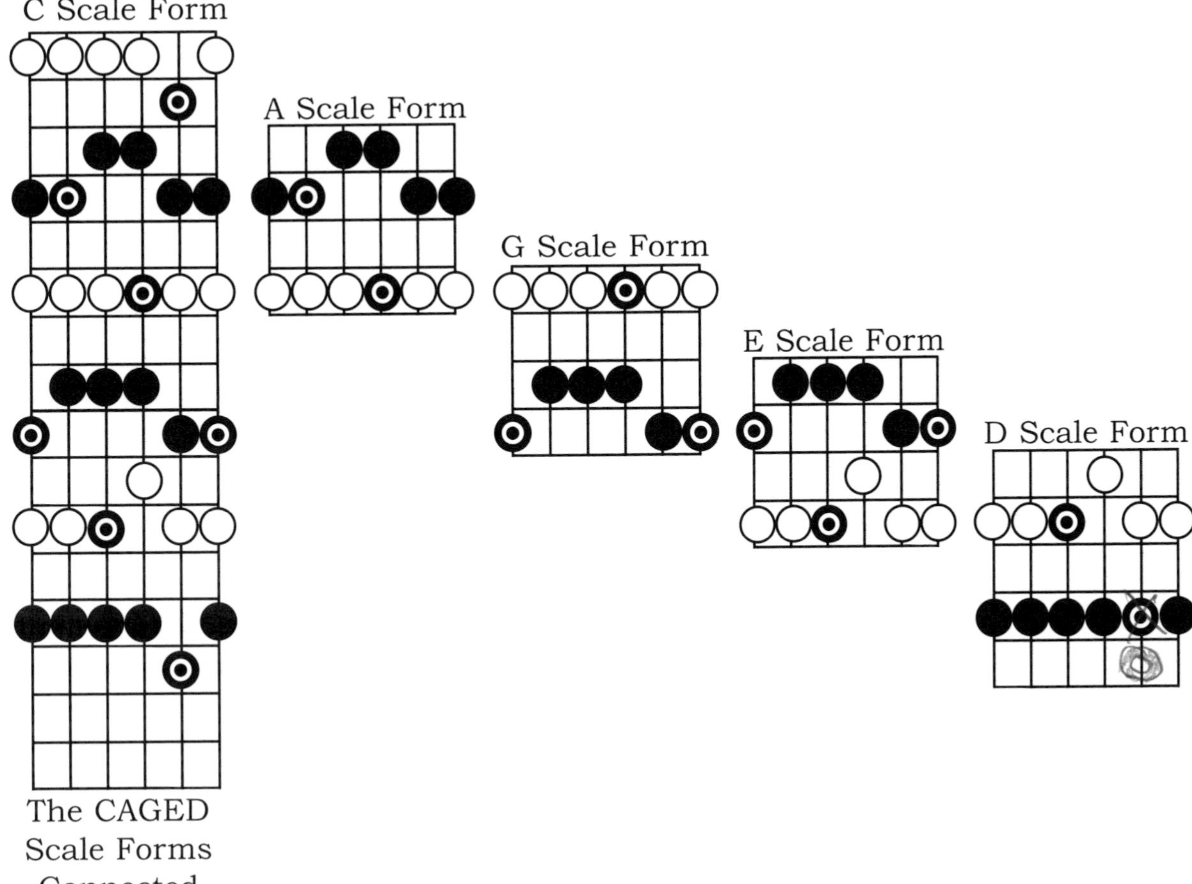

The CAGED Scale Forms Connected

This series of graphs is intended to lure you away from thinking of the scales as just five separate forms, and into seeing them also as parts of a continuous whole. Each Scale Form is the same five notes played at least twice in different positions starting with a different note.

The graphs are shaded to illustrate that the bottom of one Scale Form is the top of another. The diagram on the left shows how the Basic Scale Forms appear when connected end to end on the fretboard.

In this view, you should be able to see that the CAGED Sequence applies equally to both scales and chords. The Chord Forms are generally separate from one another. The Scale Forms all share notes with adjacent forms on either end.

This illustration introduces **Target Notes**, also known as Keynotes Tone Centers or Tonics. Unlike Chord Forms, Scale Forms are not musically accurate unless played to and from the targets. They are similar to root notes.

The G Form and the E Form provide access to two full octaves. The other three scale forms span only one octave from within the form.

Naming Scales by Form and Position

As with the chords, we established five basic forms for scales, and described them in terms of form and position. Then we viewed them as five parts of a contiguous sequence spanning more or less the length of the fretboard. Next we added target notes to produce musically accurate, five-tone scales.

Now we will identify them by name, and later (in Vol. II), by *type*. Naming scales requires the same tools that naming the chords did, and since you've gone through the procedure already, you'll find it easier, if not automatic. If you find this section difficult, it would be a good idea to go back over the section on naming chords.

To find the correct name of a Scale Form, count fret by fret using the music alphabet with either sharps ascending or flats descending starting with the letter of the form you are playing. A quick review of the music alphabet ascending starting with the letter C: C C# D D# E F F# G G# A A# B and back to C. Using flats and descending starting with E: E Eb D Db C B Bb A Ab G Gb F and back to E.

The use of sharps only, when ascending, and flats only, when descending, is a simplification for the purpose of focusing on the issues at hand. The fingering suggested is also for learning purposes only, and once you know the forms, you can substitute whatever works best for you.

Some Scale Forms cannot be played from the open position, making the counting somewhat more difficult than for chords. When in doubt, refer to the corresponding Chord Form. The graphs show the scale names of the C form in each position starting with open and ending with the 14th on the next page. Play the form in every position and name it out loud as you go.

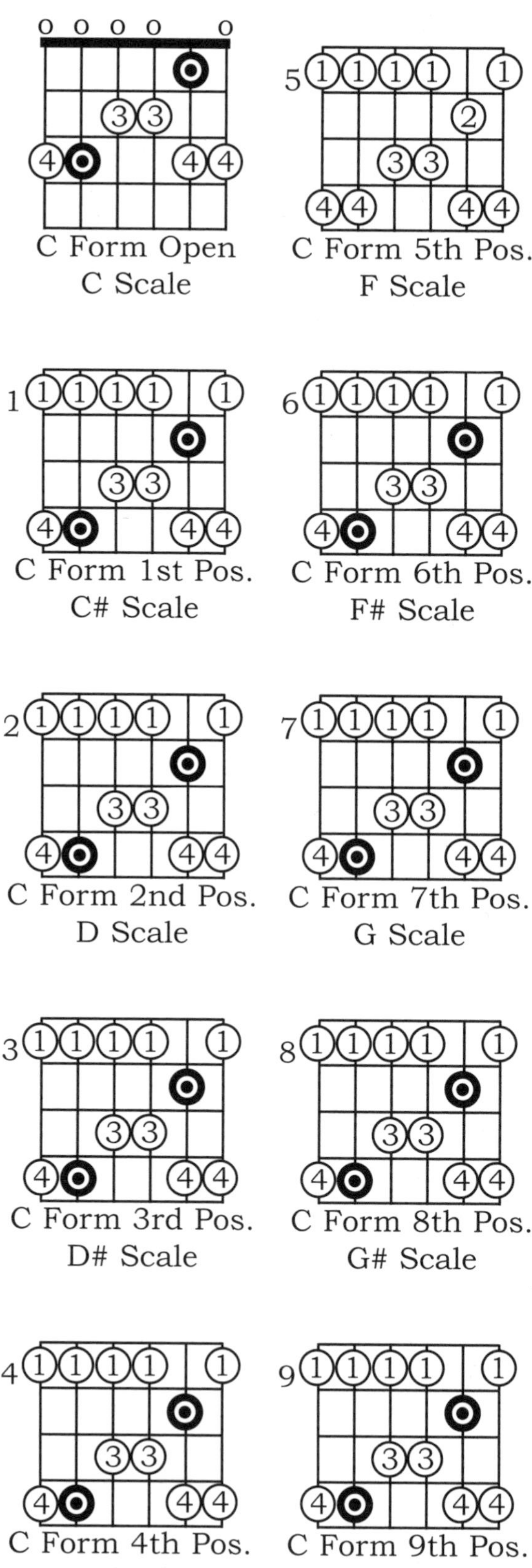

Naming Scales by Form and Position

The column on the left completes the C Scale Form circle from the previous page and continues up to the 14th fret.

The right hand column counts the A Scale Form from the 1st position to the 5th. There is no open position possible for the A form scale. Play the A form in each position and name it as you go. Don't forget that the A form and the E form treat the index finger as an extension to better follow the Chord Forms and the second or middle finger determines the relative position.

The other Scale Forms are illustrated in just a few positions rather than the entire range of the fretboard. Again, it is more useful to know how the system works than to rely on memorization. As you progress, you will automatically remember what you use the most anyway. If you are having trouble, go back to the Chord Forms and count them fret by fret, then try it with the scales again.vvvvv

> It is a decisive moment for civilization when man lays aside his arrows and devotes himself to plucking bowstrings for music. He can be very vulnerable at that point, as David discovered, in the Book of Kings, when he found himself suddenly the target of a tossed spear. But this very vulnerability is a precondition to all art, which reposes in fragile guitars rather than in swords. And thus the history of the guitar is essentially the story of some of man's best moments...
>
> Frederic V. Grunfeld

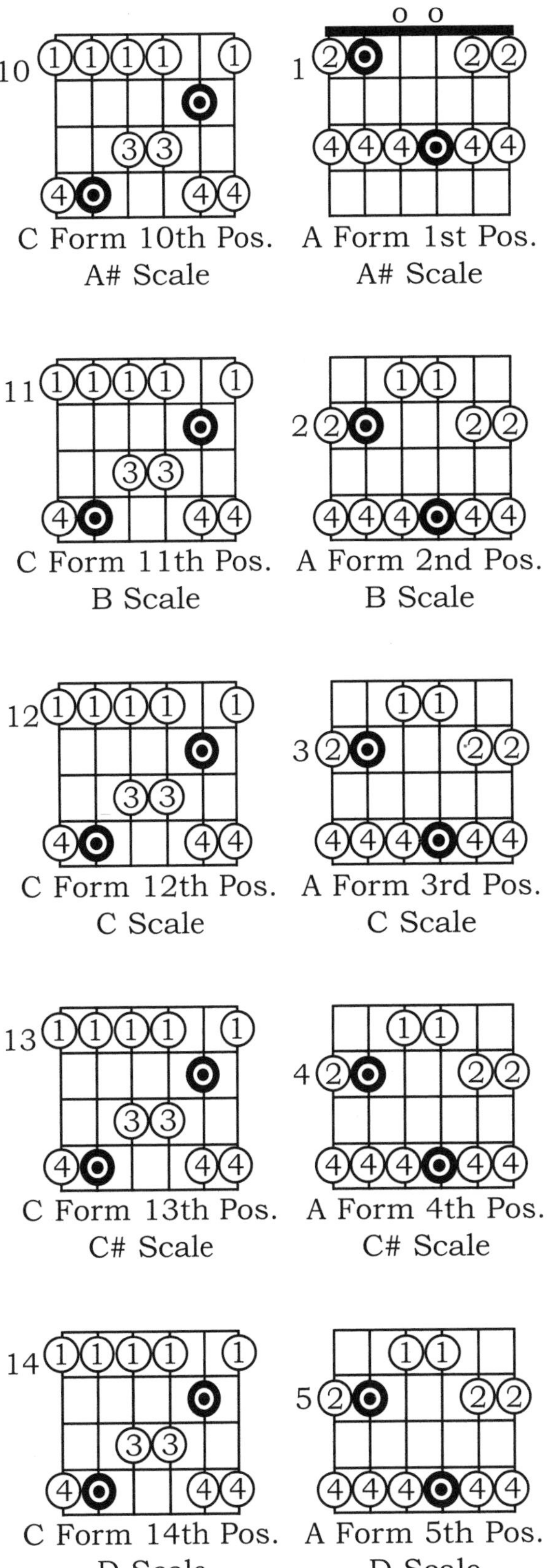

C Form 10th Pos. A# Scale — A Form 1st Pos. A# Scale

C Form 11th Pos. B Scale — A Form 2nd Pos. B Scale

C Form 12th Pos. C Scale — A Form 3rd Pos. C Scale

C Form 13th Pos. C# Scale — A Form 4th Pos. C# Scale

C Form 14th Pos. D Scale — A Form 5th Pos. D Scale

Naming Scales by Form and Position

The column on the left names each of the G Scale Forms from the open position to the 4th. Even though they aren't pictured, continue on and play through each position until it repeats at the 12th fret and see if you come back to G. If you do, you've done it right.

The right hand column shows the E Scale Forms. Here again, for naming purposes, the E Form, like the A Form, behaves as if the index were an extension, and the position is referenced by the second finger instead of the first.

Since there is no possible open E Form, the series starts in the 1st position.

As with the G Form Scale, only five positions of the E Form are illustrated, but you should again play them all the way up the neck, naming each different scale as you go.

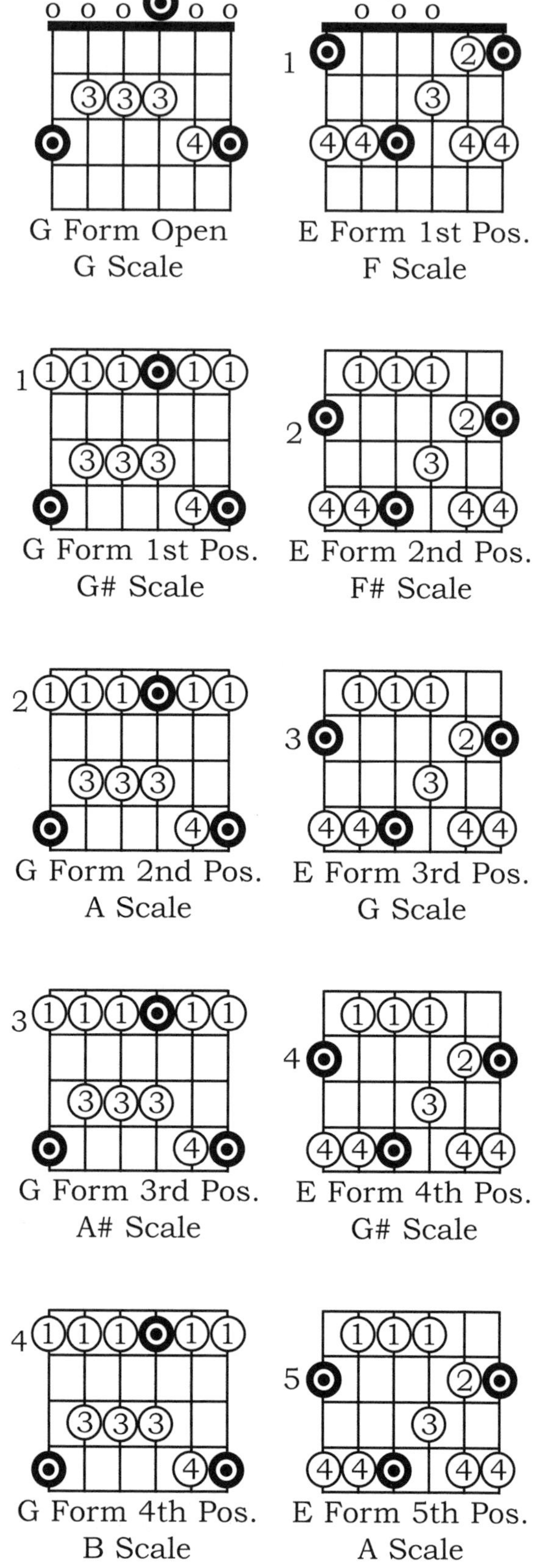

G Form Open
G Scale

E Form 1st Pos.
F Scale

G Form 1st Pos.
G# Scale

E Form 2nd Pos.
F# Scale

G Form 2nd Pos.
A Scale

E Form 3rd Pos.
G Scale

G Form 3rd Pos.
A# Scale

E Form 4th Pos.
G# Scale

G Form 4th Pos.
B Scale

E Form 5th Pos.
A Scale

Naming Scales by Form and Position

The last of the Basic Scale Forms, D Form, like the A and E, also cannot be played open, so it too will begin in the 1st position. It is illustrated such that the position is determined by the first finger, with an index extension on the third string. The series continues in the right hand column up to the ninth position.

The importance of being thoroughly familiar with *all* five Scale Forms cannot be overemphasized. Since the notes are the same five, played with different patterns, the natural tendency is to use the form or forms that are easiest to manage. Of the five, the G form is without a doubt the most often used in beginning lead playing, but this can become limiting. The different look and feel of the five forms will cause you to phrase things in a way that is more unusual and perhaps more interesting.

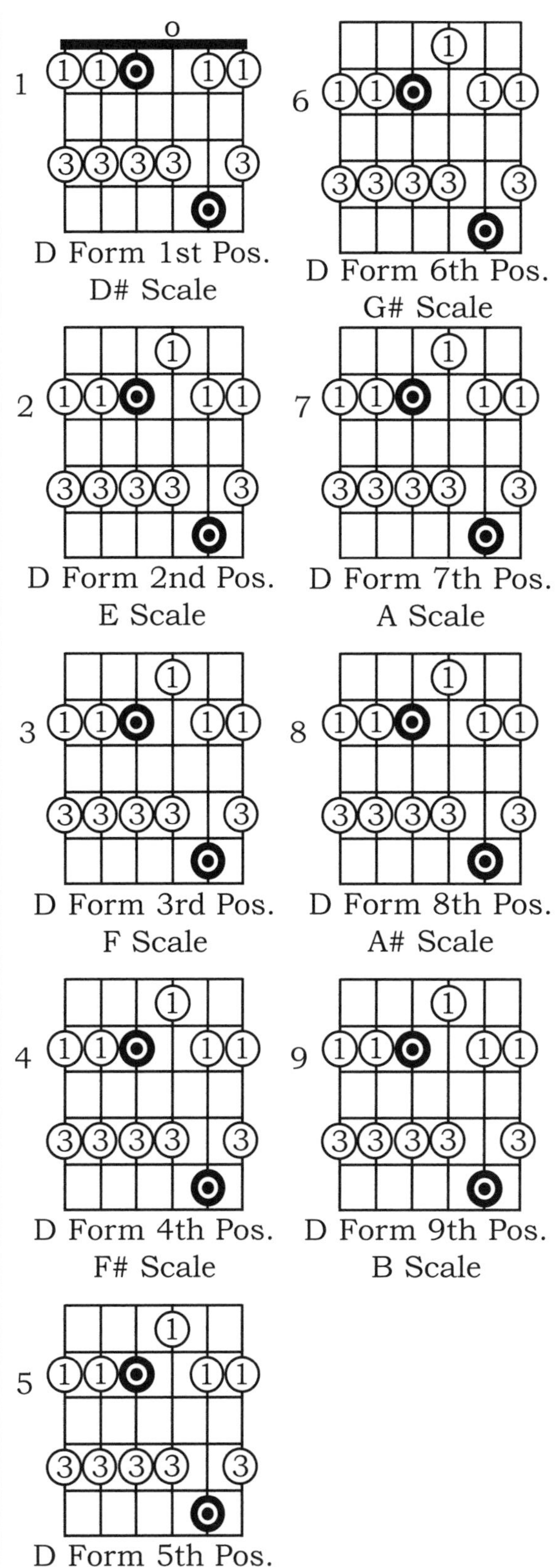

Recap

By this time you should have the same skills for the Basic Scale Forms that you acquired for the Chord Forms. You should be able to recognize and play all five Forms in any Position, visualize them in CAGED Sequence, and Name a scale by its Form and Position. Because of the relative degree of difficulty, you should expect to play the Scale Forms about 10-20 times as much as the Chord Forms to get control of them. Always distinguish between the fretboard description and the exact music name. If you are thinking the description, use the words “form and position” as in "C (Scale) Form, 2nd Position". If you are thinking key, use the name as in "D Scale." When talking to other guitar players, the physical description is useful, but other instrumentalists are only going to be aware of the musical terms.

Lead Patterns

There are Two Basic Lead Patterns which result from the guitar's tuning. This new arrangement gives us the ability to access more notes, and enables us to play things that would be impossible otherwise. The term **Lead Pattern** has been adopted primarily to distinguish these types of patterns from Scale Forms, but also to convey that they are often used in soloing, improvisation and lead playing. It is a guitar oriented name for a different form of scale, or more precisely, a symmetrical, extended, scale form which is played along the fretboard instead of across it. Whereas the Scale Forms are irregular patterns in one position, the Lead Patterns are regular patterns in several positions. (You get bonus points if you noticed that the Lead Patterns are made up of just the small or whole-step reaches of the Scale Forms.) They are illustrated first showing the notes numbered in ascending order in the left hand column. The right hand column illustrates that each Lead Pattern can be viewed as three groups of five notes with an adjustment made for the smaller interval of the 2nd and 3rd string pair. I hope you appreciate the elegance of the system when you realize that LP1 descending, is the same 3 motions string-to-string and position-to-position, as LP2 ascending. (And vice versa. See next page.) This may take a little longer to grasp, but it will be worth it.

The Lead Patterns represent the third distinct pattern type that occurs solely as a result of the guitar's tuning system.

> Visualize the lead patterns as all five Basic Scale Forms joined together, and then divided into two equal parts.

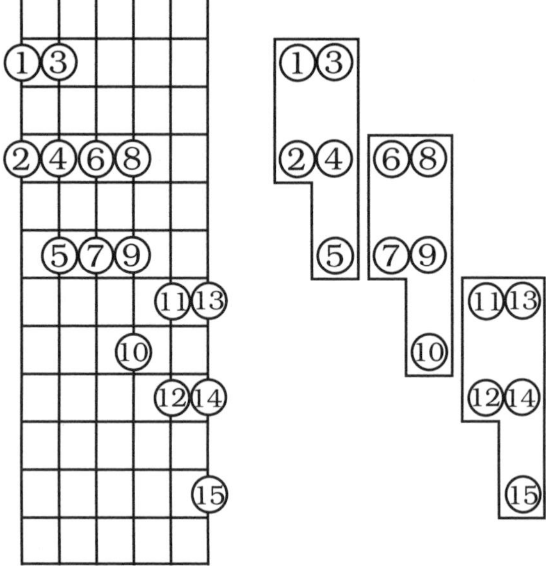

Lead Pattern 1

Lead Pattern 1 Ascending Groups

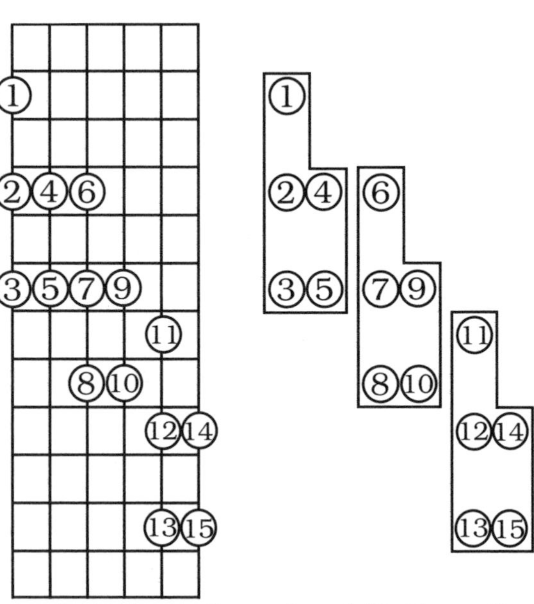

Lead Pattern 2

Lead Pattern 2 Ascending Groups

Lead Patterns

In these diagrams, the two Lead Patterns have been illustrated showing a fingering convention which is limited to the index and ring fingers only, so the player can concentrate on learning to move from position to position smoothly without having too many fingers get in the way.

The arrows indicate position changes, not *slides*, and are shown in ascending order in the top two graphs and descending order in the bottom two. The fingering, as usual, will become a matter of choice given the circumstances later on. The important thing right now is to be able to play the patterns in various positions without getting lost in the dots on the neck. One of the first things you will notice about the patterns is that they use a **stepwise,** or two fret motion. They progress in a regular fashion until they get to the 2nd and 3rd string, and then the pattern changes to a half step "finger squeeze" and then it goes back to being stepped.

The finger motion of each three fives in LP1 ascending, is to change strings then change positions. This is the same for LP2 descending. The motion of each three fives in LP2 ascending, is to change positions, then change strings. This is the same for LP1 descending. As with the Chord Forms and Scale Forms, these patterns are the basic framework for a significant portion of the organization of the fretboard. Playing these patterns is not "playing lead" per se, but it's a start. If you want to really play lead, learn these Basic Lead Patterns, and then experiment with putting the notes together into **phrases,** or musical statements, combined with other elements such as tonal groupings, coherent rhythmic statements, articulation techniques, etc. This is further discussed in Parts II and III.

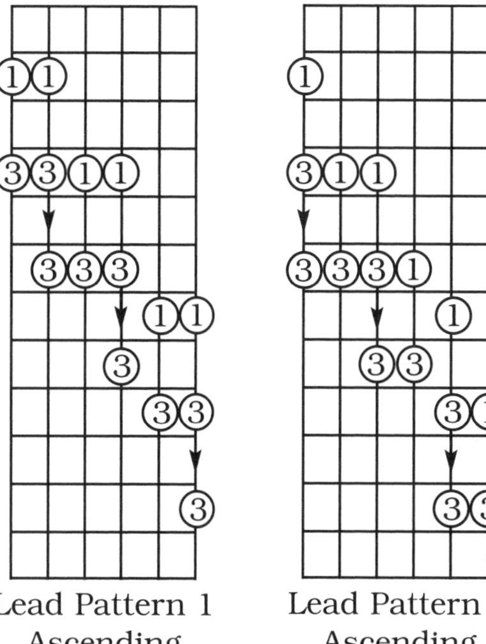

Lead Pattern 1
Ascending

Lead Pattern 2
Ascending

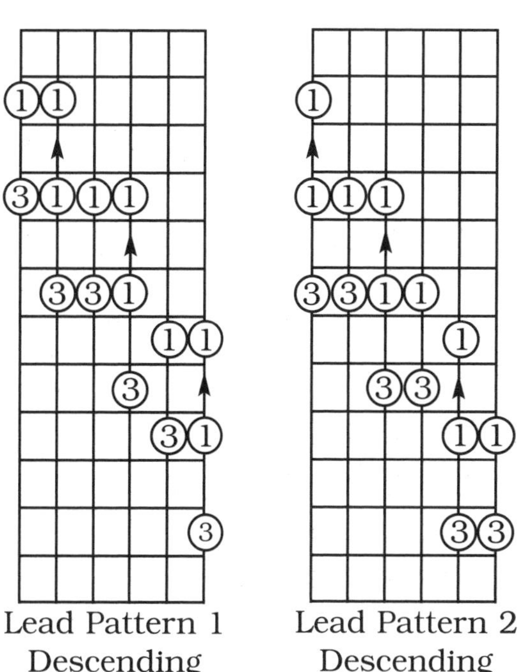

Lead Pattern 1
Descending

Lead Pattern 2
Descending

Forms and Positions - Lead Patterns

The graphs on the right illustrate the Lead Patterns' proximity to one another. In the left hand column, Lead Pattern 1 played in the 3rd position is the equivalent to Lead Pattern 2 played in the 8th position. In the right hand column, Lead Pattern 2 played in the 3rd position is the same as Lead Pattern 1 in the 10th position. (The first time you read the above, it will be about as clear as the ground water in the Love Canal, but it will make sense sooner or later.) As you play them you'll hear the similarities.

Tonally, each Lead Pattern is the same five notes played in the Scale Forms but with more range: three octaves. The primary difference is that they run lengthwise instead of widthwise relative to the fretboard. The Scale Forms are all of the available notes in one position, and the Lead Patterns are a few notes from each Scale Form in several positions. When both Lead Patterns are illustrated side by side, all of the notes of the Five Basic Scale Forms are accounted for.

The patterns should be learned well enough to be played in any position possible using either one or both. To accomplish this with Lead Patterns, it will help to be able to move as easily from position to position, as from string to string. So practice using the string itself as a guide when changing positions and don't take your finger completely off when moving. As with the Chord and Scale Forms, the use of the term position is for descriptive purposes only and pertains to a fretboard location. Saying "Lead Pattern 1 in the 4th Position" will only make sense to another guitar player. The players of the other instruments in the group will have to have it translated to a scale, a key, or number in order for it to make sense to them. This is discussed in the section entitled Naming the Lead Patterns.

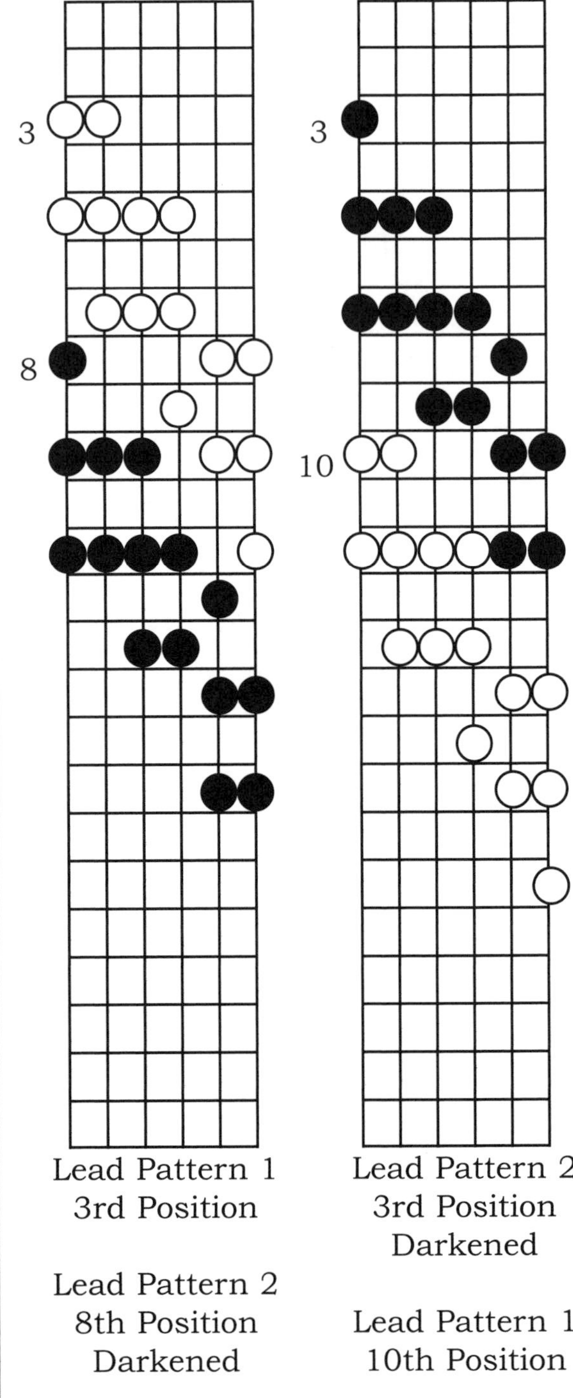

Lead Pattern 1
3rd Position

Lead Pattern 2
8th Position
Darkened

Lead Pattern 2
3rd Position
Darkened

Lead Pattern 1
10th Position

The CAGED Sequence - Lead Patterns

The diagrams to the right show the relationship between the Lead Patterns and the Five Basic Chord Forms in Sequence. The Chord Forms are darkened. Notes have been added where necessary for clarity.

By now you should be able to appreciate the pervasive nature of the CAGED Sequence on the guitar fretboard. The Chord Forms, Scale Forms and Lead Patterns are each integral to this unique arrangement. In fact, no matter what you are trying to accomplish on the fretboard, you'll be working within or without the CAGED Sequence one way or another. The more aware of this you are, the easier your job will be when it comes time to apply what you know to the instrument.

With the Lead Patterns, the sequence functions differently than with the Chord and Scale Forms. Before, each form progressed along the length of the fretboard in CAGED order. Since the Lead Patterns flow along the fretboard as opposed to across it, the CAGED Sequence becomes stationary relative to what you are playing. Its function here is more on the order of a series of guide posts along the way.

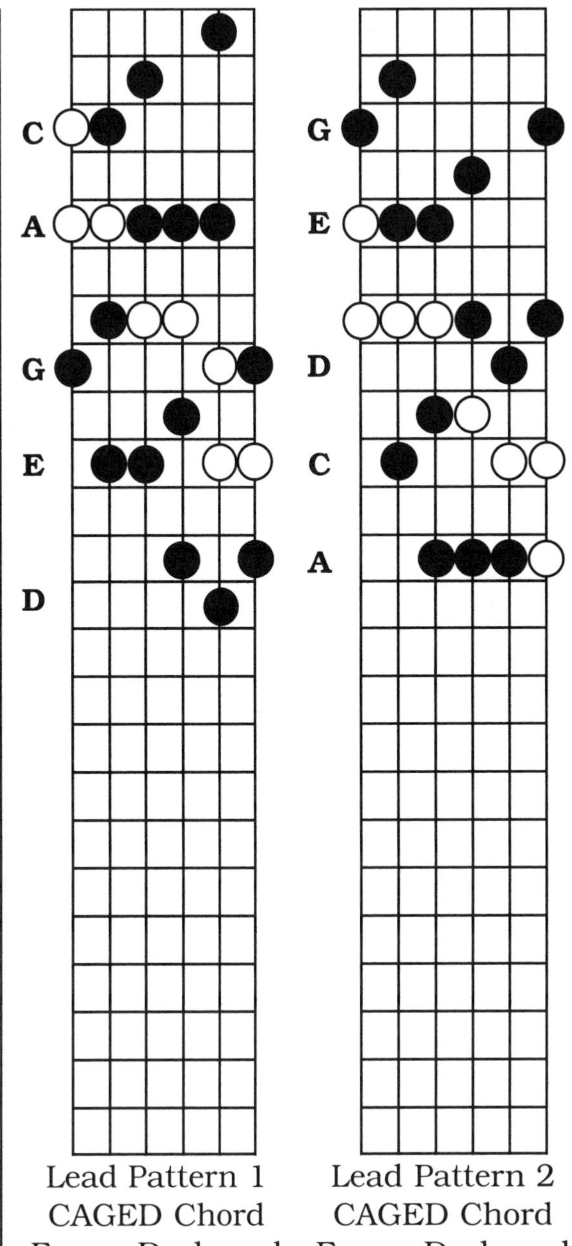

Lead Pattern 1 CAGED Chord Forms Darkened

Lead Pattern 2 CAGED Chord Forms Darkened

Naming the Lead Patterns

Naming the Lead Patterns requires one more step than naming either the Chord or Scale Forms. **The Lead Patterns are referenced by the first Chord Form of the CAGED Sequence included in the pattern.**

Lead Pattern 1 is referenced by the C Chord Form and Lead Pattern 2 is referenced by the G Chord Form. Given this, it will now be helpful to designate them as Groups - the C Group and G Group. This orientation also gives the player something more visual to grasp than the somewhat arbitrary "Lead Pattern 1" and "Lead Pattern 2" for naming purposes.

In the top left graph, LP1, or the C Group, begins on the third fret, and so it corresponds to the C Chord Form in the open position, therefore, it is in the key of C (for now). It is a C Group Lead Pattern (guitarwise) and a C Scale (musicwise).

In the top right graph, LP2, or the G Group, begins on the 3rd fret, and corresponds to the G Chord Form in the open position, and so is in the key of G, musically.

The lower graphs illustrate this in higher positions. In the graph on the bottom left, the C Group is played from the 7th position. This corresponds musically with the C Chord Form in the 4th position which is an E chord. Therefore the Lead Pattern is in the key of E, or an E scale (for now).

The bottom right hand graph shows the G Group Lead Pattern in the 7th position. This matches the G Chord Form in the 4th position which is a B chord. So this Lead Pattern is in the key of B, or a B Scale. If you can name the Chord and Scale Forms, you will also be able to name the Lead Patterns provided you remember to reference it to the correct Chord Form.

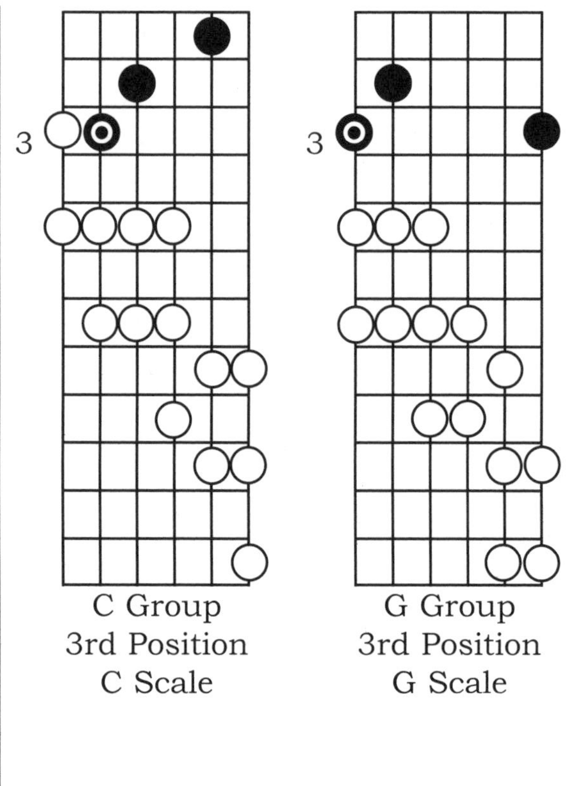

C Group 3rd Position C Scale

G Group 3rd Position G Scale

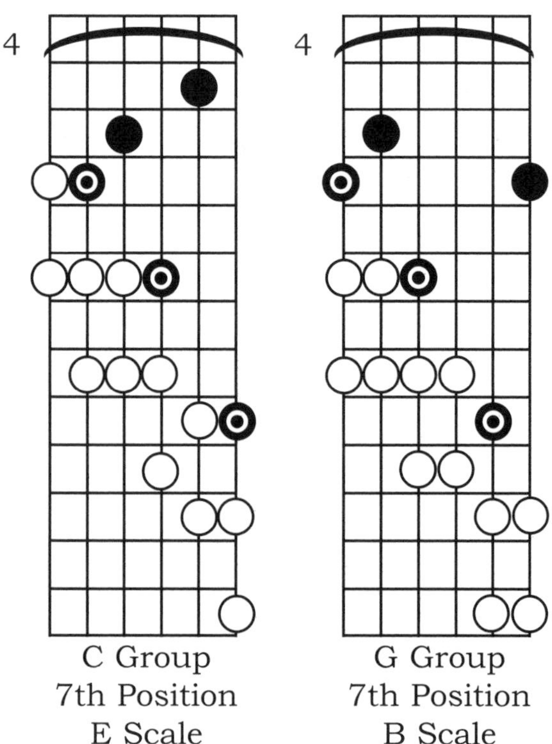

C Group 7th Position E Scale

G Group 7th Position B Scale

Naming the Lead Patterns

These graphs have been drawn to show that the naming of Lead Patterns can be done with Scale Forms, just as with the Chord Forms, so they have been matched up with their corresponding Scale Forms.

The C Group in the left column matches the C Scale Form in the 8th position so the key is Ab. The G Group in the 11th position matches the G Scale Form in the 8th position so the key is Eb. Using the Scale Forms instead of the Chord Forms for a reference isn't really as easy visually, but has been included for the sake of completeness.

At every opportunity an effort has been made to differentiate between the guitar description and the musical identity. Chords, scales and keys are music concepts common to all (polyphonic) instruments. Chord Forms, Scale Forms and Lead Patterns, as described here are specific to the guitar and are the sole result of the instrument's tuning.

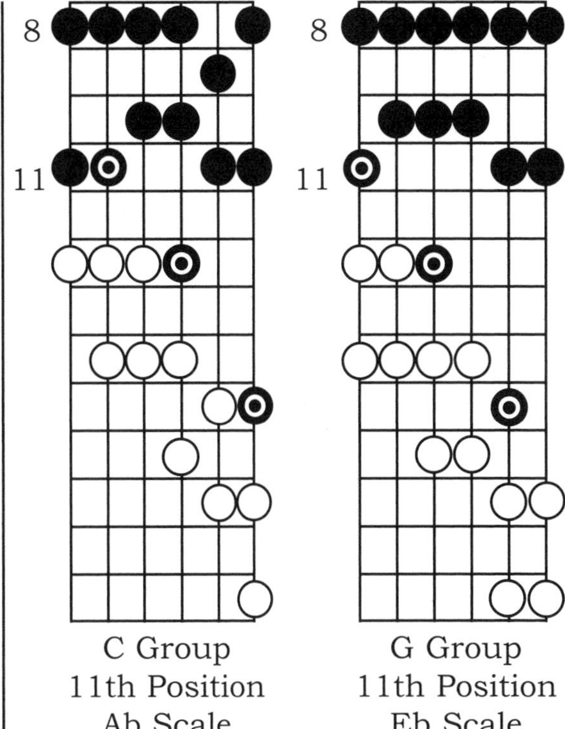

C Group
11th Position
Ab Scale

G Group
11th Position
Eb Scale

Recap

This is the end of the third section of Fretboard Logic SE Part I. By now you should be familiar with the Lead Patterns in much the same manner as the Chord and Scale Forms which preceded them. You should be able to recognize and play both Lead Patterns in any position on the fretboard. You should be able to visualize the CAGED Sequence forms in relation to each of them, and you should be able to use the C and the G Chord or Scale Forms as a reference to name them in any position. Here is another pitch to reread and replay everything from the beginning. After you've done that a time or two, take the test. Then put down the book for a while and come back to it later. See if it stuck.

Finale Part I

The Basic Chord Forms, Scale Forms, and Lead Patterns are the three fundamental components of the pattern organization of the fretboard. They result from the implementation of six strings tuned 4th, 4th, 4th, 3rd, and 4th, and evolved as a means to confer true polyphonic capabilities upon the instrument given the limitation of four fretting fingers. This fretboard organization is the interface between the guitar player and the music he or she plays. I believe its comprehension is essential to the knowledgeable application of musical ideas to the guitar. Part I focused on this pattern organization exclusively as the guitarist's first priority. Consider it just a foundation upon which to build. Without an understanding of why the instrument is tuned the way it is, learning the guitar can be unnecessarily frustrating. While the guitar's overall design and capabilities have evolved through advances in technology and changes in music styles, the tuning has remained the same. It is simple and efficient. It works perfectly. Although it is less than obvious, as you have seen, it can be learned in a short amount of time when not clouded by other issues. It is important that guitar players, even more than other instrumentalists, learn to distinguish the realm of the instrument's interface from the other areas of learning to be taken up. The fretboard relationships introduced here are merely a framework within which you can work to extract music from your guitar.

There are a total of three parts to the series. The next, Fretboard Logic SE Part II continues from this point and covers the tonal elements of music exclusively. You will learn to play different types of Chords, Scales and Arpeggios, by building them up from the basic fretboard forms. Our approach is faster, easier and more direct than either rote memorization or the cut and try approach. Groups of tones can only be expressed two ways: as played together or in succession. Chords are groups of tones played at the same time, Scales are tones played one after another, and Arpeggios are a hybrid whereby chords are played like scales. Each are presented within the context of the pattern organization discussed here.

I hope the following test provides an incentive to - you guessed it - reread and replay everything. I encourage feedback, so feel free to write with any questions, comments, criticisms or suggestions on how to improve the method. (If you want to help out, tell the folks at the store to keep us in stock.) I've put many years of work into these little books, and done countless rewrites to make them more accurate and readable (and yes, I still find typos). I truly hope they help you get more out of your guitar. The bottom line is this: You've made a good decision in your choice of an instrument. As a vehicle for self expression, the guitar is second to none. And one more thing. The only way I've ever been able to learn anything difficult is to just keep at it until it somehow sinks in. Consider that whenever something new is presented, our brains have to fit it into what is called our "frame of reference." Maybe this is a little like breaking eggs to make an omelet. I believe there is a natural resistance to changing the status quo. Anything of value will not usually be easily attained, and learning to play the guitar is no exception.

"Testing Testing..."

1) The two chords in the first column are common in many chord books. Can they also be considered basic chord forms? Explain.

2) If the E form chord is grouped on another set of strings (such as the 2nd, 3rd & 4th), will it still be an E form?

3) Describe the 5 chords in the right column in terms of form and position.

4) Give the names of the 5 diagrammed chords in question number three.

5) Which two pairs of notes do not have a sharp or flat in between them when counting fret by fret to name a chord?

6) In the CAGED sequence, which two chord forms share a note? Where?

7) What flat chord is the same as A#? What sharp chord is the same as Eb?

8) Name the scale played when the C form is in the 5th position. Name the chord.

9) What is the term for a five note scale?

10) Name the three types of patterns which occur on the fretboard as a result of the guitar's tuning system.

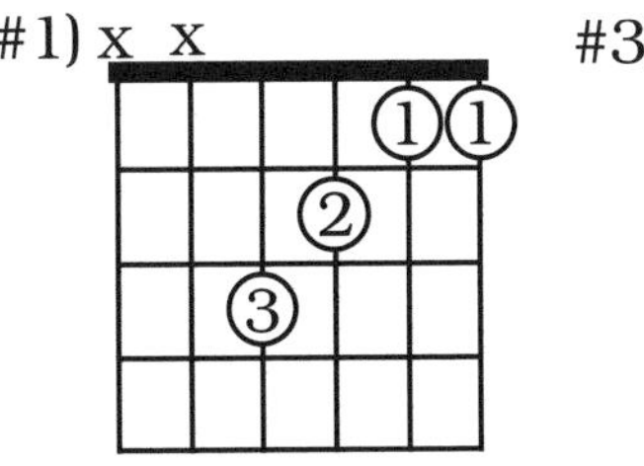

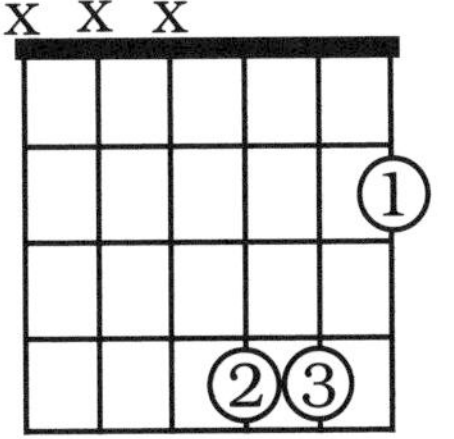

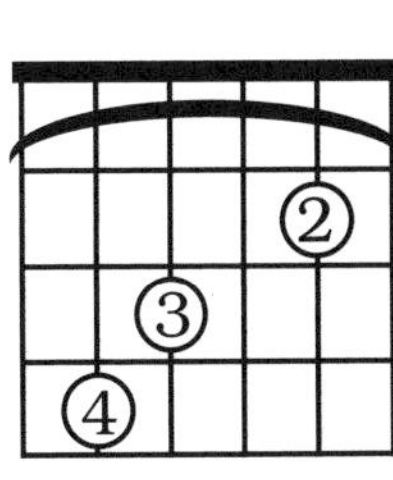

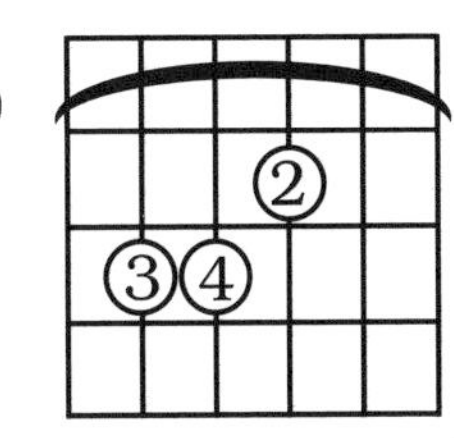

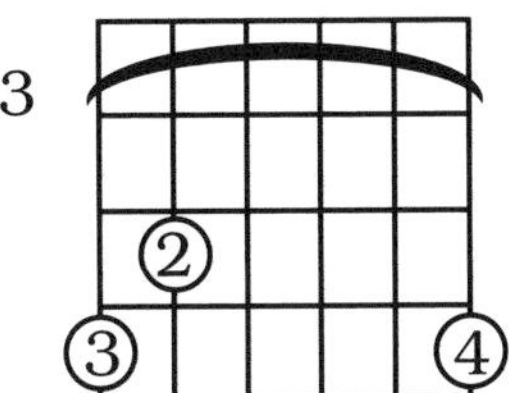

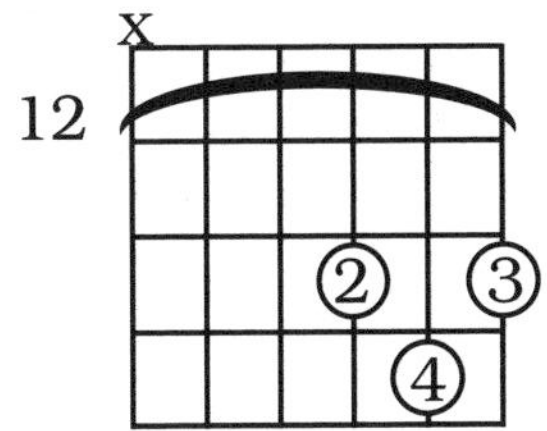

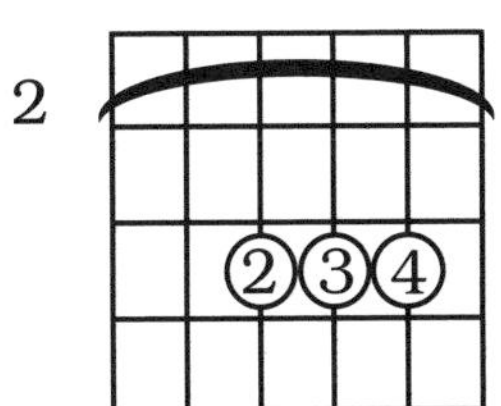

"Testing, Testing..."

11) Describe the Scale Forms in the left hand column in terms of form and position.

12) Name the scales in question 11.

13) Who is funnier, Elvis Presley or Johnny Rotten?

14) Which Scale Forms treat the index as an extension instead of the position marker in order to correspond more closely to the chord form?

15) What are the four separate ways chord forms, scale forms and lead patterns should be learned and understood?

16) Which Chord Form identifies Lead Pattern 1? Lead Pattern 2?

17) What position would you start the G Group on in order to play a B scale? (See diagrams on next page.)

18) Name the scale if you play the C Group from the 2nd fret.

19) Name the scale if you play Lead Pattern 2 from the 1st fret.

20) What fret would you start Lead Pattern 2 on to play a G# scale

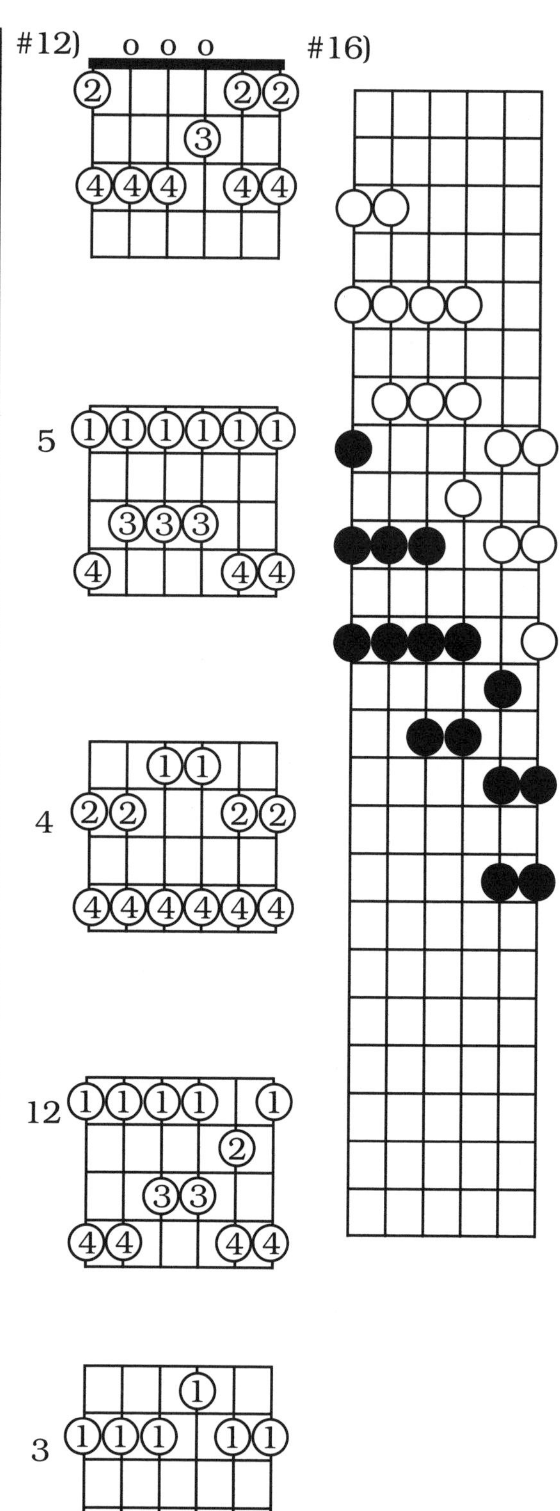

"Testing, Testing..."

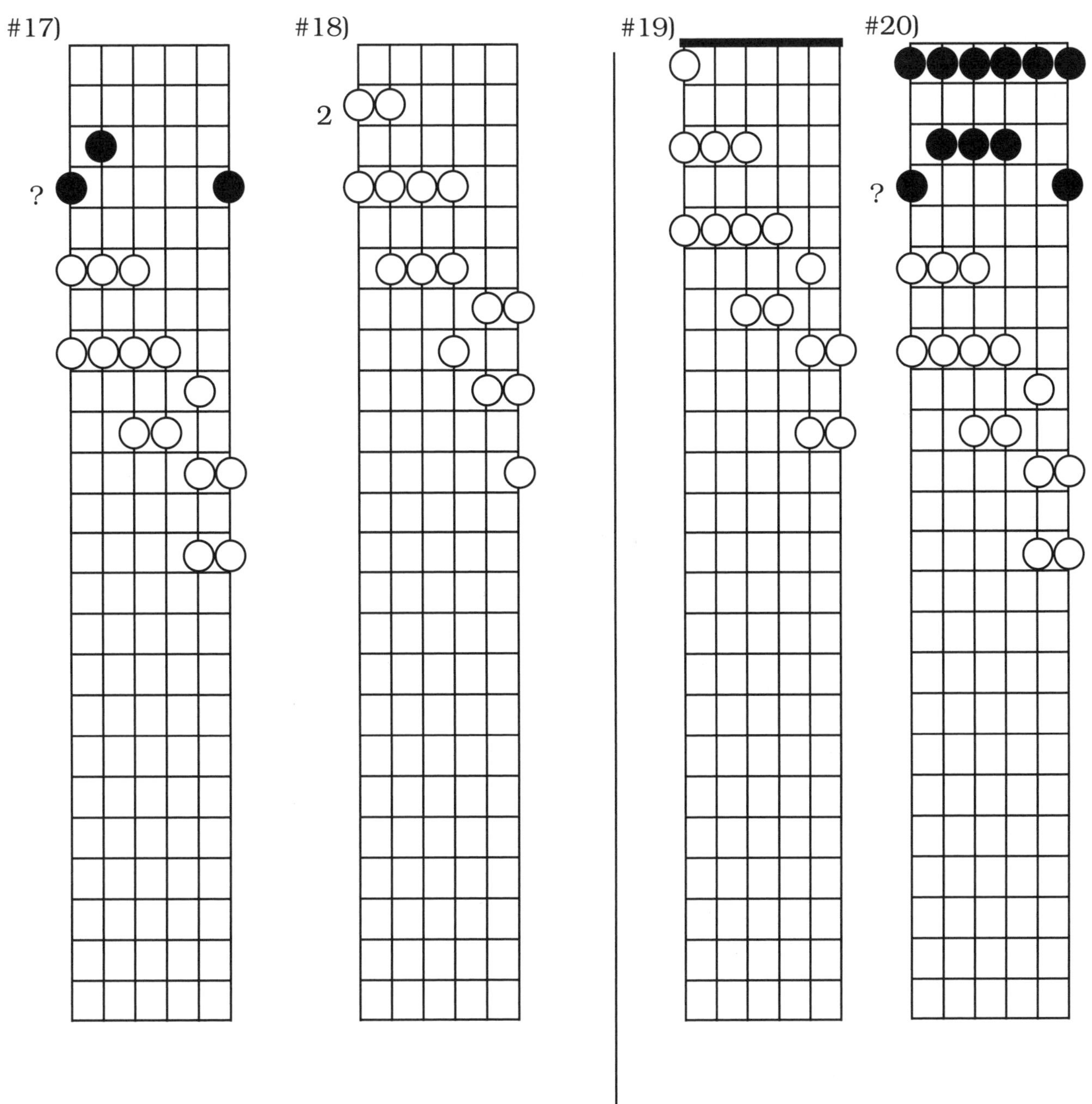

The Answers To All Your Problems

1) The F and B chords pictured are often misrepresented as basic forms. They are really only portions of other Chord Forms. The F chord pictured is a portion of the E form in the 1st position. (The B chord is a portion of the A form in the 2nd position.)

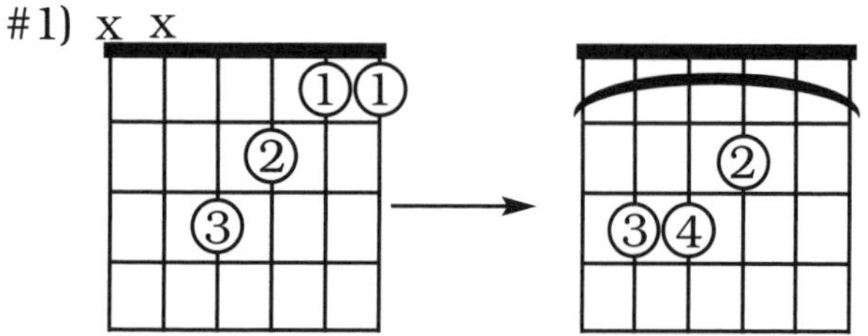

2) No. The forms retain their character only along the length of the strings, not across them. The form as described would be an A minor form.

3) C Chord Form 1st position.
E Chord Form 9th position.
G Chord Form 3rd position.
D Chord Form 12th position.
A Chord Form 2nd position.

4) C# (or Db)
C# (or Db)
A# (or Bb)
D
B

5) B and C, E and F.

6) D form and C form. 2nd string.

7) Bb. D#.

8) F scale.
F chord.

9) Pentatonic.

10) Chord Forms, Scale Forms and Lead Patterns.

11) E Scale Form 1st position.
G Scale Form 5th position.
A Scale Form 4th position.
C Scale Form 12th position.
D Scale Form 3rd position.

12) F
C
C# (or Db)
C
F

13) Wrong. Fred Grunfeld. Clearly a trick question.

14) The A scale form and E scale form.

15)
1. As Basic Forms
2. As Forms in Positions
3. Within (or without) the CAGED Sequence.
4. Named as a musical entity.

16) C form.
G form.

17) 7th position.

18) B scale.

19) F scale.

20) 4th fret.

Fretboard Logic 12 Step Program

Here it is one last time. Condensed. The reasoning behind the guitar's tuning system is to make the instrument a practical polyphonic given the limitation of four fretting fingers. Because of the tuning, EADGBE, and the resultant string to string intervals, three distinct pattern types occur on the fretboard. They are Chord Forms, Scale Forms, and Lead Patterns. They are organized and interrelated to one another as patterns and can be considered separate from typical music issues such as pitch and time.

This pattern organization can be overviewed in a series of twelve steps as illustrated below. The three pattern types each must be grasped four separate ways in order for the guitarist to have a functional understanding of the interface between the player and the music he or she plays.

The four ways each pattern type must be learned are:

1) As Basic Forms distinct from one another and from other pattern types,
2) As Forms to be used in various Positions on the fretboard,
3) As forms in CAGED Sequence along the fretboard, and
4) Identified and Named as music entities.

Five Basic Chord Forms	Five Basic Scale Forms	Two Basic Lead Patterns
Chord Forms In Positions	Scale Forms In Positions	Lead Patterns In Positions
Chord Forms In CAGED Sequence	Scale Forms In CAGED Sequence	Lead Patterns Overlying The CAGED Sequence
Chord Forms In Positions Named As Chords	Scale Forms In Positions Named As Scales	Lead Patterns In Positions Named As Scales

Alternate Placement of the "3rd" Interval

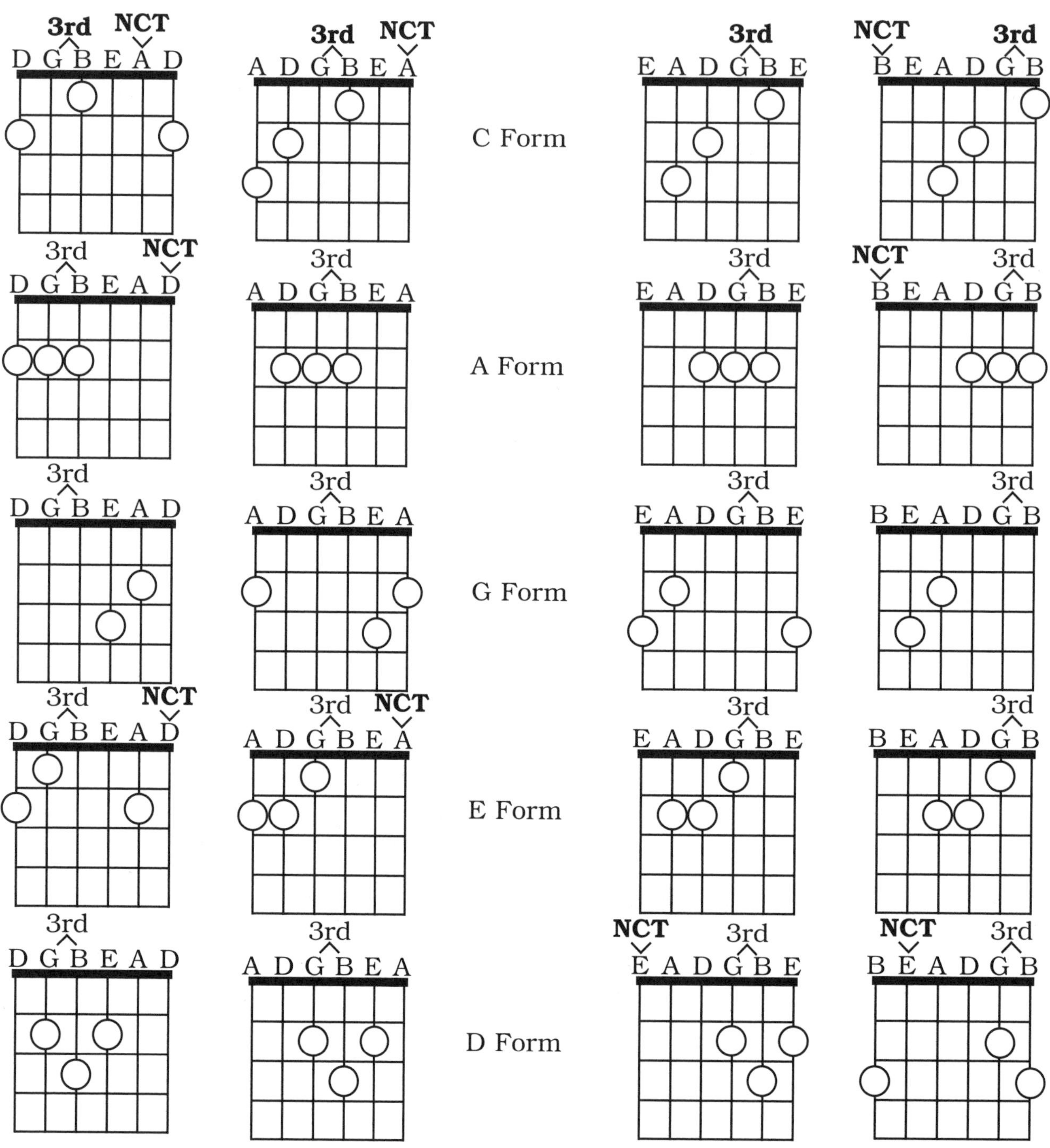

These graphs were included to illustrate that the placement of the 3rd anywhere but the 4th string pair (from the bass), produces more non-chord tones (**NCT**s), and so are less optimal given the limitation of three fretting fingers per form. The two left hand columns were common lute tunings, and are the intervallic equivalents of: CFADGC (4th 3rd 4th 4th 4th), GCFADG (4th 4th 3rd 4th 4th). The third column is standard tuning, included for comparison.

Part II

Information is anything which reduces uncertainty.

Claude Shannon

Preface

The Fretboard Logic Series began when, after years of thinking otherwise, the author finally came to see that the guitar's tuning system represented a completely separate endeavor from the typical educational requirements of other musical instruments. As it developed, he felt that it was something unique in the field of guitar methods and also very tidy, since it focused on this fretboard pattern organization to the exclusion of everything else. It distinguished itself from many earlier method books by avoiding the tendency to muddy things up by touching on many topics superficially and was, in a sense, clean and well defined.

So upon its completion, there was no intention on the part of the author, of opening up the can of worms that the next levels of involvement represented. His students and readers had other ideas, however, and they persuaded him to continue on from that point. After numerous false starts, a decision was made to limit the second effort to the subject of the tonal elements of music as viewed within the context of the pattern organization described in Part I.

As the second effort progressed, the author again became concerned with avoiding anything that would distract from the central purpose of the book. Every effort was made to prevent it from becoming one of those typical methods that talks a little bit about a lot of different subjects - usually growing enormous in the process - but one that never really nails down anything in a meaningful, original or lasting way. It was and is his intention to continue to approach the guitar in a systematic, if somewhat unorthodox, way.

As a practical matter, Part II (Vol. II) could be considered a well stocked "tonal tool box" for guitar players. The idea is to provide the basic tonal elements of music in a format that is consistent with the instrument's design. Part I dealt with the fretboard aspects of playing. Part II will focus on the tonal elements of music taught in the context of the fretboard pattern organization.

Chords, Scales and Arpeggios are not really music per se, but you will use them to make your own music and to fully understand the music of others.

Inside every fat book is a thin book trying to get out.

Anonymous

Introduction

Part II has been designed to build on the foundations established in Part I. If you have not yet completed Part I, what is written here will be more difficult and won't work as intended because the structure that supports it will not yet have been established. I can't stress strongly enough to learn the material in Part I before continuing from here. If you have just completed Part I, you'll know that one of main differences between this approach and the others is that the various components that make up music have been separated from one another so that each may be more closely examined, learned and retained. The focus of Part I was the unique and largely unappreciated reasoning behind the guitar's unusual pitch selection - EADGBE. This tuning was implemented as a way to combine simple pattern recognition with left hand efficiency. It takes a while to explain this thoroughly, but in terms of your guitar playing education, the layout of the fretboard is just the beginning.

As a guitarist, the other aspects of music, including theory, technique, and the different styles of music, must each be understood through this tuning system, otherwise you will find yourself reduced to guesswork or rote memorization much of the time. If you study theory, you are taking an intellectual approach to the pitch and time relationships in music. If you are working on technique, you are dealing with the physical requirements, and style refers to the various combinations of elements which produce music to your liking. You no doubt prefer certain types or kinds of music to others and that, too, can change from time to time. Some of the more common styles of music are rock, metal, blues, country, classical, jazz, and bluegrass. Learning music from copying records or reading could be described generally as an analytical approach, where you slowly assimilate a little bit from each different area with each piece you learn. If you write or compose, you are putting your creative faculties to use.

Fretboard Logic is, at its heart, a guitar-oriented approach. It makes no assumptions about which of the various components the player prefers to study. It does not prescribe or endorse a particular style or technique and is not music theory per se. It tries to provide information that is common to all of the aspects of guitar playing, expanding outward from the fretboard pattern organization. Illustrating the different components of music separately is to the benefit of the student two ways. It makes things easier both on the front end when learning, and later on, when applying them in various playing situations. However, as progress is made, this separation becomes more and more difficult. The lines between the styles of music, creative vs. analytic thinking, feelings and thoughts, etc., will become blurred. Words and images used to describe musical entities become less effective as their meanings overlap and become vague. Still, from a teaching standpoint, it is important to be able to distinguish them from the outset, regardless of whatever long or short term objectives the player has in mind. Just as we may value different styles at different times of our lives, the level of interest and skill in the component areas of music changes from time to time for each of us. A conscious effort was made to focus exclusively on the guitar's pattern organization in Part I. Similarly, Part II is confined to the tonal elements of music in a guitaristic orientation. Rhythmic and other elements are separated away so that the common tone groups can be more carefully examined. Part II starts by developing the different types of Chords, Scales, and Arpeggios, and ends by introducing some of the more significant components of music, with an emphasis on understanding how they work within the context of the fretboard operating system.

In the past, the learning of the tonal elements has been relegated to one of two divergent philosophical approaches. The first approach is the "bootstrap" school of thought, where chords, etc., are considered merely items of information to be learned by rote memorization, ie., without a frame of reference. Teachers of this school feel it is best to get them out of the way as soon as possible, and get on to more important matters. Unfortunately, if you happen to forget a chord or scale, for example, you must go back and memorize it over again from scratch. This occurs all too often because without supports and without integration, new information tends to get lost in our brains - the old "in one ear and out the other" effect. The net result is that guitarists retain only a small portion of what they learn and become handicapped when the time comes for more advanced activities.

The second school of thought is what is believed to be the more academic method. It considers tone groupings in terms of their most basic sub-components. In other words, chords, scales and arpeggios must be broken down into intervals and individual notes to be understood. Because of the unique nature of the guitar, I deem this to be something akin to viewing the elephant through a microscope - a reference to the five blind men and the elephant fable. This method presumes that if you know the notes on the fretboard, and also know the notes of, say, a Bbm7b5 chord, then playing it is a simple matter of combining them. No problem - if you happen to be on a *keyboard.* The problems for guitarists are many. First, the prerequisite information itself is a steep learning curve. In order to make one chord you have to know the key signature, the notes in the key, the notes in the chord, and the formula for the chord. After you have all this information then the real work begins. On a piano, there is only one of each pitch, and the notes are laid out in a line, in one dimension. On a guitar, there are multiples of most notes, and they are laid out in an irregular matrix. So after all that, you have to come to a decision about which string upon which to look for each note, and which of the available notes is going to be the most appropriate in the context of how long and strong your fingers are. As you can guess, there are a mind-boggling number of permutations of each chord within the context of a note by note approach. So it comes down to cut and try. The difficulty of this method makes the previous method of rote memorization look pretty sensible by comparison.

Do either of these approaches sound familiar? I'll bet they do. If you were frustrated by either of them, don't feel too bad. They are an example of how the dominant influences of other instruments, especially keyboards, have corrupted the teaching of the guitar for hundreds of years. It may be another hundred years before the academics and bootstrappers figure that out. For those of us who want to not only play, but understand what we're doing, there is an alternative. It boils down to looking at the guitar as if it had an interface of its own independent of the piano (or violin), which it does. The method for learning tone groups here is to combine a minimum amount of information so you can *build* them without guesswork or rote. By relying more or less on the basic fretboard forms provided by the tuning, and the formula of each tone group, you can build any tone grouping, in any key, easily.

Chords, scales and arpeggios can be considered the basic building blocks of music and they are all derived from the same origins: the notes in a *key.* The difference between them is the order in which they are taken and the way they are played. To prepare you for the process of combining fretboard and music elements, it is a good idea to make sure you are familiar with some of the basic terminology used in music, and prepare you in advance for a few of the many linguistic pitfalls that await you. Many terms in music are bandied about casually, with their meanings not very well defined. The terms note and tone, and key and scale, are good examples. Strictly speaking, a **note** is a concept which represents a pitch unit (frequency) and a **tone** is an actuality - the vibrations you hear. When you play a note, it produces a tone. In other words you can't hear notes and you can't write tones. The same relationship exists for the terms key, a concept, and scale, an actuality. However, ask just about any music teacher on the planet where the notes of chord come from, and he or she will say with absolute certainty, "From a scale." If it didn't produce logic jams later on, I'd even be willing to let it go at that, just to avoid the argument, but here's what happens. Scales have both even and odd degrees; chords have only odd degrees, and it makes all the difference in the world when building, identifying and using them for more important purposes. Using a term like Sus. 4, instead of Sus. 11, only confuses things unnecessarily. So the very words we use can lead to more or less understanding of both the more fundamental and more advanced issues in music.

A **key** is a group of related notes (or tones, if you must). The word note and tone are often used interchangeably, but again, here, tone is taken to mean the sound produced, and the note is the idea we manipulate. The concept of key normally combines three things: 1) seven notes of the twelve tone system, 2) the first seven letters of the alphabet, and 3) alterations known as sharps (#) or flats (b). For example, the notes in the key of C are: C D E F G A and B. The notes in the key of F are: F G A Bb C D and E. The notes in the key of D are: D E F# G A B and C#. Each key has at least one note different from the others designated by its **signature,** which is the number of sharps or the number of flats, given in a specific order. **Chords** are groups of three or more notes that are selected from every other degree in a key (the odd ones), and played simultaneously. A "C chord" is the notes C, E, and G played together. **Inversion** is when they are played in any other order. G C E is the same chord with the notes inverted. All the chord tones in that key are C E G B D F and A. Remember that *chords* are every other note - the odd numbers - in a key. **Scales** are groups of tones that are made up of each note in the key, but played in succession. For example, in the key of C, the C scale is: C D E F G A B and C, forward or back, one after another. **Arpeggios** are chords that are played like scales. In other words, instead of playing the chord tones all at once, you would play each tone one after the other, perhaps up and back.

Most of this section is devoted to establishing the Chords, Scales and Arpeggios from which you will learn to better understand the music of others, and experiment with your own musical ideas. It is the next logical step after you have mastered the layout of the fretboard. This should not be to the exclusion of acquiring a repertoire of pieces to play. That's the other half of the battle. Learning to build tone groups is a way of understanding an important part of what's going on. After that, other components of music will be introduced so each person will be able to choose for him or herself which direction to explore next, in order to achieve their own objectives. A few of these areas including theory, technique, style, rhythm, and lead playing, are introduced briefly at the end of the book. By the time you have finished Parts I and II, you will have been exposed to the operating system of the guitar and the basic tonal elements of music. When you examine the type of music you're interested in, you will hopefully see it in a new light and comprehend it on different levels. By the way, the work gets harder as you progress, but that is natural. Besides, if you have come this far, it is likely you have more than just a passing interest in the guitar.

One or two more observations and we'll get on with it. When most people want to teach themselves guitar, they go out and buy a chord book to learn chords from, and a songbook to learn the songs they'd like to play. It seems like all they need to do is memorize the chords one by one and add a right hand strumming or picking pattern and they'll sound pretty much like the record. If you've tried this - I sure did - then you already know that it is not that simple. There are a couple of things working against us. First of all, there are many types of chords and numerous ways to form them on the neck, and they aren't all easy to use or remember. Second, trying to make sense of the way things work on the fretboard is not exactly the easiest thing in the world. Third, the forms used in the songbook are often simplified, I believe, to keep from scaring off potential buyers, and often don't sound quite right. A common misconception about songbooks is that the artists themselves are responsible for their content and accuracy.

In Part I, we explored the basic chord and scale *forms* or shapes, as a function of the guitar's pitch selection. In Part II, the next step is to learn the chord and scale *types* as a function of the twelve tone system in music.

Chords are classified into "families" by how many different notes they have, usually either three or four. The family of three-note chords is called **Triads,** and there are four basic types: Major, Minor, Diminished, and Augmented. The five basic chord forms are all major triads. The family of four-note chords is known as the **Sevenths** because of the addition of the seventh degree, and there are six primary types: Major Seventh, Minor Seventh, Diminished Seventh, Augmented Seventh, Dominant Seventh, and Minor Seventh Flat Five.

Beyond the seventh chords are ninths, elevenths, and thirteenths which tend to become more and more esoteric as you venture farther and farther from a recognizable reference tone, or **tonic.** As you travel away from the tonic, the subject eventually changes from the discussion of chords per se, to the study of chord substitutions, for the purpose of achieving a particular harmonic effect. This becomes a matter of style and taste at some point, and no longer a purely objective discourse on chords. Just as a rock player often uses different sound effects such as distortion, chorus or delay, to give his or her music a certain type of feel, a jazz player will substitute unusual tonal material to create harmonic interest. You may have noticed that these two components of music tend to cancel each other out. In other words if the guitar has a great deal of sonic activity, then more harmonic activity just creates sonic confusion - commonly called noise. In fact, it is hard to distinguish between even a major and a minor chord if there is just distortion in the guitar sound, but, I digress.

If you learn the Triads and Sevenths, you will already have a fairly extensive chord vocabulary plus you'll know the procedure for constructing anything else you might need in the future. The first section is devoted to the building process so that you will always have them available without having to memorize a couple of hundred pages of "bits and pieces" out of an ordinary chord book. In retrospect, I'm pretty sure that some of the guys who put those books together got the idea that since we have four fretting fingers, chords should be learned as four-stringed entities - and a lot of guitar players have been baffled ever since.

After the chords, the scales and then the arpeggios will become progressively easier to understand, but harder to play.

We don’t know a millionth of one percent about anything.

Thomas Edison

Triads

In order to understand the nature of the different chord types it is helpful to take a moment and examine where they come from: keys. In western music, keys are groups of seven notes in which each is identified by a letter of the alphabet from A to G. There are basically fifteen keys and each has one or more notes that are different from the others and which are specified by a sharp (#) or a flat (b). The key of G for example, is comprised of the notes G A B C D E and F#. The difference between the key of G and the key of C is the F note. There is no F in the key of G. F# is a completely different tone although it borrows part of its name from F to confuse you.

The important thing to recognize now is that each key is equivalent to the next, as far as chord types are concerned. In order to correlate them, a number value is placed on each note or degree of the key. In the key of C, first degree is C, the second is D, the third is E, the fourth is F, the fifth is G, the sixth is A, and the seventh degree in the key of C is B. In the key of G, G=1, A=2, B=3, C=4, D=5, E=6, and F#=7. Every key is the same with respect to each note's degree. This is where chords get their musical identity. Musically, chords are made up of the odd numbered degrees in a key. Different types of chords are made by altering various degrees using sharps or flats. Any major chord, for example, is simply the first, third, and fifth degrees of a key (1 3 5). Any minor chord is the first, flatted third, and fifth degrees of a key (1 b3 5). The degrees of a chord can be "spelled" out numerically. (Hey, if you can add with letters in algebra, you can spell with numbers in music.)

These odd-numbered note groups with the various alterations that identify each chord type are called chord **formulas.** Combined with the notes in a key, they give the correct spelling for any chord. So a C major chord is spelled C E G, and a G minor chord is spelled G bB D (spoken G, B flat, D). If, from the preceding, you can spell C minor and G major yourself, you've got the basic idea. *Formulas* are the musical (tonal) side of the story, just as the CAGED System is the guitar side. In order to know the musical aspect to chords, you need to know what notes are in the key, and the chord's formula. Combine them and you understand each chord's musical nature.

To build chords on the guitar using the Fretboard Logic method, the minimum you need to know is its formula, and the order of the degrees in each of the five basic chord forms. Put these together and you can build any chord. One chord type played through each different form will sound both similar because they are the same notes, and different because of the arrangement of the tones. When chords are combined into musical statements or sequences, they become what is termed a **progression.** A more general term for how chords work is harmony. Harmony can be considered the overall vertical relationships of the notes in music. The formulas for the basic triads are as follows:

Major - 1 3 5

Minor - 1 b3 5

Augmented - 1 3 #5

Diminished - 1 b3 b5

Triads - Major; Degrees

The five basic chord forms are all Major Triads, and the formula for Major Triads is 1 3 5.

In the left hand column, the forms are illustrated as open chords with only the 1 3 5 part, or **Nucleus,** of each form shown as degrees below. There isn't a nucleus within the D form chord. These diagrams show the relationship between forms and degrees on the fretboard. It's important to recognize on which three strings each form's 1 3 5 nucleus is, as soon as possible.

The right hand column shows all the degrees below each string of the barred forms. Learn these and practice locating the equivalent tones so you can determine where the degrees are for each form by ear.

The **root,** or (lowest) first degree of the chord, is marked with an **R**. The root for the G and E forms is on the sixth string, the root for the C and A is on the fifth, the the root for the D form is on the fourth string.

> In music theory, the term **Inversion** is used to refer to changing the order of the notes in a chord so that a degree other than the root is the lowest note. The first inversion has the third in the bass. The second inversion has the fifth in the bass and so on. The term for an "uninverted" chord is "root position," since, on a piano, changing position and inverting the chord are inseparable. However the term *position* has a completely different meaning for the guitar so a different descriptive term is called for. The term we will adopt for an adjacent string 1 3 5 tone group is **nucleus.**

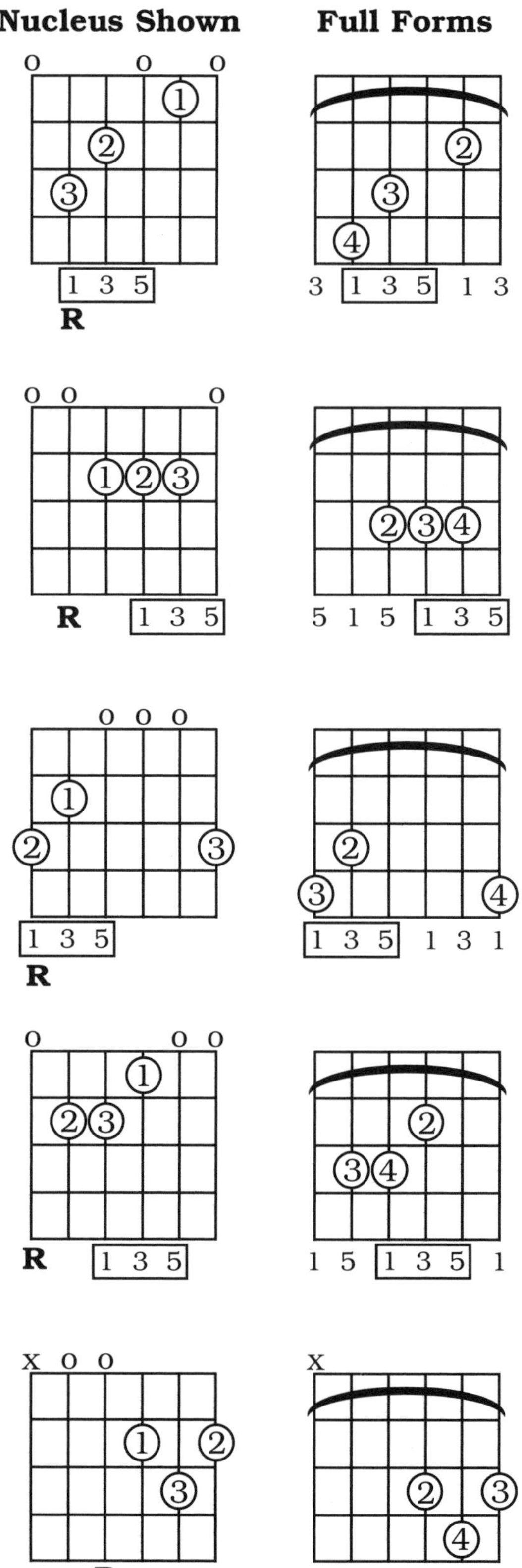

Triads - Alterations

The left side graphs show the nuclear forms, so that the rest of the notes of the form are omitted. It might be hard to recognize them at first, but they are taken directly from the forms on the preceding page *but not necessarily the same positions.* Again, some forms can't be played open. When the chord forms are stripped down like this, it's easier to observe the process of alteration which produces the different chord types. This is the heart of the Fretboard Logic method of combining a music formula with a fretboard form to build the different types of chords.

The term **alteration** pertains to changing a degree other than the root, in half step increments. By raising or lowering (sharping or flatting) the chord tones, you change the type of the chord. Each chord type's formula specifies the alterations. For example, the formula for a minor is 1 b3 5. That requires that you alter the 3rd by lowering it, meaning play the string one fret lower in pitch (toward the headstock). When you sharp a note, you move one fret closer to the guitar body.

The graphs on the right are examples of alterations that produce the minor nuclear forms. When alterations are made, the fingering is adjusted in each case to allow for the most comfortable grip. The G Form Nucleus is on strings 6, 5, & 4; the C Form Nucleus is on 5,4, & 3; the E Form Nucleus is on strings 4, 3, & 2; and the A Form Nucleus is on 3, 2, & 1. Again, there is no D form Nucleus.

By now you should be able to appreciate that attempts to grasp these relationships by assimilation from playing by ear, reading music or by rote memorization from ordinary chord books can lead to wasted time and bad craziness.

Nuclear Forms | **Alterations**

1 3 5

C Form Nucleus
Strings 5 4 & 3

1 b3 5

C Minor Form
Altered 3rd

1 3 5

A Form Nucleus
Strings 3 2 & 1

1 b3 5

A Minor Form
Altered 3rd

1 3 5

G Form Nucleus
Strings 6 5 & 4

1 b3 5

G Minor Form
Altered 3rd

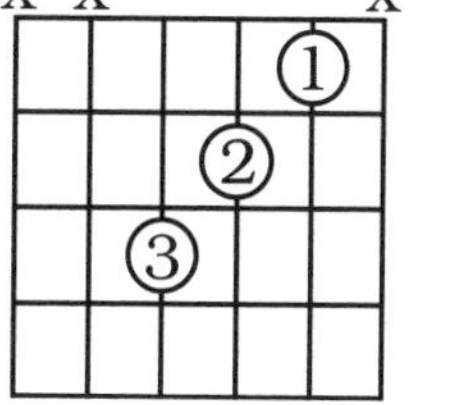

1 3 5

E Form Nucleus
Strings 4 3 & 2

1 b3 5

E Minor Form
Altered 3rd

Triads - Minor

So far, in order to demonstrate the alterations that produce the various chord types, the forms were reduced to the bare minimum. In common practice, the basic chord forms are altered in their entirety to make the different chord types. For learning purposes, both ways are used throughout this section - the left column more for instruction, the right more for common usage. The formula for Minor chords is 1 b3 5. The common abbreviations are min. or m, as in A min. or Cm.

The left hand column illustrates the Minor Triads as nuclear forms with the basic degree relationship shown below. The right hand column shows full forms using a bar with the complete degree relationship given. If you want to play, say, an open A minor, you can use the barred form (without the bar) in the open position. The same goes for the G E and D forms.

In practical application, we must decide which of the available forms is appropriate. Some forms are going to be easy and some will seem like they are more trouble than they're worth. Having a grasp of the mechanics of chord building and a larger chord vocabulary means you are going to have more choices. You can always play through the five forms and then choose which sounds or works the best. Sooner or later you will see that there are other possible variations for the different chord types, especially if you don't mind stretching across the "borders" and borrowing tones from two adjacent forms, or using portions of basic forms. It doesn't make any sense to try to illustrate or explain every possible combination (unless of course, you're trying to sell a thick book). Instead, you should experiment with the basic ideas and come up with variations and usages on your own.

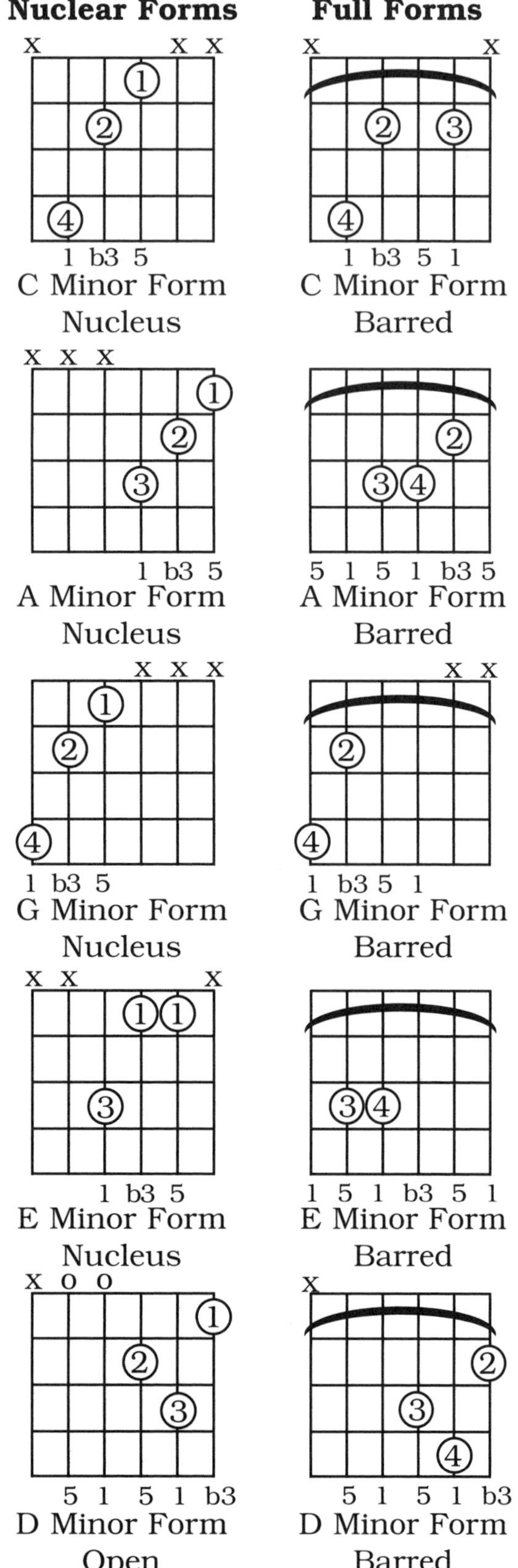

Triads - Augmented

The formula for Augmented Triads is 1 3 #5. The common abbreviations for augmented are aug., and +, as in G aug. or F+.

The Augmented chords are one of what are termed the **symmetrical** chords since the distance from each tone to the next is the same in half steps or frets. This is not easy to visualize on a fretboard, by the way. Each note is four frets (five frets inclusive), or a major third interval from the other. An **interval** is two notes specified by the distance between them in terms of half steps.

On most instruments, especially the piano, intervals are considered the primary sub-components of chords, but on the guitar, there is a good reason to think of the different types of chords in terms of how they relate to the pattern organization instead. Intervals per se will be explored in Volume III (Part III).

An Augmented chord's symmetry creates a similarity in the forms. Usually the forms are distinct from each other in terms of their shape, but symmetrical chords often look exactly alike, although they are derived from different basic forms on the guitar. An interesting result of their symmetry is that they can be identified by any note in the chord. For example the C aug. chord contains the notes C, E, and G#. It can also be correctly called E aug., G# aug. or even Ab aug. Another result of this is that there are actually only four (musically) different Augmented chords.

The left hand column shows the nuclear forms which were made by raising the fifth degree. Only the root, third, and sharped fifth degrees are given.

The right hand column shows the forms as either barred or extended forms with each degree given below.

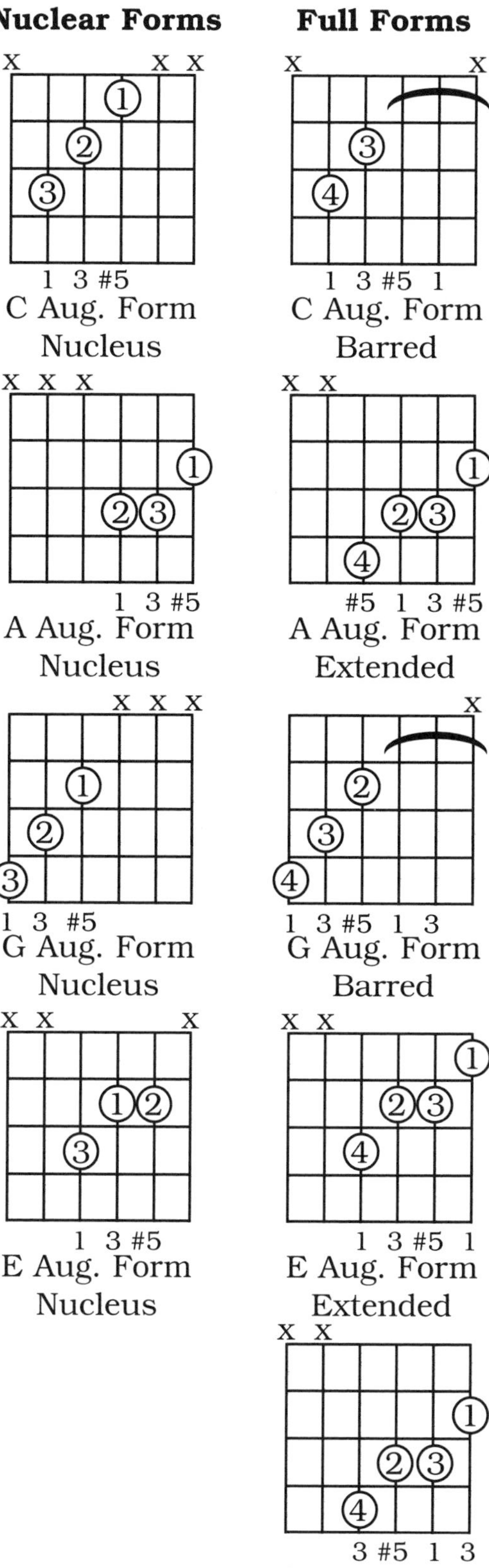

Triads - Diminished

The formula for the Diminished Triads is 1 b3 b5. The abbreviations are dim. and °, as in C dim. or F°. Like the augmented chords, Diminished chords are symmetrical in that the distance from one note to the next is the same in terms of half steps. Each note is three frets (four inclusive), or a minor third interval from the other. Any note in the chord can correctly identify or name the chord, and this allows for only three completely different Diminished chords.

The left column illustrates the nuclear forms with root, flatted third, and flatted fifth shown.

The right side column shows the Diminished chords as barred forms. As before, the degrees are given for each string that has a chord tone.

With the Diminished chords, there is little practical difference between the triads and sevenths.

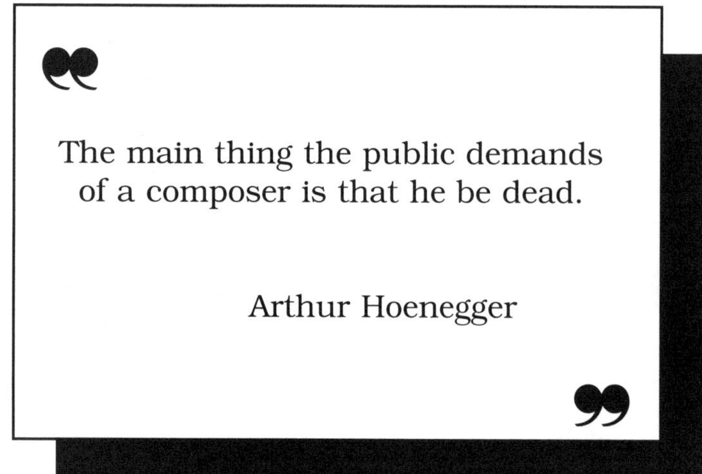

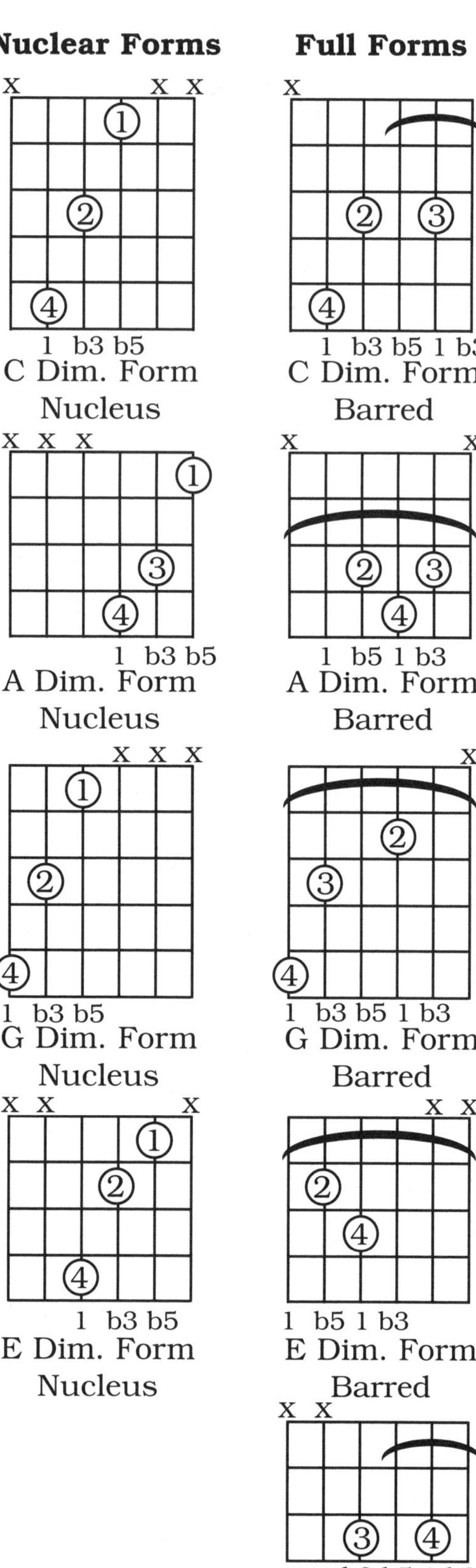

Major Seventh

Seventh Chords

The Seventh chords are four-note chords comprised of the 1st, 3rd, 5th, and 7th degrees of a key. As with the triads, alterations produce the different chord types. The Sevenths and their formulas are:

Major Seventh: 1 3 5 7
Minor Seventh: 1 b3 5 b7
Augmented Seventh: 1 3 #5 b7
Diminished Seventh: 1 b3 b5 bb7
Dominant Seventh: 1 3 5 b7
Minor Seventh Flat Five: 1 b3 b5 b7

The common abbreviations for Major Seventh are Maj. 7 and M7, as in E Maj. 7 and Eb M7. Here again, for the sake of clarity and consistency, the chord types will be described using the three letter abbreviations adding degrees and alterations when necessary.

The diagrams to the right are the Major Sevenths. The left side column shows them uninverted. Only three Major Sevenths are able to be played as nuclear forms: C, G, and E. The C form nucleus is actually played with a three-string, or half bar.

The right column illustrates the barred forms with each degree shown. The G Maj. 7 form is not able to be played with a bar and so was omitted. As we progress into building the different Seventh chords, you'll realize that there will be fewer patterns that are easy to recognize as derived from a basic form. By now you should be familiar enough with the method of combining the music formula with the guitar form to be able to construct them yourself anyway. By learning to build them on your own, you won't have to stop what you're doing and reach for a book, chart, or gizmo, every time you are searching for just the right sound. This makes creative experimentation more accessible.

Nuclear Forms

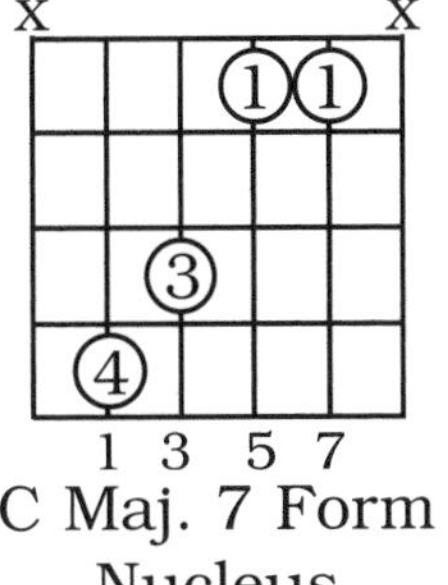

C Maj. 7 Form
Nucleus

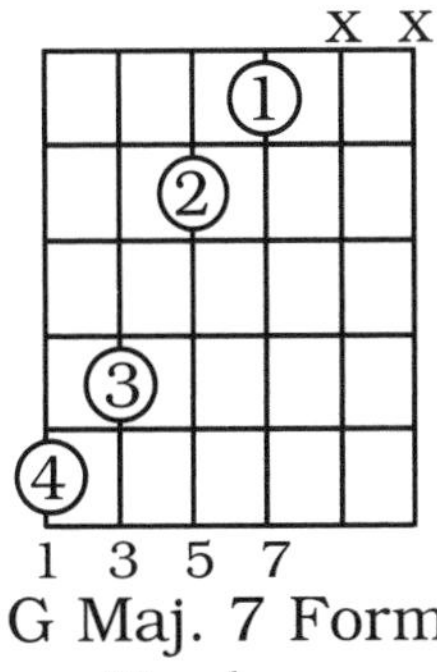

G Maj. 7 Form
Nucleus

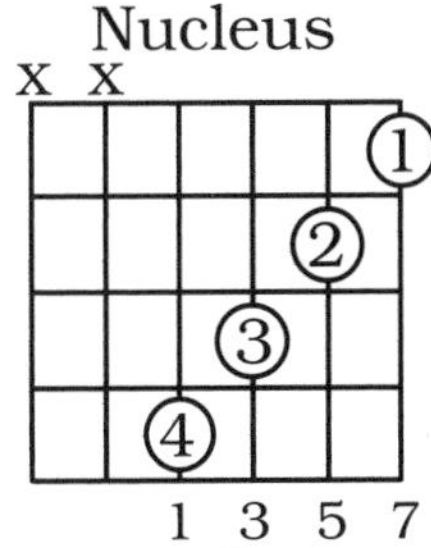

E Maj. 7 Form
Nucleus

Full Forms

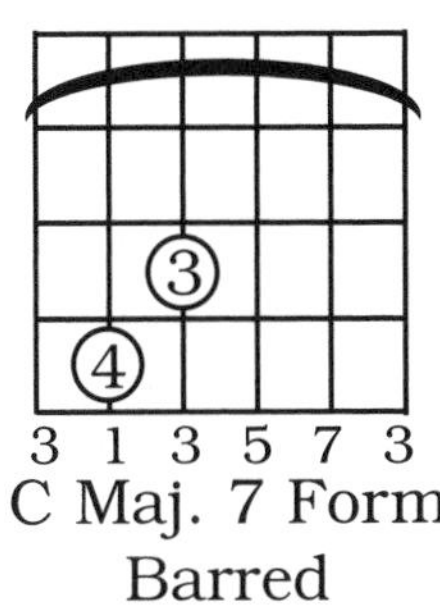

C Maj. 7 Form
Barred

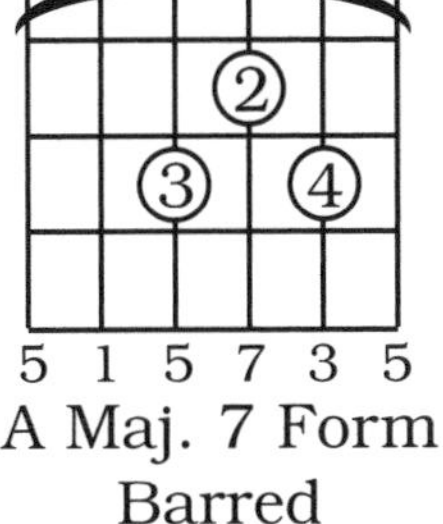

A Maj. 7 Form
Barred

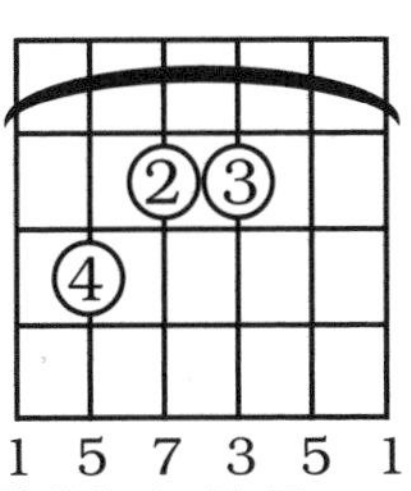

E Maj. 7 Form
Barred

D Maj. 7 Form
Barred

Sevenths - Minor Seventh

The formula for Minor Seventh chords is 1 b3 5 b7. The common abbreviations are min. 7 and m7.

The left side column shows the nuclear forms of all but the A min. 7 and the D min. 7 forms. As you can tell, some of these are a long stretch. The G min. 7 form seems almost unplayable but was included anyway for completeness.

The right side column illustrates the barred forms of the Minor Sevenths with each degree shown.

In order to acquire the b7 in the barred forms, a root is lowered two frets. Lowering it one fret makes a seventh degree, lowering two is then a flat seven.

Triads are so named for having three separate tones. Seventh chords, on the other hand, are named by the addition of the seventh degree. This semantic distinction has prompted some music educators to refer to the sevenths as *quatrads* or *tetrads* to better follow the designation for three note chords (as opposed to, say, calling triads "fifths.") You mayhaps will encounter such terminological obfuscation and/or disparity in the field of music which you must henceforth eschew. The term for this is, um, embafflement. Just don't ask me what a tritone is.

?

Nuclear Forms

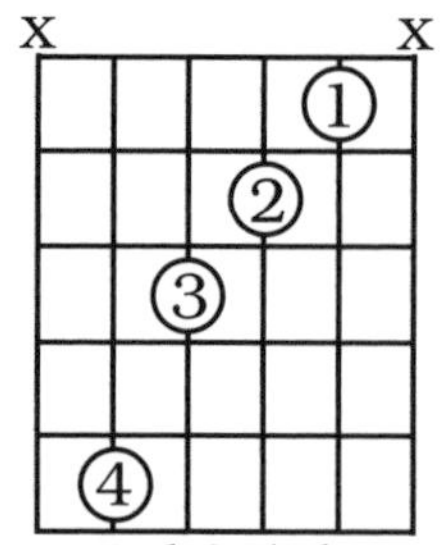

1 b3 5 b7
C Min. 7 Form
Nucleus

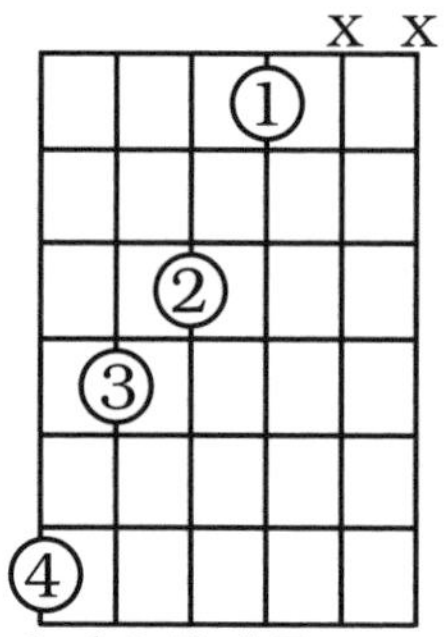

1 b3 5 b7
G Min. 7 Form
Nucleus

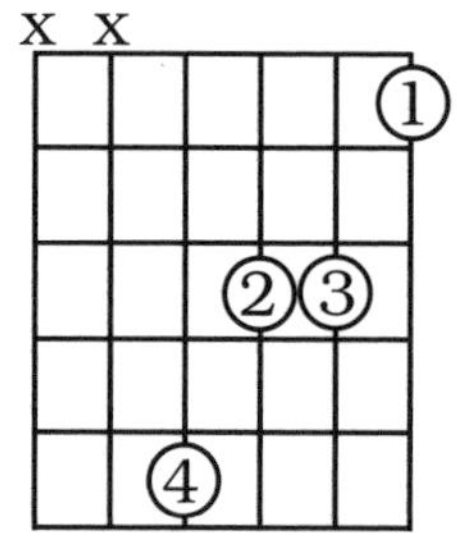

1 b3 5 b7
E Min. 7 Form
Nucleus

Full Forms

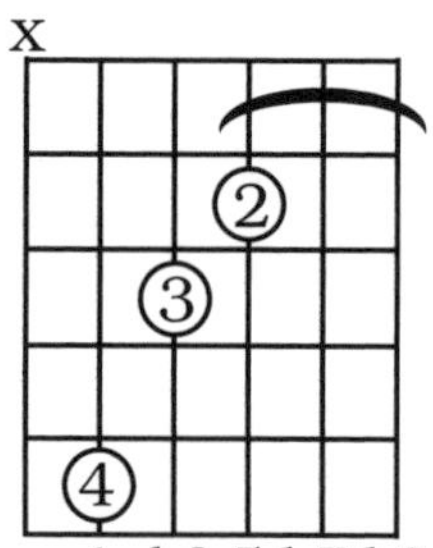

1 b3 5 b7 b3
C Min. 7 Form
Barred

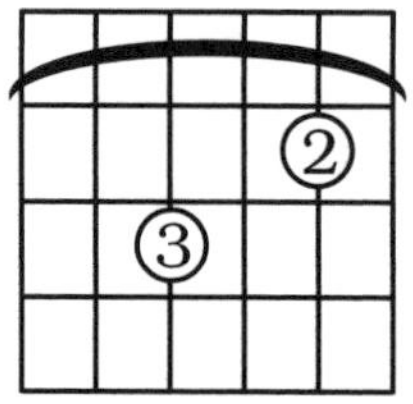

5 1 5 b7 b3 5
A Min. 7 Form
Barred

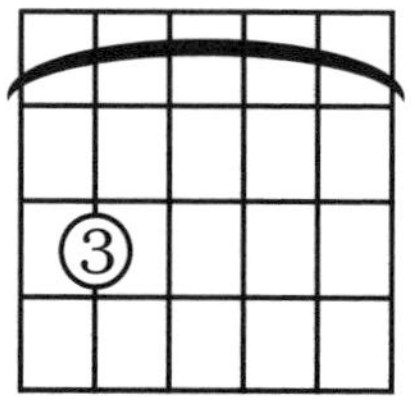

1 5 b7 b3 5 1
E Min. 7 Form
Barred

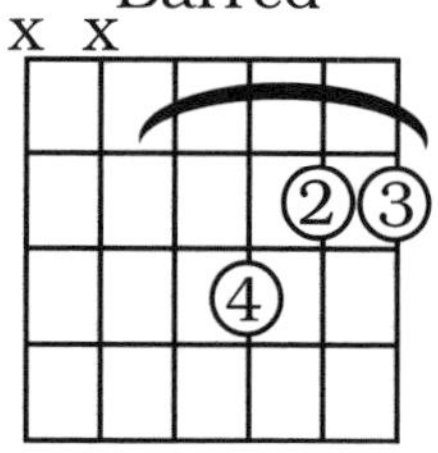

1 5 b7 b3
D Min. 7 Form
Barred

Sevenths - Augmented Seventh

The formula for the Augmented Sevenths is 1 3 #5 b7. This is the same as adding a flatted seventh degree to an augmented triad. The common abbreviations are aug. 7 and +7, as in G# aug. 7 and Eb +7.

The column on the left illustrates the nucleus forms and again, only the C G and E forms are available. This is due to the greater number of strings required by the nucleus itself.

The column on the right shows the barred forms, and here only the A and D forms are possible.

You've probably noticed by now that some things that are easy to understand are hard to play, and vice versa. For example, it is easy to see how to derive the G aug. 7th form, but it is ridiculous reach, and won't get used much for that reason.

"No, no, no! What are you doing?... Fifth leg! Fifth leg!"

Nuclear Forms **Full Forms**

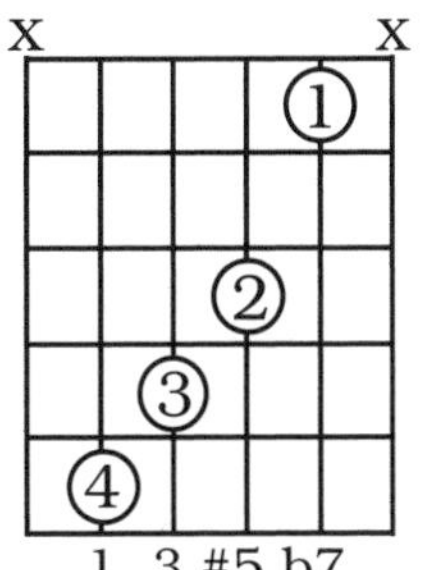

C Aug. 7 Form
Nucleus

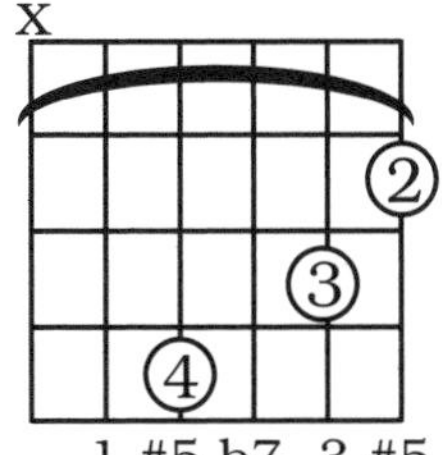

A Aug. 7 Form
Barred

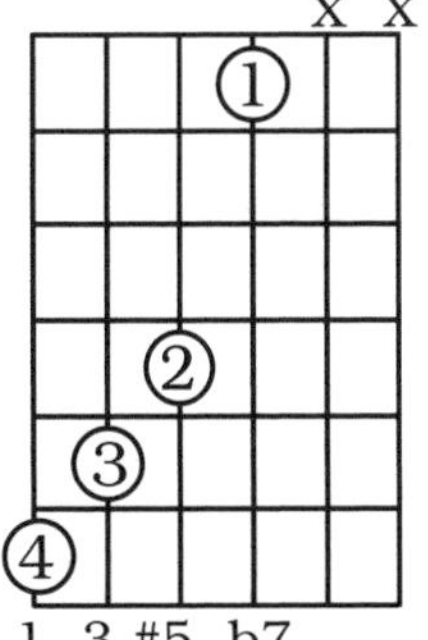

G Aug. 7 Form
Nucleus

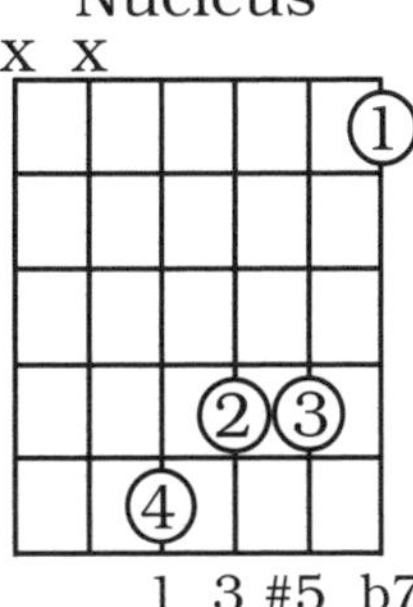

E Aug. 7 Form
Nucleus

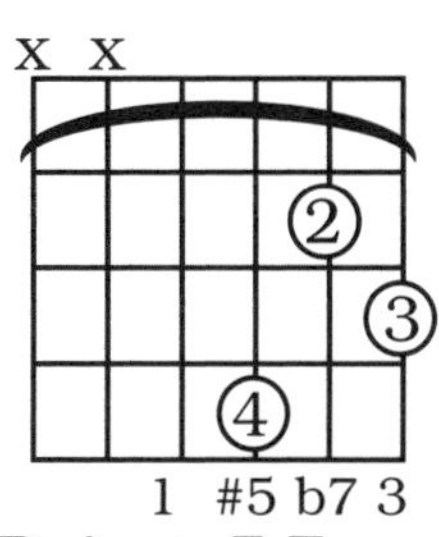

D Aug. 7 Form
Barred

Sevenths - Diminished Seventh

The formula for the Diminished Seventh chords is 1 b3 b5 bb7 (spoken double flat 7). The abbreviations are dim. 7 and °7. The double flat seventh degree might seem unusual at first but it is nothing more complicated than lowering a b7 degree one more fret. You will probably notice that it changes to the next note in the music alphabet. For example, an Abb is the same note as G **enharmonically,** (its tonal equivalent) but it is incorrect to call it G in this context.

The left side diagrams are some world class reaches that were included for the sake of completeness. It's no loss if you can't make these forms. Most people can only reach them above the 12th fret if at all.

The full forms are easier to manage and will be no trouble to play. The Diminished Sevenths, like the Diminished Triads, are symmetrical. In fact, these Triads and Sevenths can be considered interchangeable since there is no functional difference between them in any musical context.

At this stage, you might be feeling like the study of chords on the guitar is getting, um, out of hand. Many of the nuclear forms are too long to reach plus the barred and extended chords don't necessarily follow the basic forms. Not only that, there's hardly any consistency changing from a nucleus to a barred form. Don't worry about it. Remember these are symmetrical chords. This method of learning chords from the basic forms combined with each chord's formula is designed to provide you with options and overall coherence. You get to decide what is right for each situation. As you go back over everything, the approach becomes more sensible. Besides, after the Diminished 7ths, the hardest part is over, so quit complaining. Geez.

Nuclear Forms

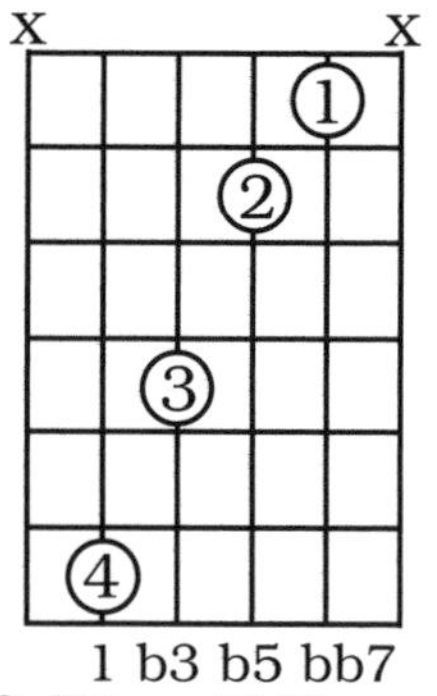

C Dim. 7 Form
Nucleus

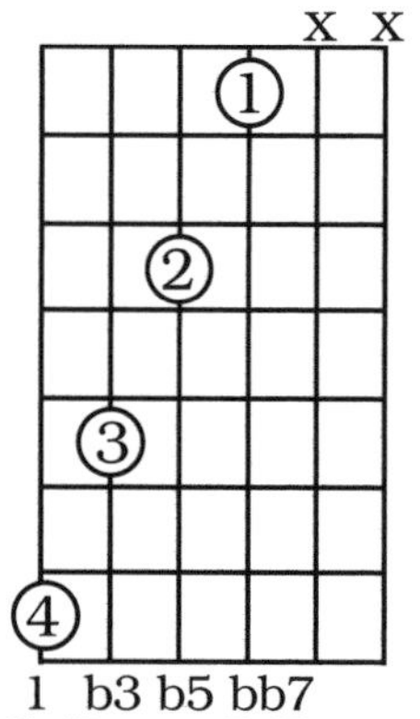

G Dim. 7 Form
Nucleus

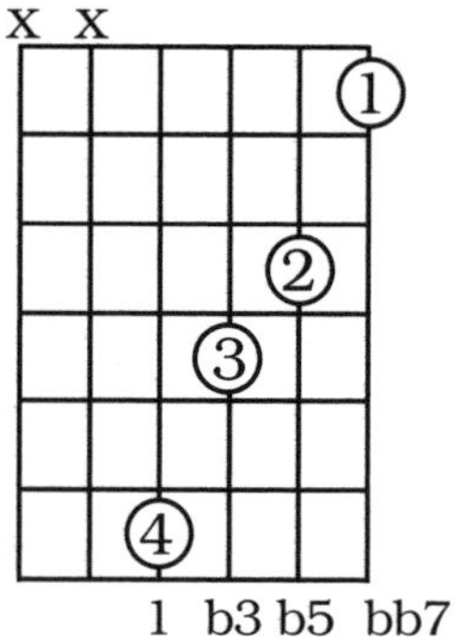

E Dim. 7 Form
Nucleus

Full Forms

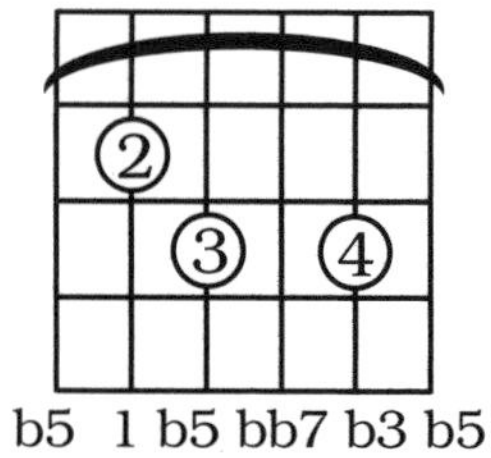

A Dim. 7 Form
Barred

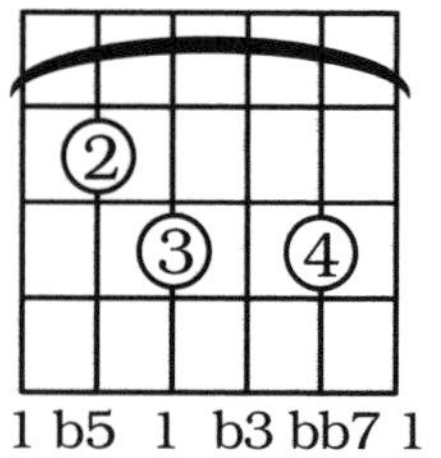

E Dim. 7 Form
Barred

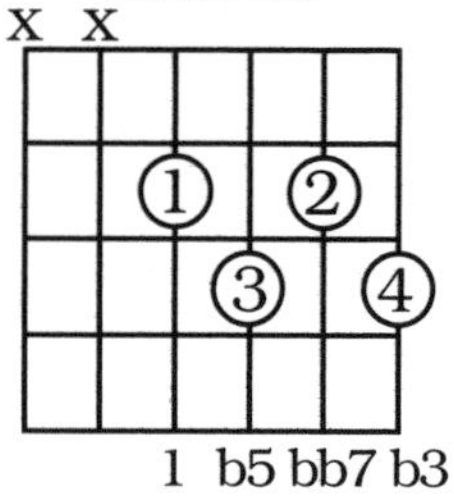

D Dim. 7 Form

Sevenths - Dominant Seventh

The formula for Dominant Sevenths, which are also referred to as just Sevenths, is 1 3 5 b7. The abbreviations are dom. 7 and 7, as in A dom. 7 and C7.

The Dominant Sevenths are easier to deal with than the Augmented or Diminished Sevenths, and one reason is that they follow the basic forms more closely. However, with the Dominant Seventh chords, the chord tones become completely scrambled, and nuclear forms are impossible. You may have noticed that it became more and more difficult to make the nuclear forms as we progressed.

The open and barred forms, are presented in the left and right columns. In two of the forms, the open C dom. 7 and the barred G dom. 7, a less important chord tone has been omitted. Eliminating unnecessary chord tones is an important concept in chord building, and applies later to what are commonly known as *altered* and *extended* chords. In the left hand column, the first form is the open C dom. 7. There is no 5th degree in the chord at all. It can be left out because it is the least important to the overall character of the chord. Leaving it out also allows the C form to be played comfortably. In the right column are either the barred or moveable versions of the same chords. You'll notice that the C dom. 7 form is not able to be barred and is played with the end strings muted or unplayed. The G dom. 7 form is different from the open form in that the flat seventh degree is played on the fourth string instead of the first. In many of these forms, the order of the notes or the chord's voicing can be changed. For example, in the A dom. 7th form, the b7 can also be played on the first string, third fret. Knowing where the degrees of each form are makes other things possible later.

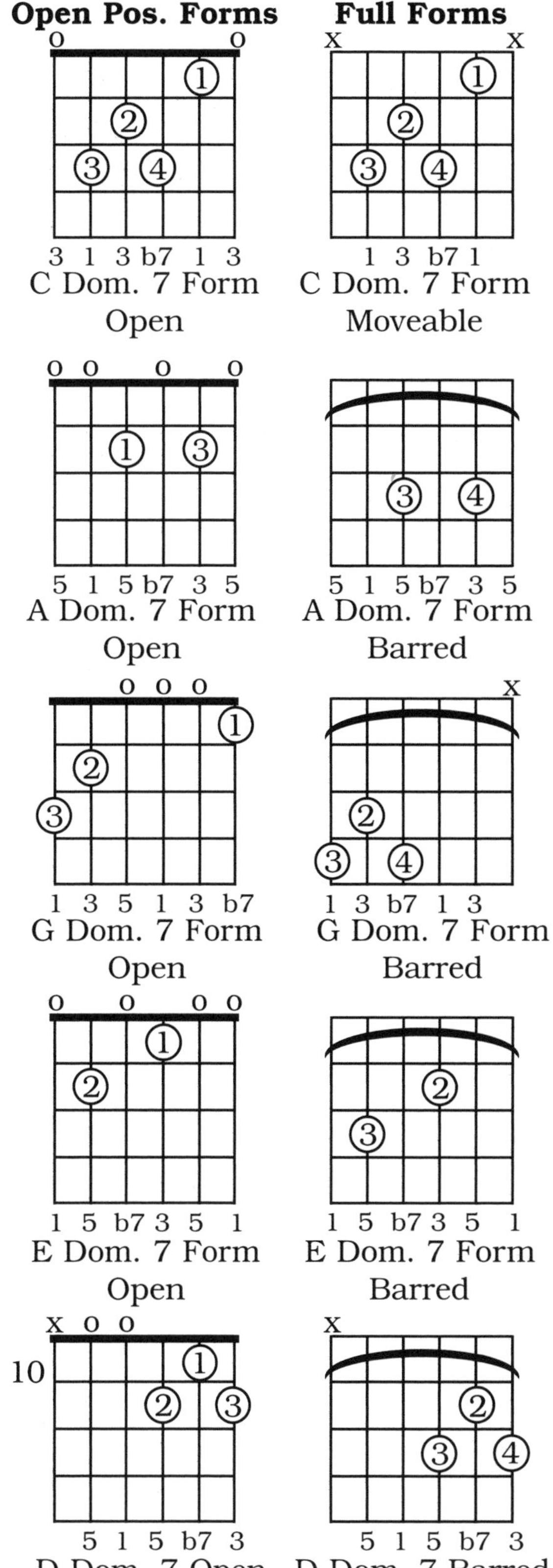

Sevenths - Minor Seventh Flat Five

The formula for the Minor Seventh Flat Five is 1 b3 b5 b7. The more common abbreviations are min.7 b5, or m7 b5. This chord was once called Half-Diminished but that term is seldom used anymore since it behaves in the context of a progression more like an altered Minor than a Diminished chord. The term for this "behavior" of chords is *function,* and is explored in detail in Vol. III in the section on Progressions. One of the goals of this approach is to free you from the tyranny of memorization so you can progress to understanding how things work together. That's when it starts to get a lot more interesting and productive. The left column shows the min.7 b5 chords as either nuclear or open forms. The C min.7 b5 and the E min.7 b5 forms are the only two that have a nucleus. The right hand side illustrates the full barred versions for the C, A and D forms. The D form employs a double bar using the index and third fingers.

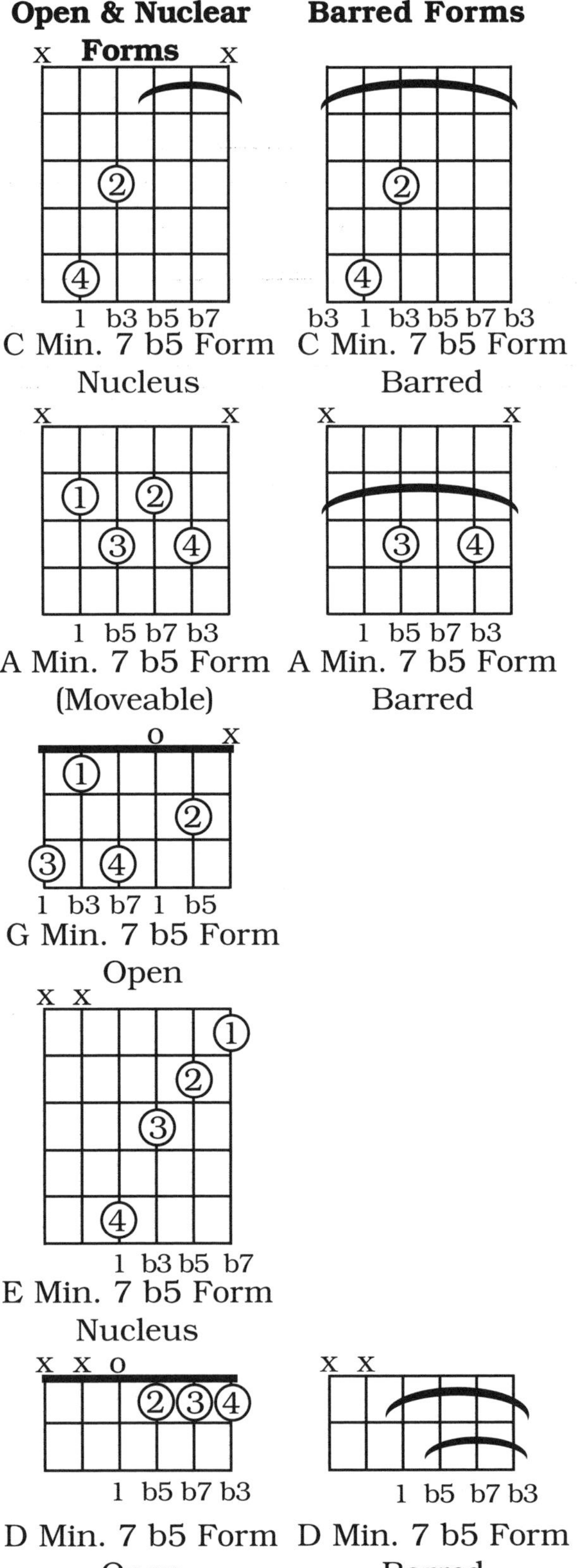

Recap

Chords can be grouped generally by the number of different notes they have, and specifically by their formulas. Triads have three notes and seventh chords have four. A formula is each chord type's unique fingerprint of altered degrees. There are four Triads and six Sevenths, and together, they comprise a large portion of what actually gets used in most kinds of music. In order to build the different types of chords on guitar, we apply the music formula to the fretboard form. On the fretboard, the C A G E or D form is altered by moving a fretting finger up or down to correspond to the chord's formula. When learning, the nuclear forms are easiest to grasp, but in actual usage, the full or barred forms tend to get used the most.

Scales

In Part I, the smallest Scale type, the Pentatonic, was introduced and illustrated as a pattern extension or continuation of the basic chord forms, as opposed to a completely independent grouping. The Diatonic Scales are seven note groups which can also be viewed as extensions or continuations of both the Pentatonic scales and the basic chord forms. Contrast the difference in the meaning of the terms "pattern extension" and "finger extension." They're not the same.

The left hand column is a review of the five basic scale forms, showing the integral chord forms darkened. All the Pentatonic scale forms except the D form are able to be played within the standard four finger - four fret position. The D form requires a finger extension in that a finger is extended beyond that four fret area.

The right hand column illustrates the five Diatonic scale forms. Now the A, G and D forms span more than four frets. In some cases, the fingerings given for the Diatonic scale forms differ completely from pentatonics, and sometimes the patterns just seem to have notes added. Learn the diatonic patterns by playing them in different positions on the neck and count the frets to name the Scale. It is important to also play them in CAGED Sequence as you did with the pentatonics. The Diatonics are somewhat more difficult than the Pentatonics, and may take a little longer to learn.

Again, please don't confuse these fretboard patterns with *modes*. This is a common error even among teachers and guitar method authors. The mode is a musical (tonal) orientation, and the fretboard form is a guitar (pattern) orientation. A mode cannot be determined until certain constraints are imposed. This is discussed further starting on page 68.

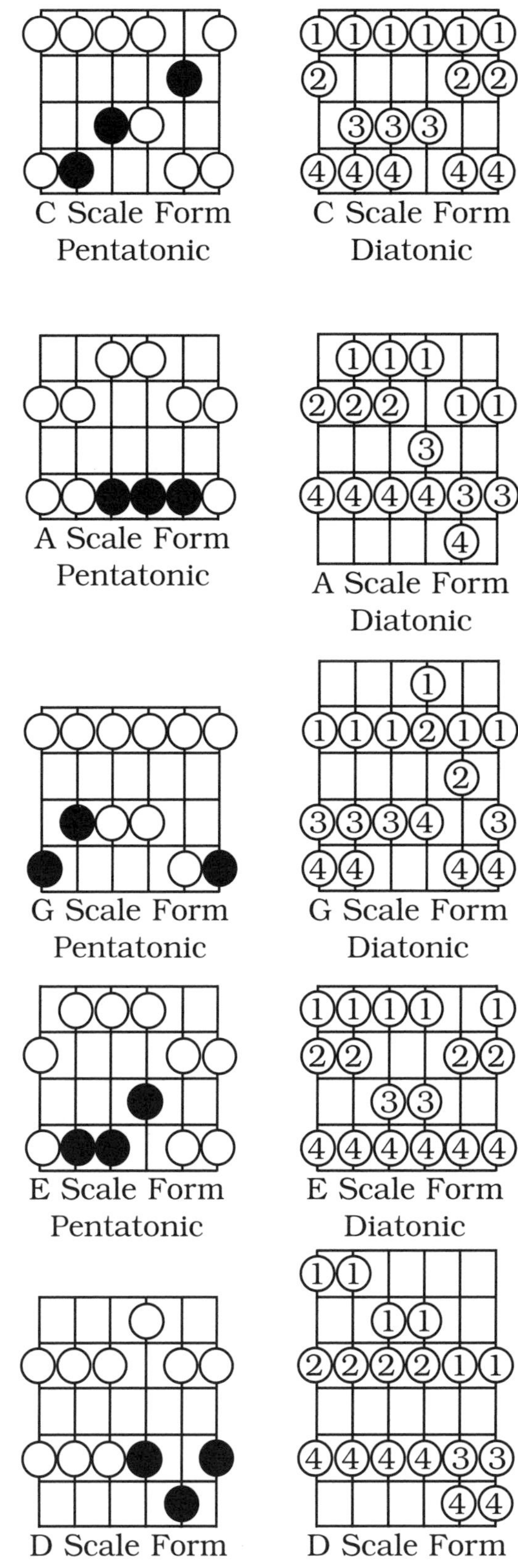

Scales - Diatonic

In the right hand column, the pentatonic scale forms have been darkened to expose the additional notes that make the diatonics, usually one per string. As presented, each Diatonic Scale Form will give access to a little over two **octaves,** or spans of eight notes, across the width of the neck. As with the pentatonics, these scale forms will later be connected together into more symmetrical groupings known as lead patterns to allow continuous access along the length of the neck as well as across it. This will enable the guitarist to span three or even four octaves on guitars with enough access.

The ability to visualize the available notes in any part of the fretboard is a primary part of being able to function in the various playing situations you will encounter. Knowing the forms is one part. Learning how they are used in combination with other elements of music is what will get you really stoked.

More embafflement. The term Diatonic means "two-toned" as in dialogue. This pertains to the two types of motion - half step and whole step - from one scale degree to the next. It has also been defined "dia" as in diameter - meaning *through* the tones. These derivations should be contrasted with the meaning of pentatonic as five-toned. This particular inconsistency has caused some people to refer to the Diatonic scales as **Heptatonic** or seven-toned, to better follow the more straight forward term Pentatonic.

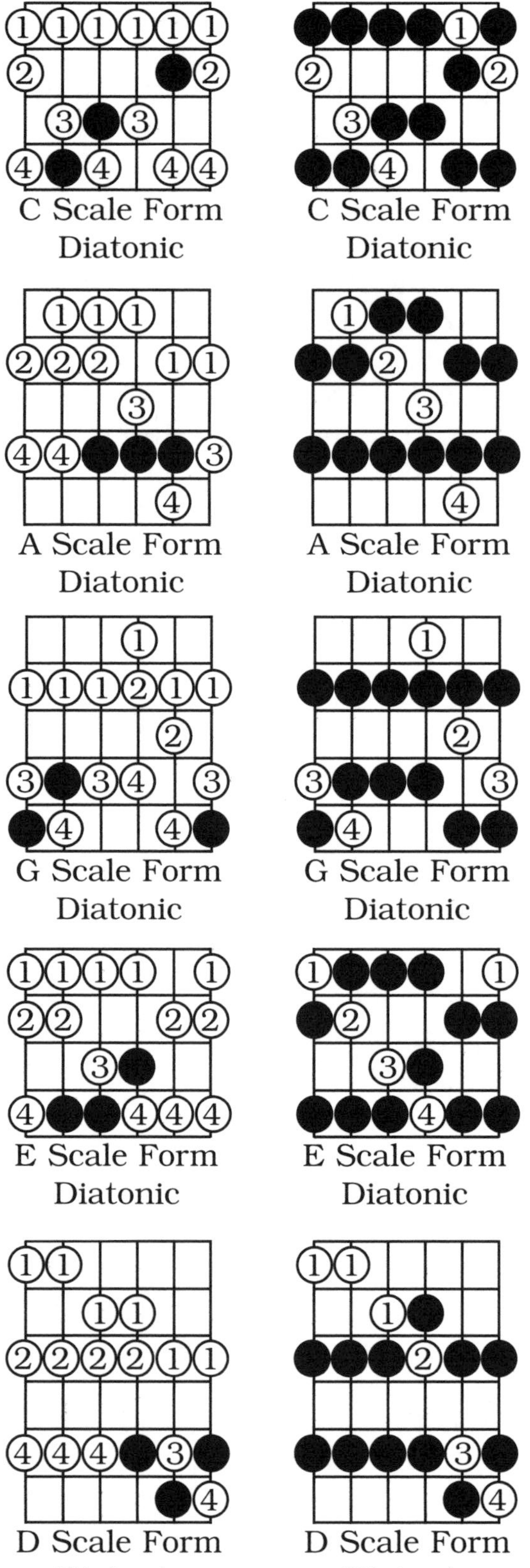

Scales - Diatonic

In a number of cases, there were various alternatives to choose from when deciding which notes should belong to which string in the scale forms. For example, the G form diatonic has a note on the third string that might just as easily be played on the fourth string with a pinky extension. There is also the question of which notes to include at the beginning and end of the scale form itself. The choices illustrated were made so as to best follow the same organization as the pentatonics, where the end of one scale form is the beginning of the next. This method helps the guitarist in the direction of visualizing the continuity of the forms along the length of the fretboard.

Learning the forms *across* the neck enables us to get to where we can also see the patterns *along* the neck. One benefit of this approach is that it can help the player avoid the habit of always playing the same scale form from the same degree on the same string resulting in a "scaley" and predictable type of sound when improvising. Guitarists, for some reason, tend to get hooked on the patterns themselves, and may have a harder time seeing the differences between practicing scales and true improvisation than other instrumentalists. The differences are taken up in an introductory fashion in the section on lead playing and in greater detail in Video I and Book III. The illustrations in the right hand column show that the end of one form is the same as the beginning of the next. In other words, each two adjacent forms have a row of notes in common. The left side graphs were included for the purpose of visual comparison. Practice every form until you can play each one by description in any position. For example, E form Diatonic, 3rd position, or D form Diatonic, 9th position and so on.

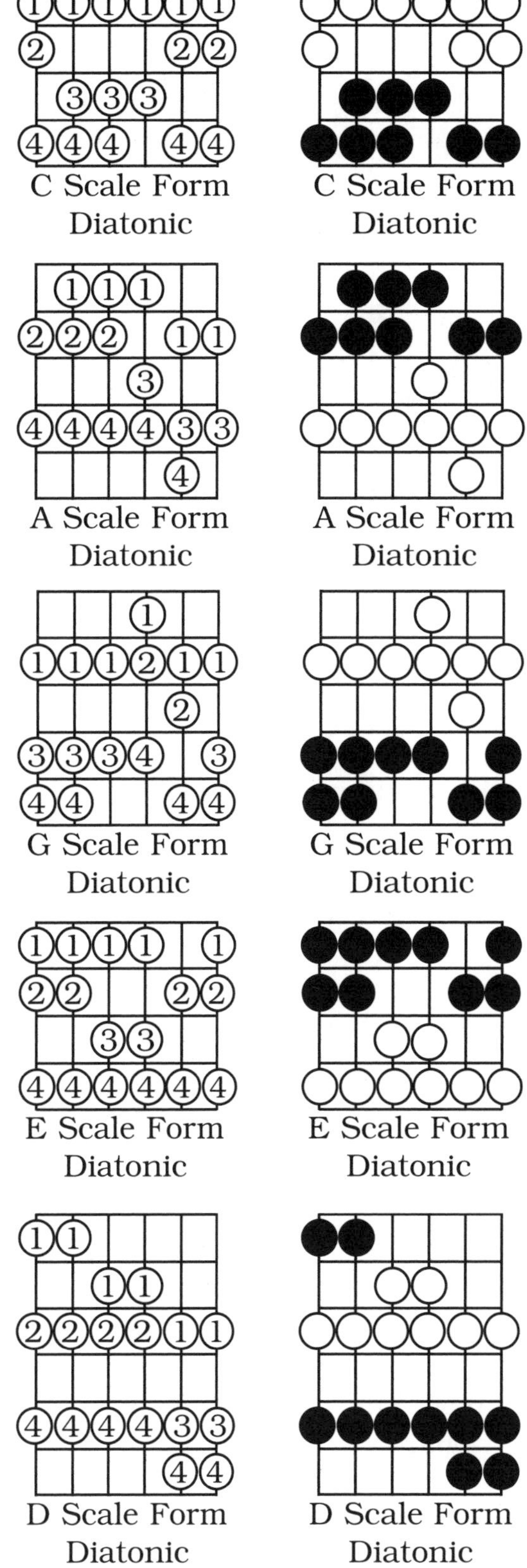

C Scale Form Diatonic — C Scale Form Diatonic

A Scale Form Diatonic — A Scale Form Diatonic

G Scale Form Diatonic — G Scale Form Diatonic

E Scale Form Diatonic — E Scale Form Diatonic

D Scale Form Diatonic — D Scale Form Diatonic

The CAGED Sequence - Diatonics

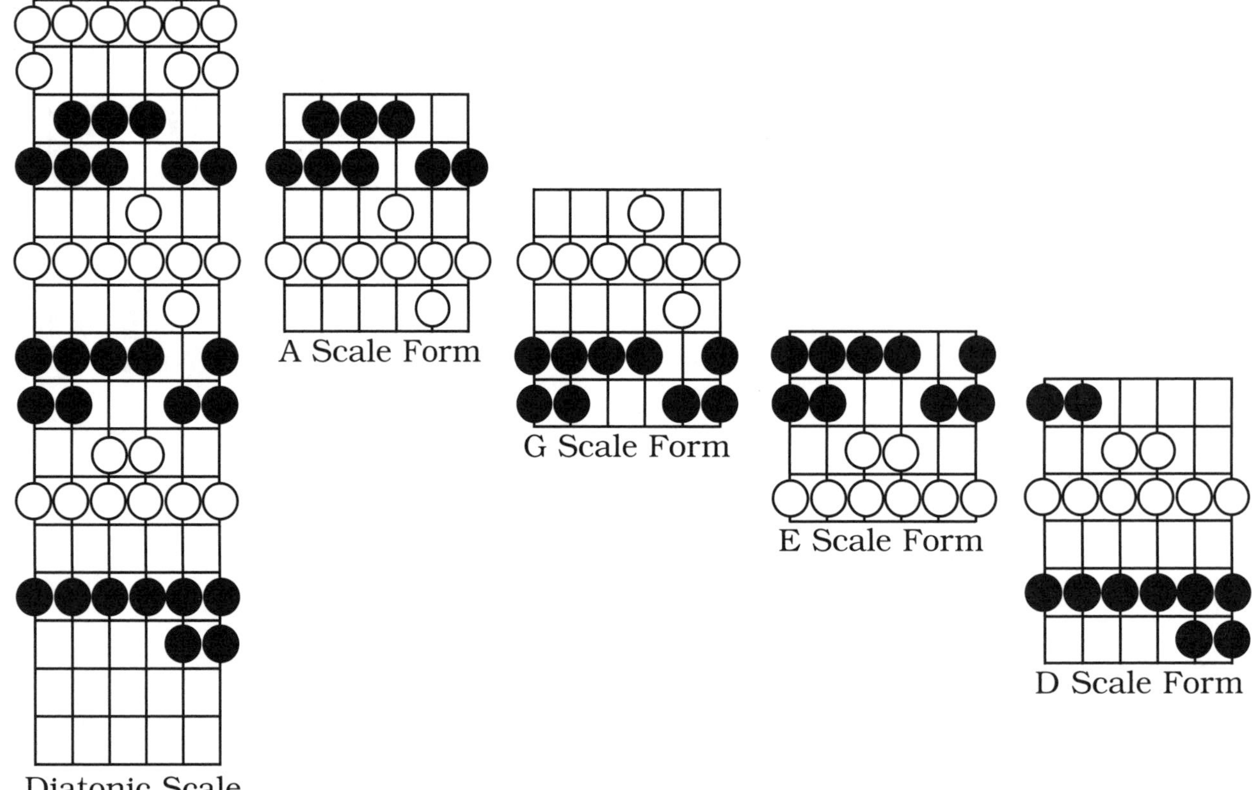

Diatonic Scale Forms End to End

When joined end to end, the Diatonic Scale Forms create a contiguous pattern of notes along the fretboard as depicted in the leftmost graph. As with the pentatonics, this view is intended as a bridge to enable you to visualize the scale forms and lead patterns as parts of the same whole.

In order for the player to make use of the entire range of these notes, they must again be reorganized to permit fluid motion from one position to another. This enables us to use a variety of techniques and combinations that would not otherwise be possible and also allows for greater access to the fretboard.

The next step is to divide the notes into more playable groupings based on the most regular or symmetrical groupings.

Since more notes are available with the diatonic scales than with the pentatonics, there are also more combinations possible.

There's some good news in the technical department, also. The diatonics provide a physical advantage to the guitarist in the way of notes per string. With respect to velocity and picking technique, what was relatively difficult to negotiate because of changing strings after only two notes with the pentatonic scale forms, will now be somewhat easier since the diatonics generally have three notes per string.

Diatonic Lead Patterns

The two basic Diatonic Lead Patterns are shown in the left hand column. On the right side, each has been divided into smaller sub-groupings. The sub-groups illustrate the three repeating seven note patterns of which each lead pattern is comprised. To extend the series to three complete octaves, three more notes have been added to each showing where the pattern repeats again, provided your fretboard has the real estate.

With the DLPs, and in order to access the third octave, a new technique will also be introduced to enable the move from one position to another on the same string. We will designate it a *crossover* since the fretting hand completely crosses over its previous position. This is detailed further on the next page along with the fingering recommendations.

In developing each Diatonic Lead Pattern and its variations, we are looking for the maximum symmetry in our choice of note groupings. The ones that are easiest to play and remember will get the most use. Diatonic Lead Patterns I and II correspond with the Pentatonic Lead Patterns, naturally. Where the pentatonics have five notes in each sub-group, the Diatonics have seven. When DLP I and II are combined, as with the pentatonics, they account for every note in the five basic Diatonic Scale Forms.

The numbers in the left hand graphs are the notes in order ascending, and the numbers in the right column show the seven notes of each sub-group.

> The scale forms are *irregular* string patterns in a single position. The lead patterns are *regular* string patterns in many positions.

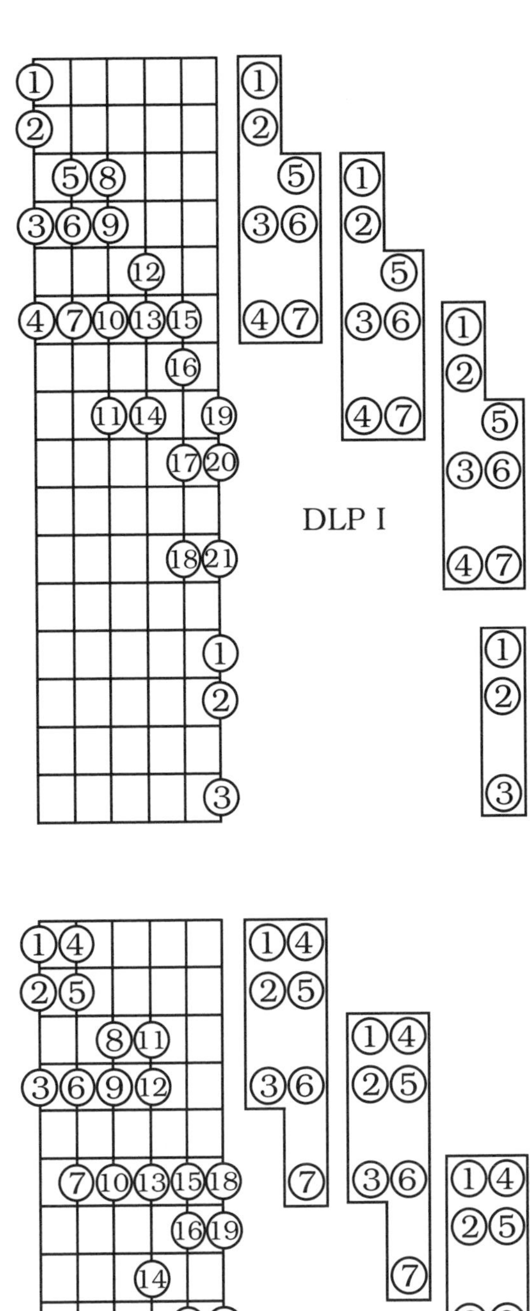

Lead Patterns - DLP I

These graphs illustrate Diatonic Lead Pattern I with appropriate fingerings and position changes as indicated by the numbers and arrows. Since only the index, middle, and pinky fingers of the fretting hand are used, certain combinations are more logical than others. The graph on the left side is DLP I ascending, and the one on the right is the descending combinations.

As with the pentatonics, when changing positions, you slide your finger (without fretting) along the string to the next position, play the note, and then continue on the next string. Lead patterns rely upon smooth position changes to work, without which, you become limited to the range of notes within one position, ie., scale forms.

Now might be a good time to remember that the way the notes are grouped on the fretboard as patterns is not necessarily going to be conducive to good musicianship. In fact, sometimes they can get in the way of our musical sensibilities. The ways phrases are constructed in a rhythmic and melodic sense are separate issues from these fundamental fretboard patterns. The patterns provide us with a structured way to get around the fretboard - that's all.

To access the guitar's three octave range, at some point we will have to change positions on the same string. This **crossover** technique means you take your hand completely off the fretboard and continue on to the next note on the same string. It takes practice, but this is another technique which is essential to gaining access to the entire fretboard as a whole. The alternative is to face countless possible combinations of finger patterns and position changes. The nature of the lead patterns suggests that the crossovers take place on the first string.

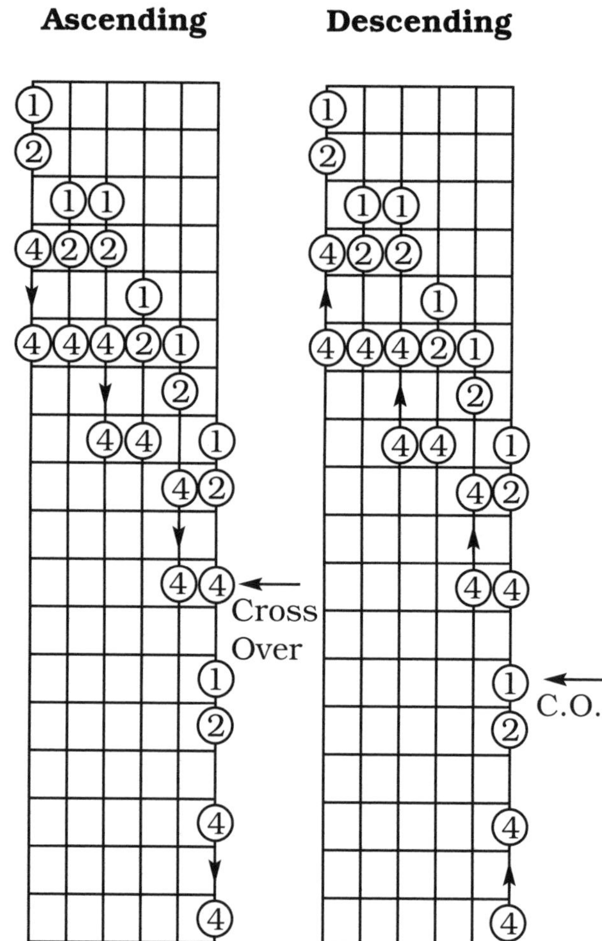

Lead Patterns - DLP II

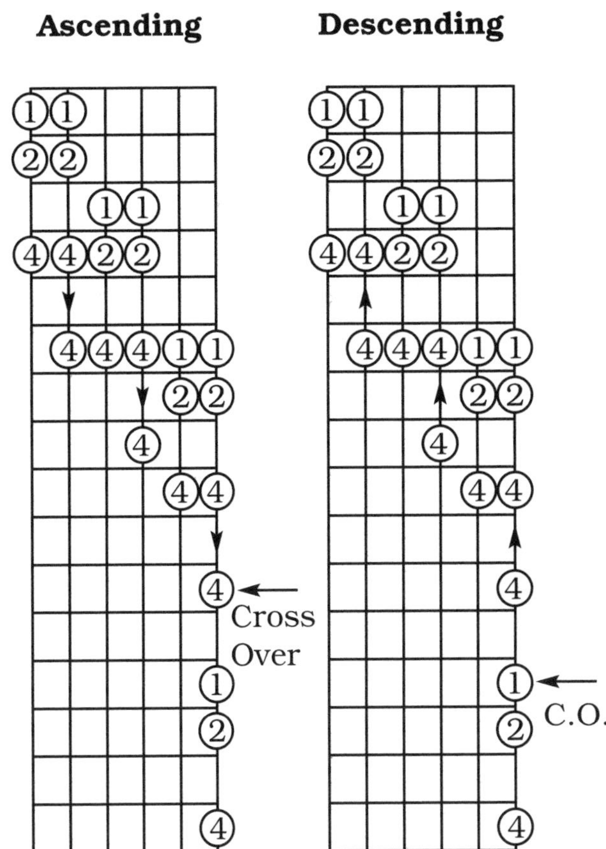

The fingerings and position changes for Diatonic Lead Pattern II are illustrated in the graphs on the right.

For learning purposes and overall coherence, the important thing is that the sub-groupings be symmetrical and repeatable.

The elegance of the tuning system can here again be realized by seeing that the basic string to position relationship of the sub-groups for DLP I ascending, is the opposite for DLP II ascending, and vice versa. In each sub-group of DLP I ascending, you play three notes, then change positions, then change strings and play three more notes. In DLP II ascending, the order is reversed. This time, you play three notes, change strings, play three more notes, then change positions. In other words, given a pattern and direction, you'll change strings first, then positions, or the other way around. It should be easy to appreciate this since you already saw it with the smaller PLPs in Part I.

As with Diatonic Lead Pattern I, a crossover on the first string is necessary to access a full three octaves worth of notes. Try to practice the DLPs slowly enough at first so the crossover notes are blended in with the rest of the scale tones and don't stand out.

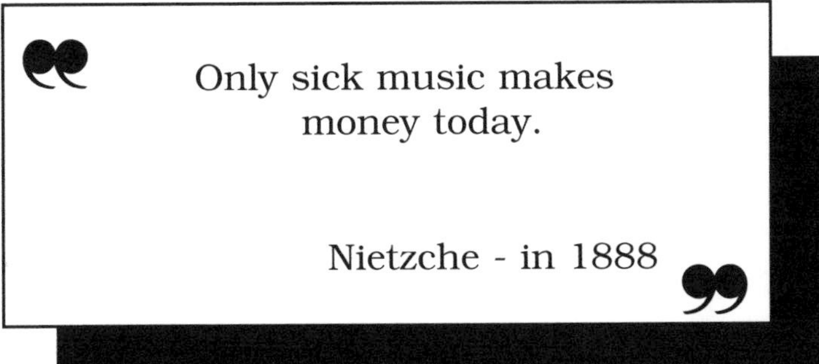

Lead Patterns - DLP I Variation

If you have an experimental nature, you will soon find that there are a variety of ways to get from one end of the fretboard to the other diatonically. But without some kind of strategy you are likely to encounter some frustration along the way.

There are a couple of obstacles both the fretboard and these types of patterns pose to the process of trial and error. The irregular placement of the marker dots and the smaller interval on the second and third string pair, make traversing the fretboard consistently inconsistent.

In addition, a significant difference between the lead patterns and the scale forms is that with the scale forms, you are only moving across the fretboard in one position and must only deal with usually one or two markers at a time. With the lead patterns, you are moving across the fretboard both widthwise and lengthwise. The number of these "helpful" dots becomes multiplied posing something of a visual challenge. Plus, every time you move across the G-B string pair, you have to compensate for the smaller interval with a position shift of one fret. For these reasons, the variations presented are limited and have been selected for their overall coherence and regularity.

Of the numerous possibilities, only two variations are being presented based upon their relative symmetry and easiness to learn. One for DLP I and one for DLP II.

The variation of DLP I at the right makes use of the third fretting finger. Beyond that, the position changes, fingering, and crossovers are the same as the preceding ones.

If you want to experiment, try position shifts and changing the fingerings. Sometimes it is easier to make the position shift on the first finger when descending.

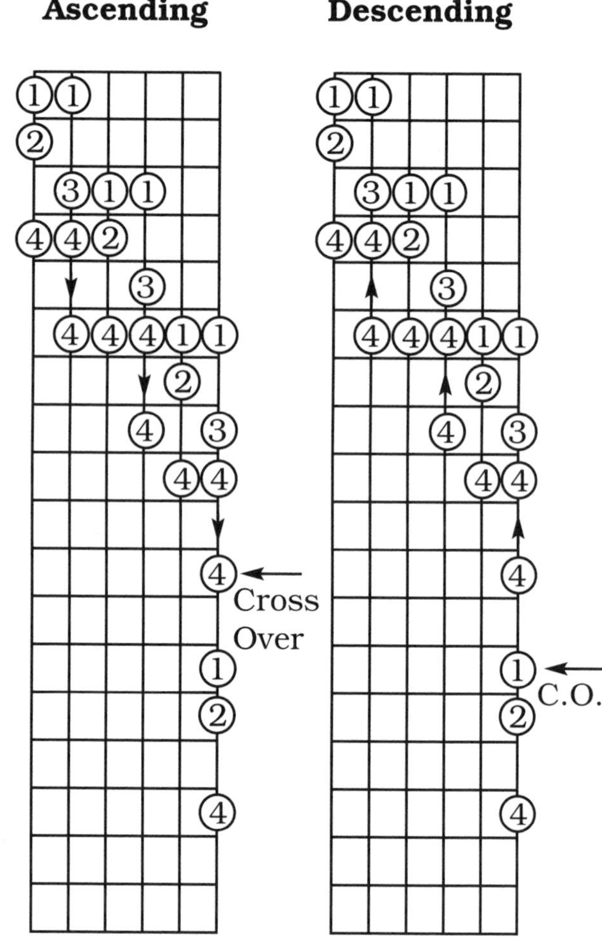

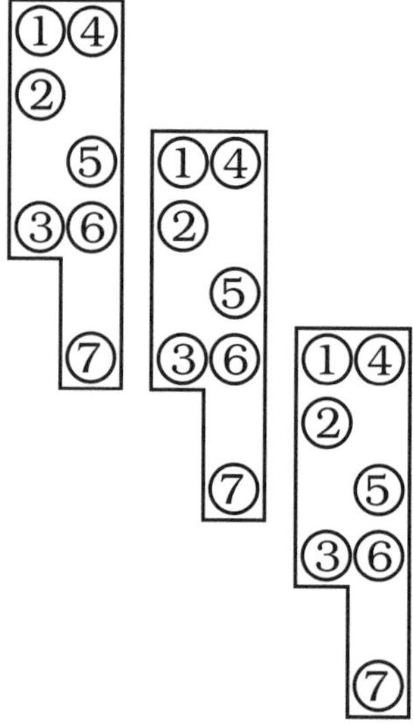

Lead Patterns - DLP II Variation

A nice variation of DLP II is illustrated on the right. An interesting aspect of this variation is that its sub-groups consist entirely of whole-steps. It is one of the most symmetrical forms possible on the guitar.

The top left graph shows the variation ascending, again using the fourth finger as the guide for the position changes. The right side is the same descending. It is also possible to substitute the third finger for the second in this pattern. As with the scale forms, the tonality or modality of the lead patterns is dependent on factors other than the fretboard form. A scale's tonal orientation, major, minor, etc., is normally going to be determined by the beginning and ending notes and the intervals in between them. What is presented so far has been the guitaristic orientation. **The notes you choose to begin and end on are independent of the pattern.** In other words, if you start the DLP II variation on the right, and play in eight note groupings, it will come out musically as a major scale or tonal orientation. If you opt to play the same pattern from the second degree, then the tonal orientation becomes Dorian, while the pattern remains the same. The same applies for the more musically coherent series of notes termed a phrase or melody. A melody is more complex and interesting than a simple scale, and its tonality or modality is equally independent of the fretboard pattern. You can play the same melody using a variety of scale forms or lead patterns.

The conflict between what is meant by mode on the guitar stems at least in part to the fact that most patterns played ascending and descending begin and end on the sixth string. I guess that alone, in the minds of a some folks, is enough to determine the tonal orientation.

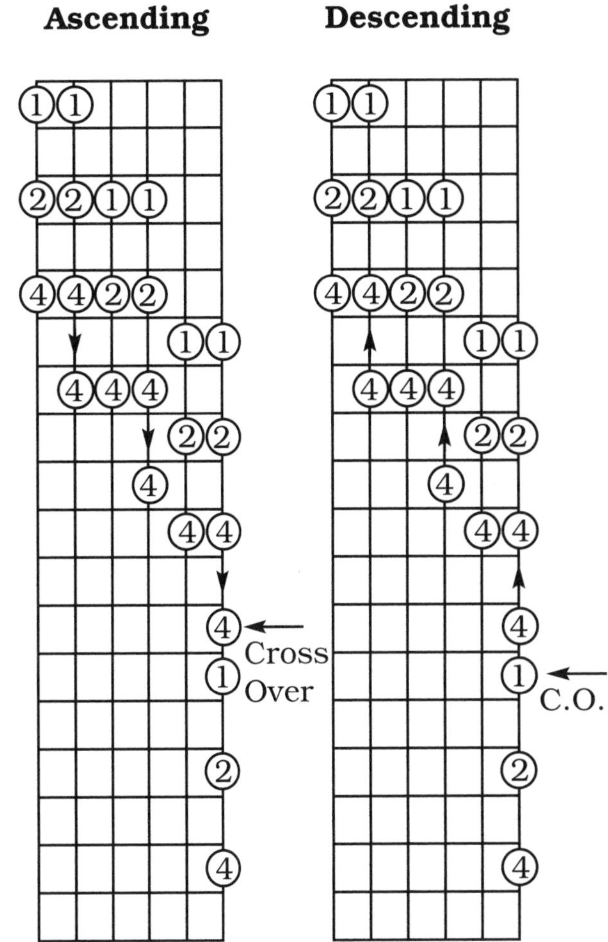

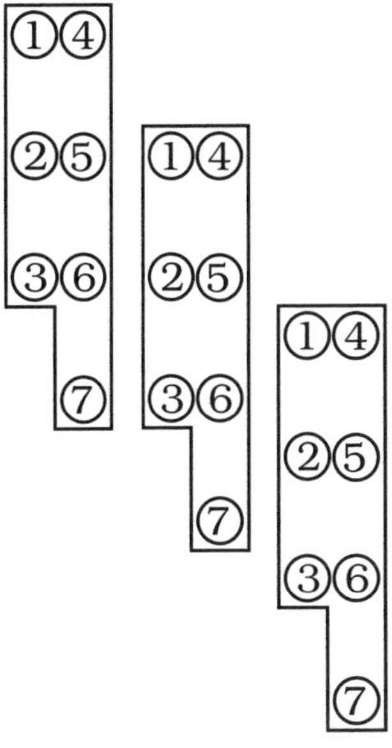

Naming the Diatonic Lead Patterns

The method of naming the Diatonic Lead Patterns is slightly different from the one used for the pentatonics. The Diatonics are still referenced by specific chord forms, but DLP I is more directly located with respect to the reference form. This makes naming the scale one step easier than with the pentatonics.

As before, DLP I is referenced with respect to the C chord form as shaded in the left side graph. A partial bar symbol has been included as a visual aid. If you count up the C form to the fourth position properly, you will get the E Chord. Therefore Diatonic Lead Pattern 1 from the same position is also in the key of E when phrased appropriately. For this purpose, tone centers, have been provided. The targets represent the tone centers (or roots) for the Major tonal orientation.

In the right side graph, Pentatonic Lead Pattern I has been darkened to illustrate where it is in relation to the Diatonic Lead Pattern.

The notes with an "X" belong to the Pentatonic Lead Pattern, but they are not shared with the Diatonic due to pattern inconsistencies. Since DLP 1 is referenced by the C form chord, again it will be designated as the C Diatonic Group.

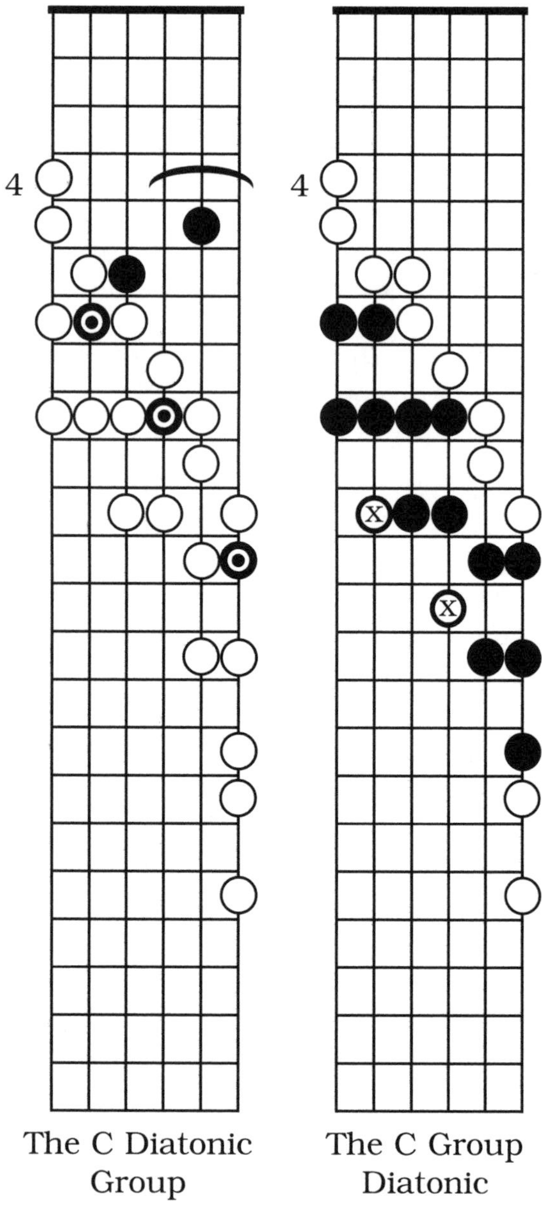

The C Diatonic Group

Reference Form Darkened

The C Group Diatonic

PLP I Darkened

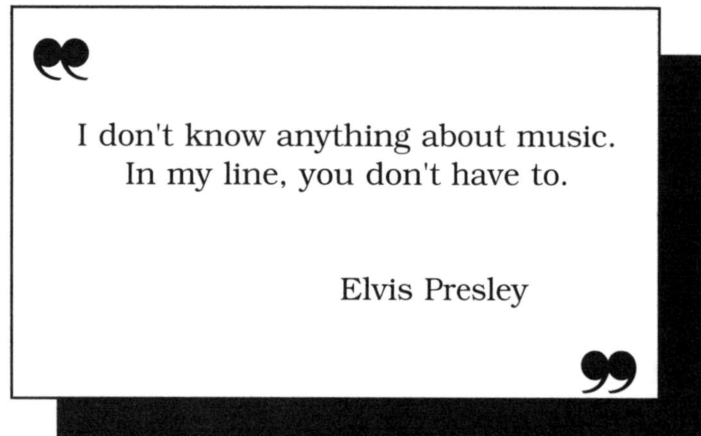

Naming the Diatonic Lead Patterns

Diatonic Lead Pattern II is referenced by the G chord form as shaded in the left side graph. However, as with the pentatonics, the reference form is offset from the bar position. In contrast with DLP I, the pattern does not actually start at the bar where the chord form derives its position for naming purposes. If you count up a G chord form to the second position, you will arrive at the A chord. Therefore DLP II from the same reference area, which is the 4th position, is also in the key of A. The targets provide the **tonics,** or tone centers, for the Major mode.

Remember that when playing scales, it is customary to start and end on a tonic. When phrasing or producing melodies, you don't have to start or end on the tonic necessarily, but a phrase or melody must be constructed in a way such that it has tonal orientation. Sometimes this means starting it on one tone center, and ending on another to better follow the progression of chords. What this implies is a kind of tonal "target," better known as a **target note**. In actual usage, the fretboard patterns become little more than a vehicle for reliably finding your way around the guitar neck while you develop combinations of rhythmic, melodic, articulative, iterative and other more musical elements. Or, perhaps just search for target notes to arrive at on time. This process of constructing different types of phrases from various *components* is taken up in detail in Vol. III.

In the right side graph, PLP II has been darkened to illustrate where it is in relation to the Diatonic Lead Pattern. Again, the "x" notes belong to the pentatonic form, but they are not used in the same position in the Diatonic because of inconsistencies in the patterns. Since DLP 2 is referenced by the G chord form, it will, of course, be designated as the G (Diatonic) Group.

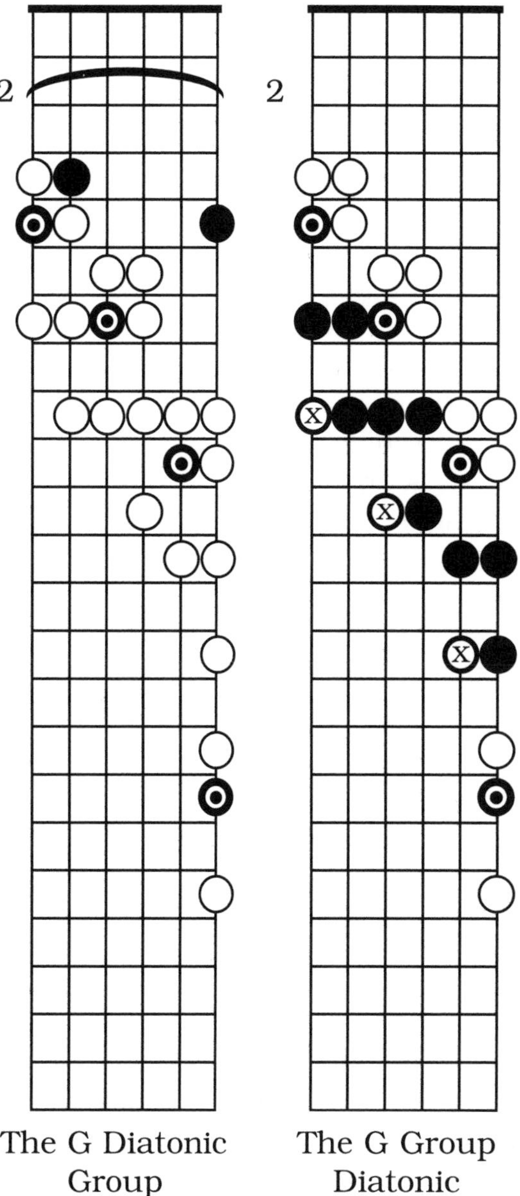

The G Diatonic Group — Reference Form Darkened

The G Group Diatonic — PLP II Darkened

Major

Modes

With the introduction of Modes, we move further away from thinking in terms of fretboard forms, and toward specific tonal orientations. The shape and symmetry of the pattern is now subordinate to the formula and target notes. Given the seven notes of the Diatonic Scale, there are seven Modes. The two most common are Major (Ionian) and Minor (Aeolian). As with chords, the Major Mode is considered a reference, and the other modes' formulas are discussed in terms of how they relate to it. The formula is more theoretical, and the targets are more practical. The formula for the Major Mode is 1, 2, 3, 4, 5, 6 and 7, or no alterations, of a key.

The guitar's tuning provides two fundamentally different approaches to playing in the different Modes: scale forms and lead patterns. In order to play in a Mode, one or the other must be oriented (targeted) toward a particular degree. That tone center combined with the form and position produces an identifiable Mode *relative to the patterns.*

The following are examples of Modes *relative to a key.* In C Major, C is the tonic and the key signature has no accidentals. The notes in C Major are C D E F G A & B. In A (relative) Minor, the tonic is A, and the key signature is also no sharps or flats. The notes in A Minor are A B C D E F & G. In D Dorian, the tone center is D, and the key signature is the same. The notes in D Dorian are D E F G A B & C. In each case, the notes are all the same but the tone center, and the intervals between each note changes, therefore, the Mode changes. At the right are examples of the Major Mode in the key of C played through both the scale forms and lead patterns. The idea at this point is to play from and toward the target notes, which are illustrated appropriately.

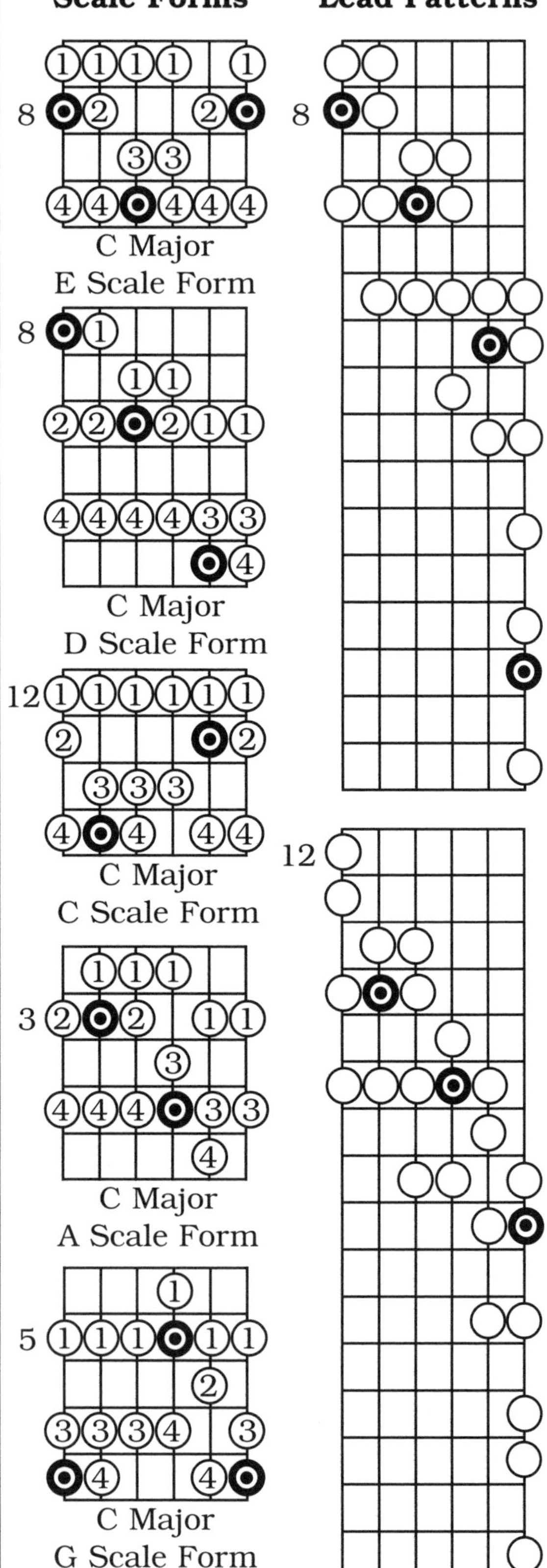

Natural Minor

The next most common mode is the Natural Minor with its variations Harmonic and Melodic Minor.

Relative to Major, the formula for Natural Minor is 1, 2, b3, 4, 5, b6, & b7 (or just b3 b6 & b7). With Major as the reference point, Minor can be considered the sixth of seven Modes. As with the Majors, you can play a Minor Scale using any of the scale forms or lead patterns if you start and end on the correct target note. In other words, what makes it a Minor, or any other Mode, is less a matter of which guitar pattern you use, than how you use it. This is a fairly important concept, and one that tends to distinguish Fretboard Logic from many (perhaps most) other guitar methods.

The Major and Minor Modes are so closely related in practical application, that the corresponding one is termed **relative.** For G Major, E Minor is termed the Relative Minor and vice versa. Further material on keys and key signatures has been reserved for later and takes up an entire section.

For the examples on the right, we'll use a new key to go along with the new Mode. Starting with G Major as our reference, the tonic is G, and the key signature is F#. The notes in G Major would be G A B C D E and F#. In E (relative) Minor, the tonic is E and the key signature is the same as G Major (F#). That makes the notes in E Minor, E F# G A B C and D as shown in the examples on the right. *Don't forget that the target is degree 1, the next note is degree 2, etc.*

The conventions for ascending and descending the lead patterns vary, but what makes the most sense is to consistently use a whole step for the position change. There are a number of variations for the Natural Minor lead patterns, and a little experimentation will produce them.

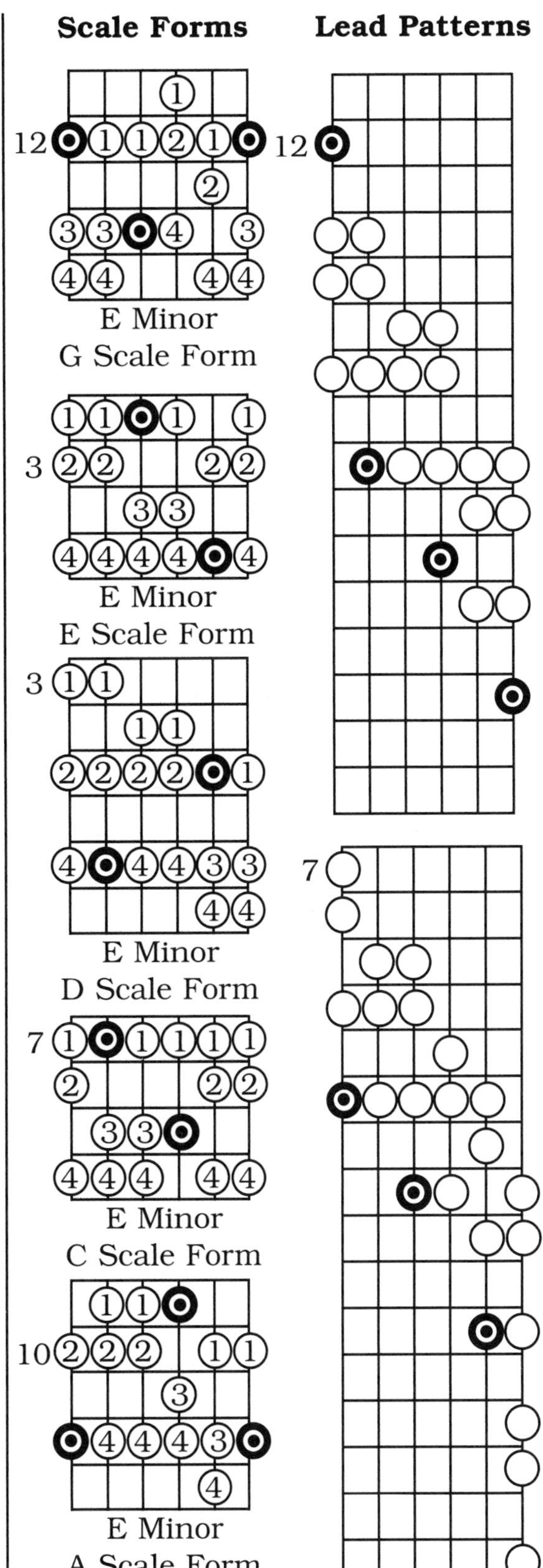

Harmonic Minor

The Harmonic Minor is one of the more exotic sounding variations. It has a character that is interpreted by many as a classical or neo-classical type of sound.

Relative to Major, the formula for Harmonic Minor is 1 2 b3 4 5 b6 & 7 (b3 & b6). However, relative to Natural Minor, we've "raised" the 7th degree. This is not unlike ending a Minor Scale on a Major note, or *interval*, to be more precise. This apparent change in tonality is what gives Harmonic Minor its spice. The raised seventh also produces advantages when building chords upon the scale tones which is also discussed in the last book in a section on chords in progression. The examples on the right are in the key of F# (Harmonic) Minor. The relative key of A Major has a key signature of F# C# and G# with the A as tonic. F# Natural Minor has the same key signature, F# C# and G# with a tone center of F#. From there, the Harmonic Minor additionally raises the seventh degree from E, to E# (not F). So the notes in F# Harmonic Minor are F# G# A B C# D and E#. On the right, each of the scale forms has been altered so that the pattern reflects this #7. In some cases the change is enough so it makes it difficult to tell the scale form from which it was derived. From a technical standpoint, the scale forms are fairly irregular and therefore somewhat more difficult than average. Also, with the D and C forms, there is a certain amount of pattern overlap, which is unavoidable. Both lead patterns have an interesting and elegant symmetry of alternating fours and threes on adjacent string pairs. Again, variations can be derived with a little experimentation. The ones presented have been chosen either for their coherence within the context of the fretboard's pattern organization, or because of their inherent symmetry.

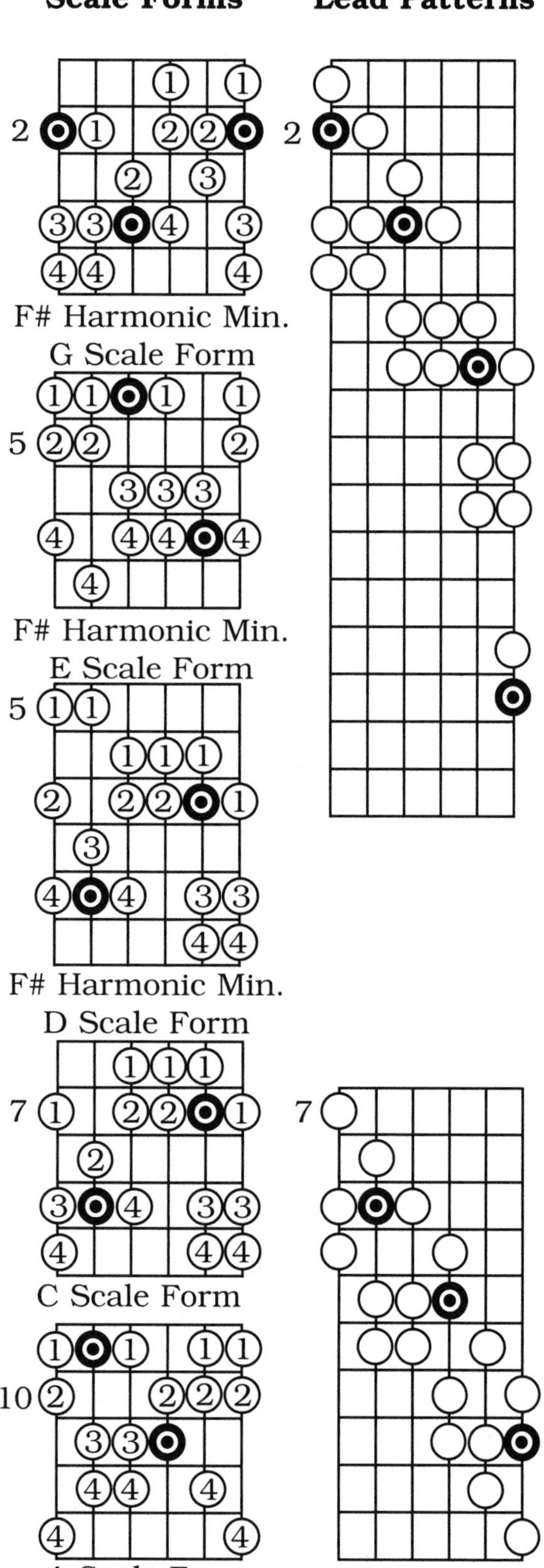

Melodic Minor

The first thing to know about Melodic Minor is that it is played differently ascending and descending. Relative to the Natural Minor, it is altered during ascent, but unaltered in descent. Relative to Major, its formula ascending is 1 2 b3 4 5 6 & 7 (or b3 only). Relative to Natural Minor, both the sixth and seventh degrees are raised. This makes it even more Major-influenced than the Harmonic Minor, since now the last three notes are part of a Major tonal orientation. It is this dual nature that makes the Melodic Minor so rich and yet versatile. Descending, it is exactly the same as Natural Minor. For that reason, **only the ascending part with the altered scale tones is illustrated.** The descending Natural Minor forms will be the same as on page 69. In order to make the connection between the ascending and descending forms, the ones on the right have been rendered in the same key and mode as before: E Minor.

Because of the alterations and the difference in the descending tones, the Melodic Minor might be considered slightly more difficult than the average Scale or Mode. So if you're having trouble with them, you might limit yourself to just a couple of the easier forms at first. The lead patterns are nicely symmetrical as were the Harmonic Minors, and should not present too much in the way of difficulty except for the reaches.

Major and Minor tonal orientations dominate western, or twelve-toned, music. Major is generally interpreted as happy or lighthearted, and Minor is usually interpreted as sad, serious or somber. To the western ear, other Modes may sound exotic, foreign, or even somewhat off center tonally, depending on the listener. The result is that most of us tend to hear other Modes as either (more or less) Major or Minor sounding.

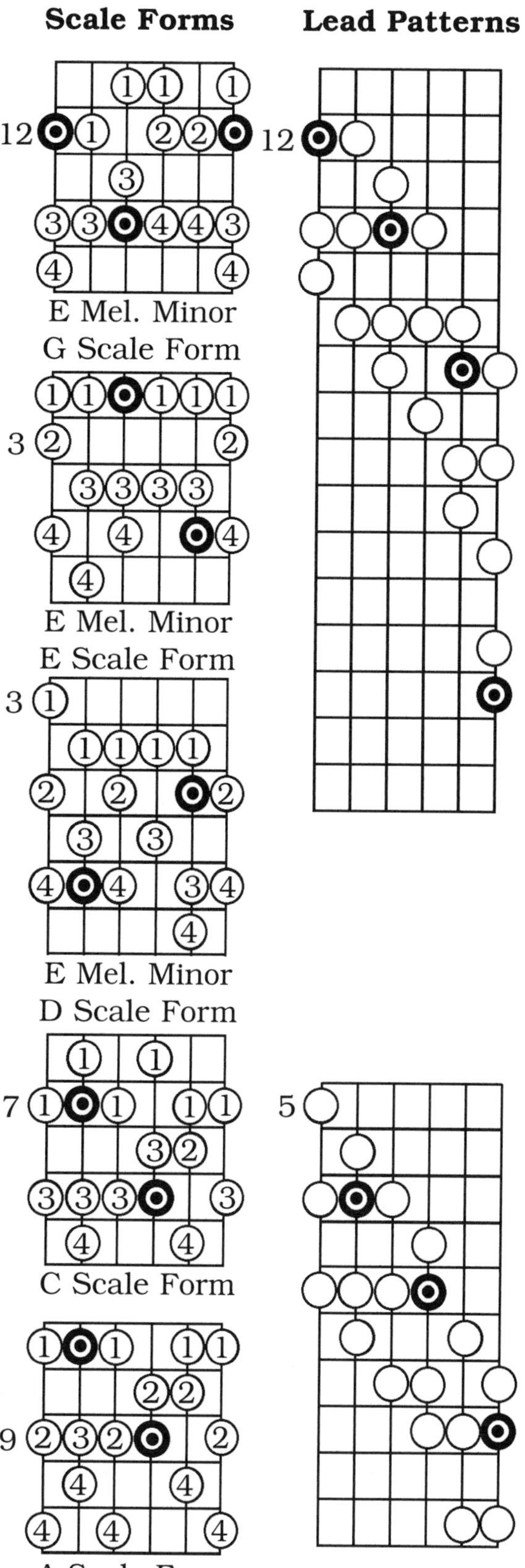

Dorian

In academic discussions on the subject, the Major and Minor tonal orientations should not deemed to be precisely *modal* in nature. The terms Modal and Modes have come to refer to tonal orientations other than Major and Minor, which are deemed *tonalities*. In other words, Dorian, Phrygian, Lydian, Mixolydian and Locrian are usually what is meant when someone refers to a Mode or a Modal sound.

The formula for Dorian, again, relative to Major, is 1 2 b3 4 5 6 & b7 (or b3 and b7). Relative to minor, the formula for the Dorian mode is #6.

Using Major as a reference, or degree number one, we consider a Mode to be one where the tonal orientation is toward a degree other than the first. That being the case, given a Major key, the tonal orientation of the Dorian mode will be toward degree number two; the tonal orientation of the Phrygian mode will be toward degree number three; Lydian will be targeted toward degree number four; Mixolydian is oriented toward degree number five; Aeolian (natural minor) is oriented degree number six; and the Locrian mode will be targeted toward degree number seven.

As discussed previously, counting up a scale form to a position produces the name of a scale and key with respect to Major. For example, if you count the E Diatonic scale form to the third position (don't forget the second finger reference) you have the key of G - which was assumed to be Major. By playing the same scale form starting from the second degree, or the fourth finger, and back toward the same degree, you have changed the tonal orientation and Mode to A Dorian you still have the same scale form, but now a different Mode and target note. This is what is illustrated on the right.

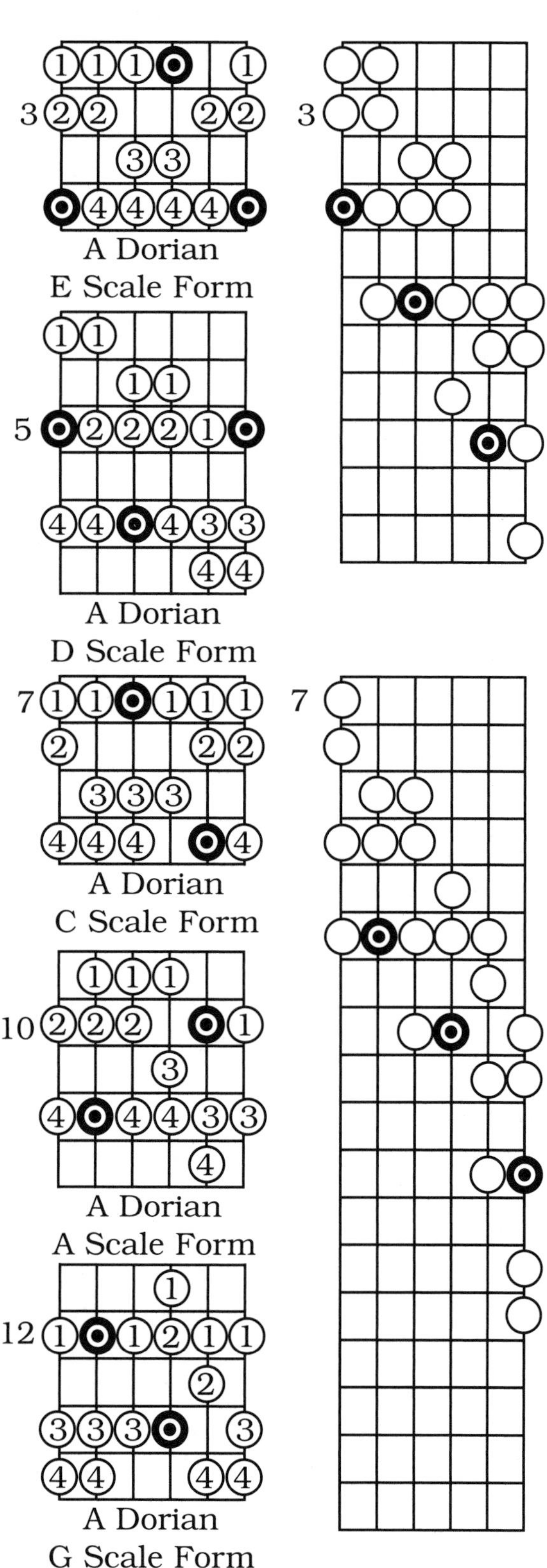

Phrygian

The formula for Phrygian, relative to Major is 1 b2 b3 4 5 b6 & b7. Keeping the same key signature, F#, and moving the tonic up one more degree produces the B Phrygian mode. As stated before, the modes tend to line up as either more Major or minor sounding. I suspect the last interval, (leading tone to tonic) has most impact on this determination. If the last interval is a whole step, then the mode comes across as minor sounding. If the interval is a half step, then it sounds more Major.

The previous mode, Dorian, is the easiest to classify this way. It has a whole step for the final interval, and a distinctly minor flavor.

The Phrygian mode also sports the whole step interval prior to tonic, and has a minor feel to it. It is interesting to note a melodic/harmonic contrast in practical application. The so-called "Spanish Minor" gets its effect from playing a Phrygian melodic modality against a Major harmonic backing chord. (Yes, that is an oversimplification.) But it is not unlike the so-called "Blues Minor" effect of playing pentatonic minor with a b5 against Major one, four and five chords in a key, but, as usual, we're getting ahead of ourselves.

The Lydian mode has the half step interval, and so comes across as Major-sounding. Mixolydian seems like melodic minor in reverse. It starts out with a definite major sound but ends up with the whole step interval, so draw your own conclusions.

Locrian has the whole step interval at the end, and so comes off sounding minor. To demonstrate this effect, play a Major chord and then one of the Major sounding modes, say, Lydian. Then try a minor chord, with, say, Dorian. Reverse this and you'll see they don't match up as well.

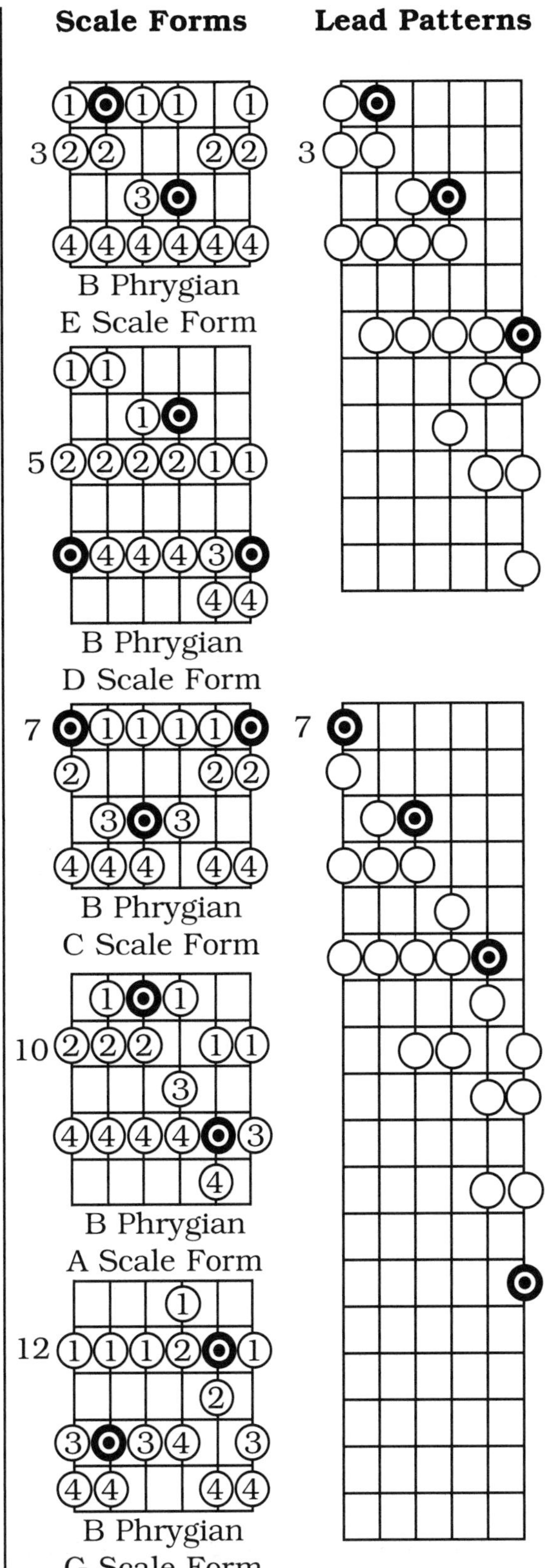

Lydian

The formula for Lydian is 1 2 3 #4 5 6 &7 (or just #4). Again, retaining the same key signature and moving the tonic up one more degree produces the C Lydian mode. This time you may have noticed that the next degree was only a half step from the last, but it is the fourth degree with respect to G Major nevertheless.

Because they are often used interchangeably in other method books, the meanings of the terms Scale and Mode should be contrasted. A Scale is a succession of notes of a Key, as opposed to a Chord which is the simultaneous sounding of the notes of a key. A Mode differs from a Scale in that a tonal orientation is specified instead of assumed. Think of it like this. Someone says "The song's in G." Without further explanation, we would all assume G with a Major tonality. However, if the key was G and the tonal orientation was stipulated as Dorian, then it is considered to be a Mode as opposed to just a Scale (as in series of notes played) or Key (as in group of notes specified by a key signature).

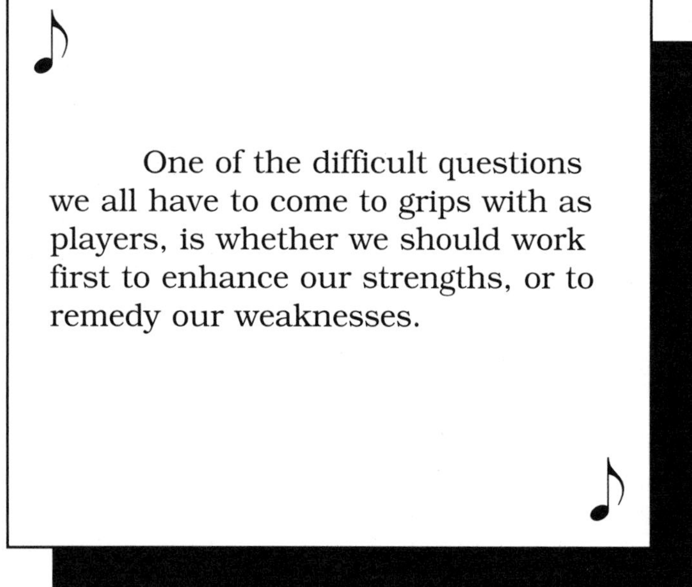

One of the difficult questions we all have to come to grips with as players, is whether we should work first to enhance our strengths, or to remedy our weaknesses.

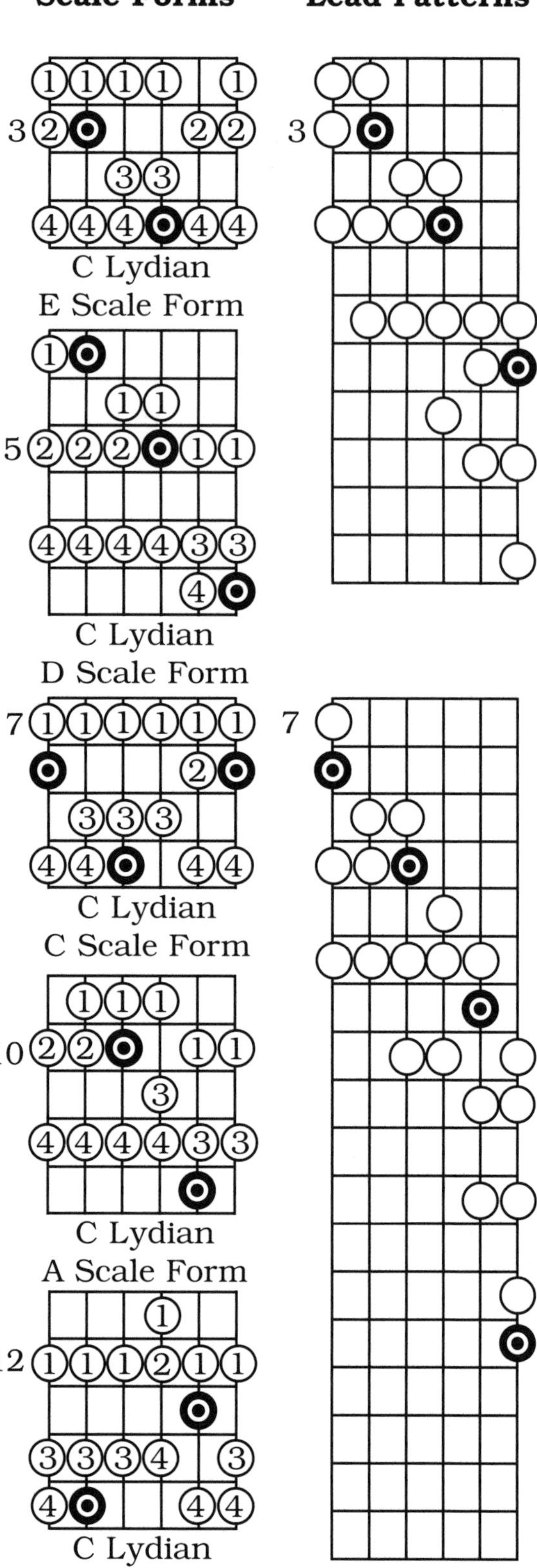

C Lydian
E Scale Form

C Lydian
D Scale Form

C Lydian
C Scale Form

C Lydian
A Scale Form

C Lydian
G Scale Form

Mixolydian

The formula for Mixolydian is 1 2 3 4 5 6 & b7 (or just b7). Playing with a key signature of F# and a tonal orientation of the fifth degree relative to Major produces the Mixolydian Mode. The ambiguous nature of this Mode makes it useful as a contrast to Major. The ending of the Pachelbel Canon in D (DVD II v 2.0) has an interesting example of Mixolydian working within a Major environment. It makes you take notice.

The question asked most when students become able to function with the scale forms and lead patterns is "What scale form goes with what chord form(s)?" This question, although natural to ask, is a gross oversimplification. It is something akin to asking "What colors go well together on a canvas to make a painting?" It is a matter of style, taste, technique, objective, etc.

An obvious response would be to say "Play Major sounding melodic material in a Major key, and minor against minor. It isn't wrong, it just avoids dealing with more complex and interesting issues. It is brought up right now, because most students, when they get to this point in the proceedings, want to cut to the chase and start tearing up the fretboard as a lead player. And don't let me or anyone else stop you, either. But my job is to keep some kind of coherence and structure to each book, so the subject of lead playing is reserved for Volume III and the videos. At least part of the problem is that the question begs for some conditions, such as a stylistic determination. In this section it would be premature to start associating with artists, techniques or styles and would no doubt lessen the focus. If you experiment a little, you will find many things that work. But to really answer the question without putting too fine a point on it, if it sounds right, then it is right.

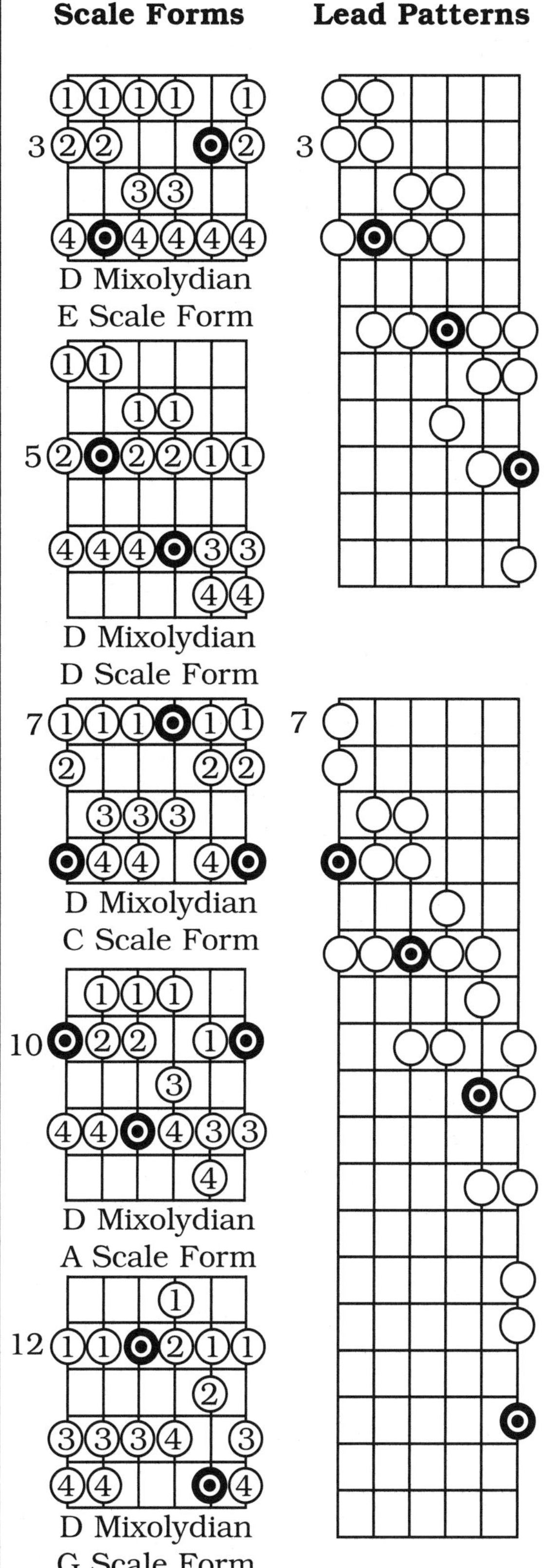

D Mixolydian
E Scale Form

D Mixolydian
D Scale Form

D Mixolydian
C Scale Form

D Mixolydian
A Scale Form

D Mixolydian
G Scale Form

Locrian

Aeolian was discussed under the name Minor, so the next and last Mode is Locrian. The formula is 1 b2 b3 4 b5 b6 & b7. As you might imagine, through the centuries and around the world, different Modalities have gone in and out of fashion. The Locrian tonal orientation is one that doesn't seem to get used much nowadays, but that can change. Again, you can access each degree of a mode by simply counting from one note to the next within a form starting with the target note.

Recap

As patterns, the Diatonic Scale Forms extend the Pentatonics just as they were pattern extensions of the five basic chord forms. The Diatonic Scale Forms can also be combined and divided into symmetric halves to produce lead patterns as before. The Diatonic Lead Patterns are referenced for naming by the C and G chord forms, just as with the Pentatonics.

In contrast to this patternistic orientation, the scales can have specific notes targeted so that a tonal orientation overrides the fretboard forms in terms of precedence. This tonal orientation is usually termed *tonality* when referring to Major or Minor or *modality* when referring to Dorian, Phrygian, Lydian, Mixolydian or Locrian. Natural minor has two common variations called Harmonic and Melodic Minor. Although the formulas for the modes are relative to Major as a rule, the formulas for Harmonic and Melodic minor are often referenced relative to natural minor.

As with the different styles of music, the way Modes are perceived by the listener varies with each person. Depending on the ear of the beholder, each Mode will have a more or less Major or Minor sound.

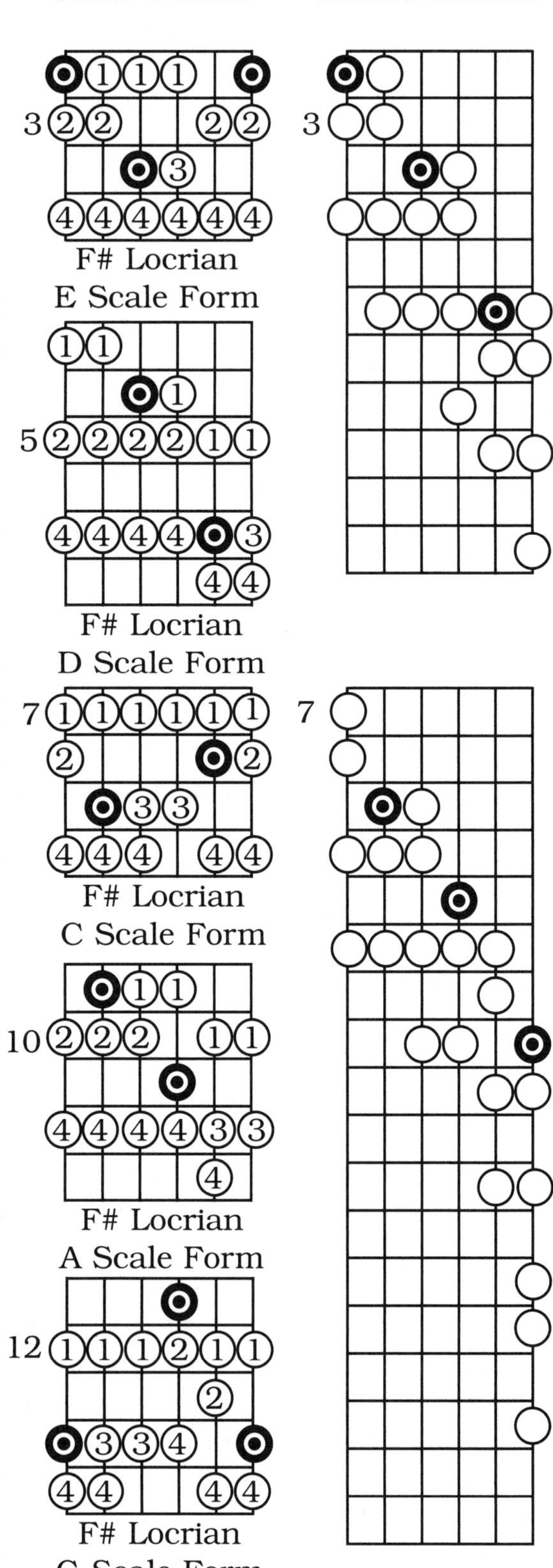

Arpeggios

Arpeggios are hybrid tone groupings. They can be thought of as chords that are played like scales, one note after another. Their formulas do not differ from chords, and so are not iterated in this section. On the guitar they are derived both from individual chord forms, often with finger extensions, and from connecting adjacent forms. The term many pick-style guitarists now use for them is *sweeps*, based on the action of the pick "sweeping" across the strings, but the method of right hand execution is up to the individual player. The Arpeggios presented in this section are illustrated only once for both ascending and descending order. Whenever two notes occur on the same string, the execution strategy is to hammer-on or pull-off the following note depending on the direction. This enables the right hand to pick or pluck each string only one time each way. The arrow groupings indicate the distance in frets for position changes.

Virtually any chord form can be an Arpeggio, so some constraints have been applied. Rather than duplicate every chord form previously illustrated, we will use only the triads and sevenths that naturally lend themselves to arpeggiation. The best ones are those that provide more than one complete octave and are reasonably easy to execute. The D major form, in contrast, starts on the fourth string and spans only one octave even with a position change. So it is not included here as an example of a form that is ideally arpeggiated per se. The forms that best lend themselves to arpeggiation are C, A, G, and E. Barred forms have been drawn as individual notes. The tonics are represented by the darker circles. In the right hand column, several forms are combined in a manner similar to the lead patterns to provide a range of three octaves.

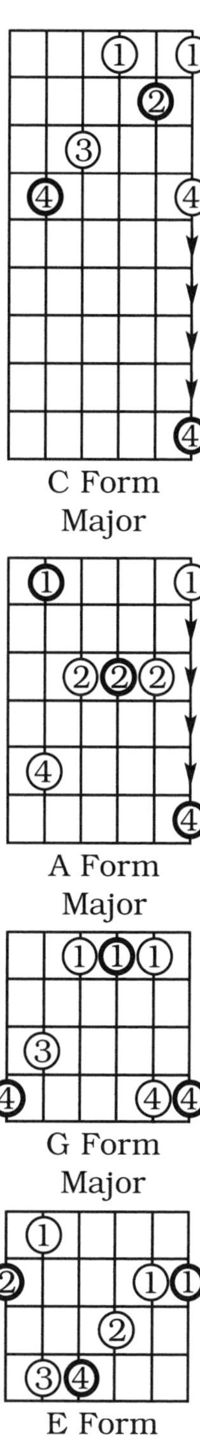

C Form Major

A Form Major

G Form Major

E Form Major

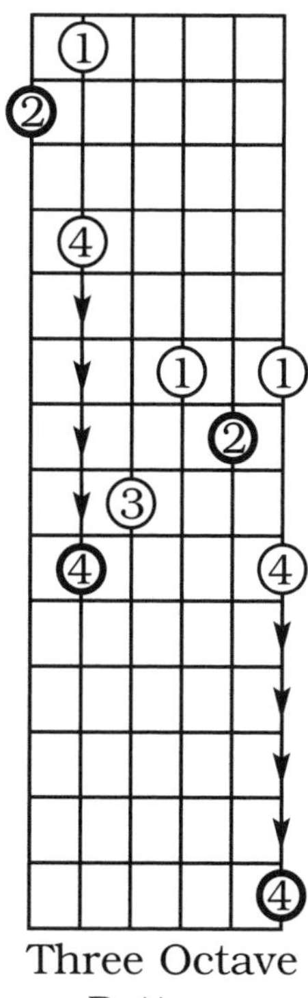

Three Octave Pattern

Arpeggios - Minors

The two-octave Minor Arpeggios are illustrated in the graphs on the left and are based on the C A G and E Minor chord forms.

With the C and A Minor forms, the arpeggiation begins on the 5th string and concludes with a four fret position change on the first string.

You may have noticed by now that many Arpeggio forms are heavily reliant on the pinky finger. The index and especially the pinky are in key locations since they are on each end of the fretting hand. As a result they are often called upon to make reaches and jumps that the middle ones aren't in a position to.

The G minor form uses both a four-string index bar and a three-string pinky bar. Don't forget that when two or more adjacent notes are shown with the same finger it implies a bar covering the included notes. They are drawn individually to better convey how they're played.

Again, it usually helps to increase overall playability to hammer-on and pull-off notes that are on the same string when playing arpeggios. For example, with the G minor form, a hammer-on would occur on the third string ascending, and a pull-off when descending.

The E minor form can be barred with the index finger across all six strings, and you will probably find this form to be the easiest to play and use at first.

The graph on the top right is a three-octave minor arpeggio pattern. It should be emphasized again that almost any chord form can be expressed as a one-octave arpeggio. There are numerous single octave arpeggio forms that can be derived from parts of the ones presented, which are not illustrated. Think first three strings.

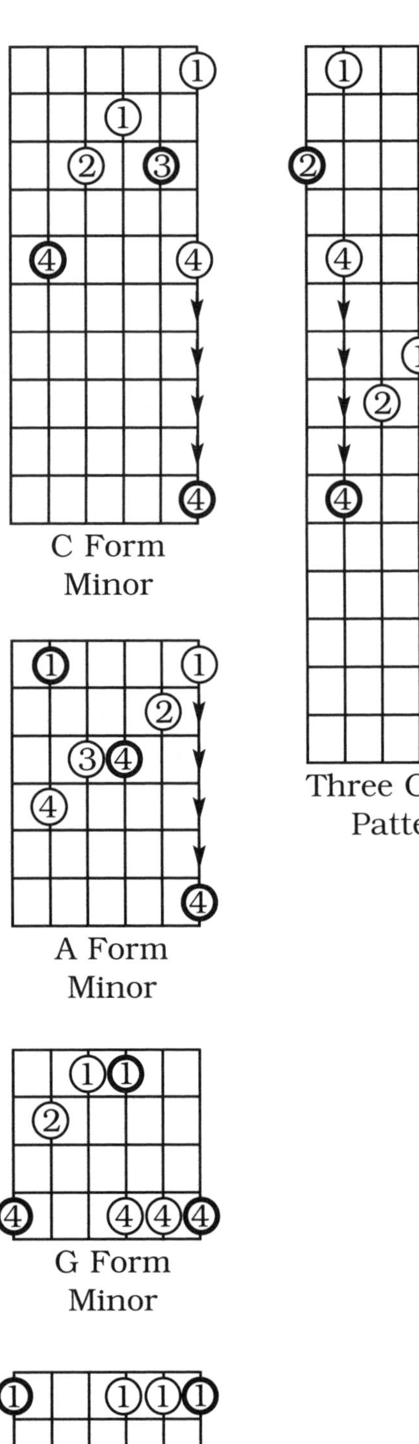

Arpeggios - Diminished

You should recall that the Diminished chords were termed symmetrical since the distance from each note to the other is the same. This symmetry causes limitations in the note groupings for the purposes of arpeggiation. In other words there are not very many practical forms for the Diminished Arpeggios, and like the Diminished chord forms, they don't relate well as variations to the CAGED forms.

In the graphs on the left, four forms of Diminished Arpeggios are illustrated. These don't even span the distance of an octave, but you will hear them used often, and they are pretty easy to play.

On the right side is an extended form, and the one you will probably use most. The extended form illustrates well the symmetry of the diminished intervals and also the lack of symmetry of the guitar's tuning with respect to the second and third string pair. A note has been added to the first string to allow this extended pattern to span three complete octaves.

If the fingering shown for the extended Diminished Arpeggio is uncomfortable or difficult, try substituting the third finger for the pinky.

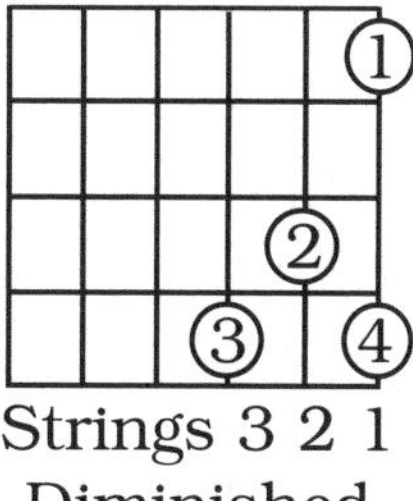

Strings 3 2 1
Diminished

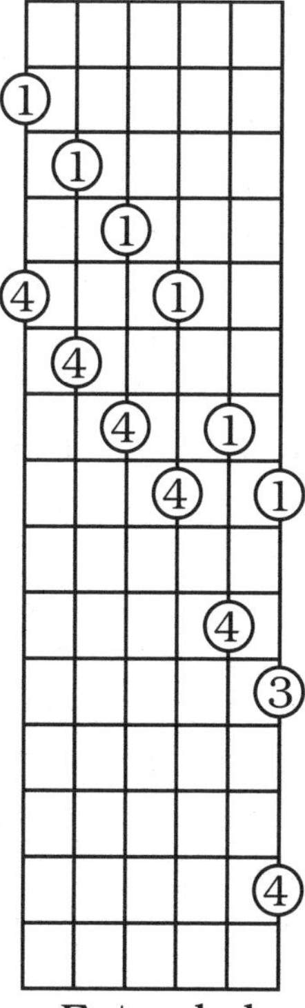

Extended
Pattern

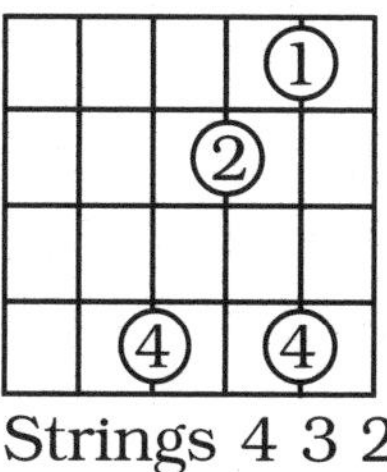

Strings 4 3 2
Diminished

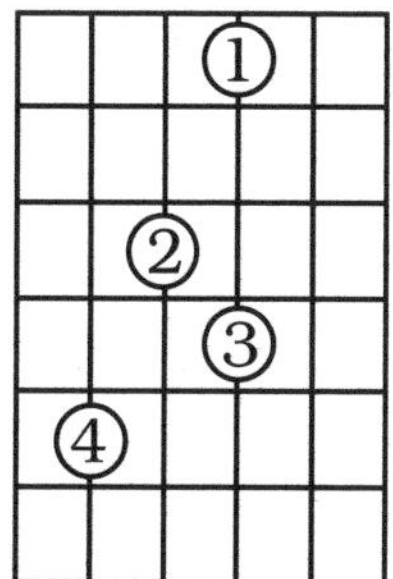

Strings 5 4 3
Diminished

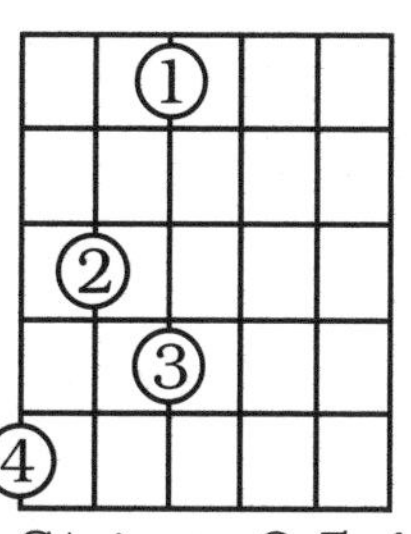

Strings 6 5 4
Diminished

Arpeggios - Augmented

As with the Diminished, the symmetrical nature of the Augmented intervals provides only a few possibilities for arpeggiation. You probably won't hear the Augmented Arpeggios used too often anyway.

With respect to tonics and the Augmented and Diminished Arpeggios, you can think of it two ways: either there is no real target note, or every note is a target note. For that reason there isn't a darker circle in these forms to show a starting or ending suggestion.

Major, minor, diminished and augmented arpeggios are triadic. When learning these three-note Arpeggios for the first time, *accent* the first of each three-note group when playing. In two-octave Arpeggios, up and back, this will translate to:

Up - **Strong** weak weak
Strong weak weak
Back - **Strong** weak weak
Strong weak weak
Strong.

Virgil's Philosophy of Life

Life is like playing electric guitar through a 100 watt stack in public... and learning the instrument as you go.

So Crank It Up.

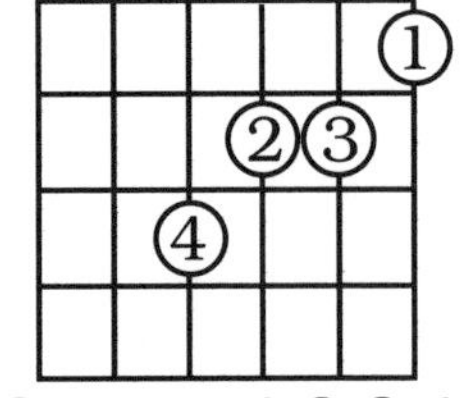

Strings 4 3 2 1
Augmented

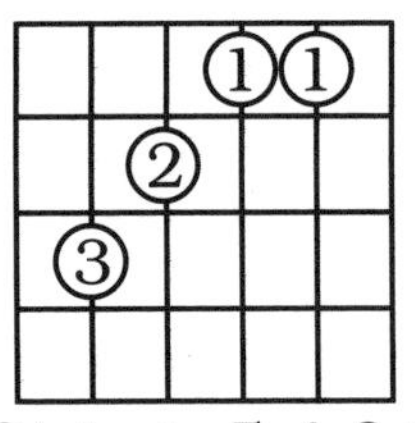

Strings 5 4 3 2
Augmented

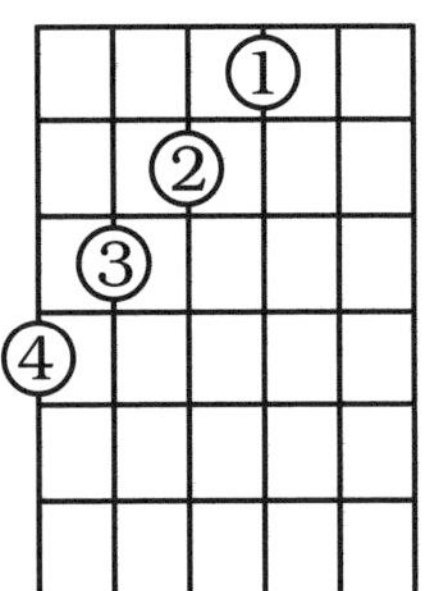

Strings 6 5 4 3
Augmented

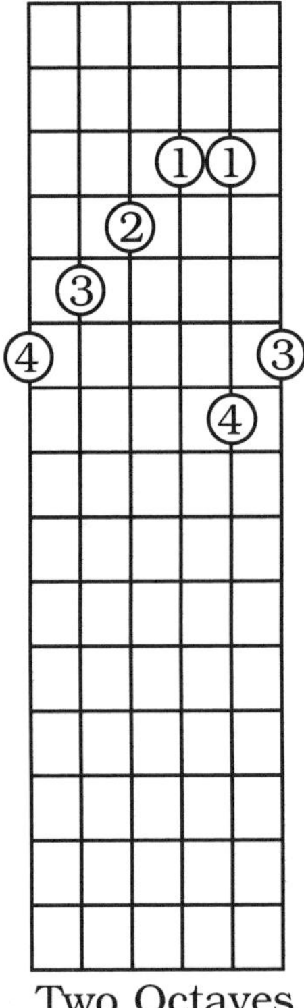

Two Octaves
Augmented

Arpeggios - Major Seventh

The first four-note Arpeggio taken up is the Major Seventh. When learning these for the first time, accent the first note of each four-note group. In two-octave Arpeggios, up and back, this will translate to:

Up - **Strong** weak weak weak
Strong weak weak weak
Back - **Strong** weak weak weak
Strong weak weak weak
Strong.

In the left hand column, the two-octave Major Seventh Arpeggios are drawn based upon the A, G, and E chord forms.

In the right column, two three-octave Major Seventh Arpeggio patterns are shown.

As more notes are added to the forms, the fingering combinations become more difficult and will require more patience and practice. In fact, this can be said of almost all the Arpeggios. Compared to the even the more difficult chords and scales, the Arpeggios will be harder to master as a rule. They require more from both hands in terms of fretting accuracy and synchronization. In light of that, these most difficult patterns were saved for last.

On the other hand, arpeggios are among the most effective and easily applied musical resources you can have at your disposal. They work well in a lot of improvisational situations.

With the Major Seventh Arpeggios, you should be able to appreciate from the character of the patterns, how each form draws from both the chord forms and the scale forms. To visualize this you might consider practicing each form of the chord, scale and arpeggio, one after another from memory once you have learned them.

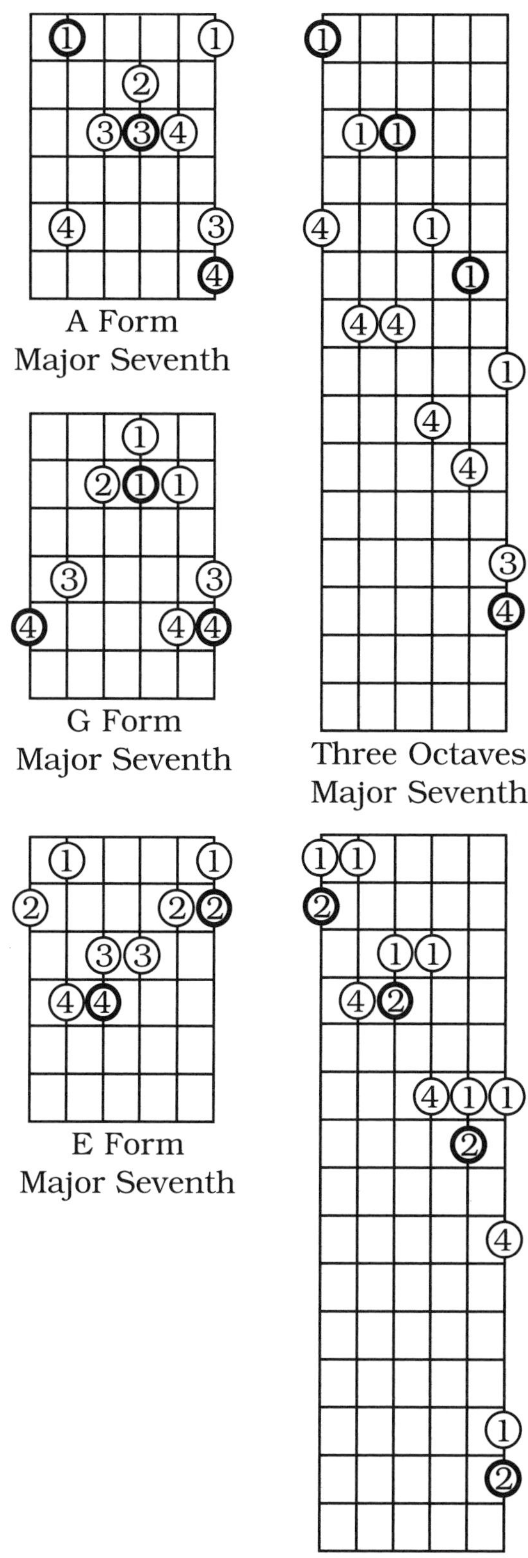
A Form Major Seventh

G Form Major Seventh

E Form Major Seventh

Three Octaves Major Seventh

Three Octaves Major Seventh

Arpeggios - Minor Seventh

The two-octave Minor Seventh Arpeggios are shown in the left side column and are based upon the A, G, and E chord and scale forms.

In the right column, a three octave pattern is illustrated.

Don't forget to experiment with alternate fingering strategies. Those illustrated throughout the book represent only what seem to be the most workable solutions, and are by no means suggested as the only appropriate ones. The same goes for the patterns themselves. There are ways other than the ones illustrated to accomplish the same thing, and it is recommended that you look for viable alternatives as a matter of course.

?

Q: How many guitarists does it take to change a light bulb?

A: A lot. One to climb the ladder and the rest to sit in the audience telling each other they could have done it better.

?

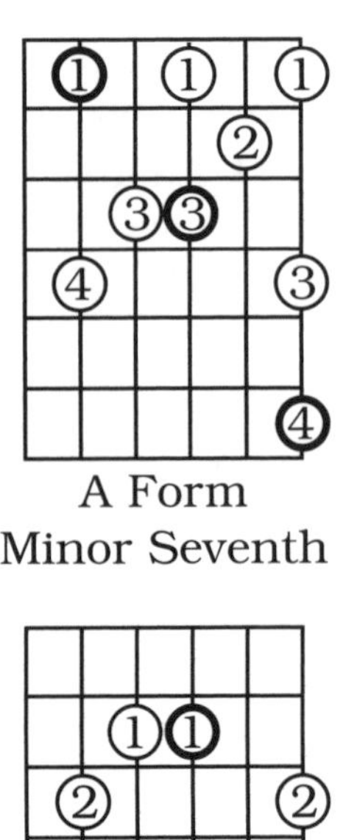
A Form
Minor Seventh

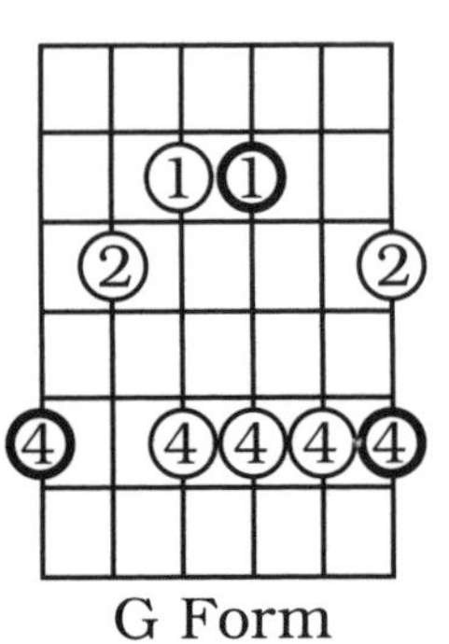
G Form
Minor Seventh

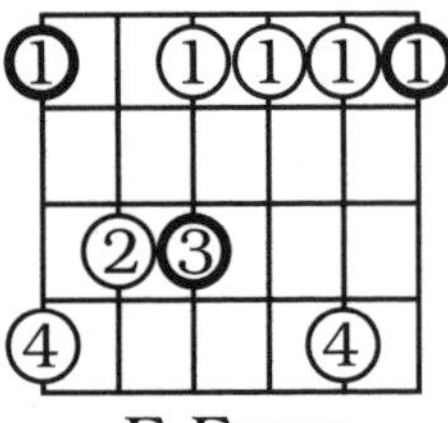
E Form
Minor Seventh

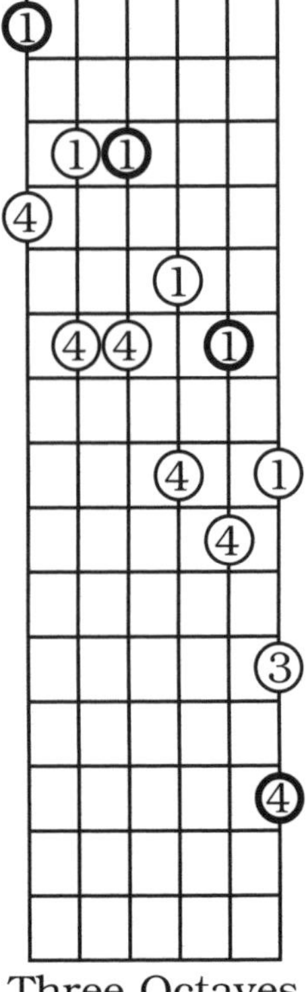
Three Octaves
Minor Seventh

Arpeggios - Dominant Seventh

The last chord type to be patterned for arpeggiation is the Dominant Seventh. In the left column, it is illustrated based upon the A, G, and E chord forms, with a three octave version at the bottom.

In the right column are two more three-octave arpeggiations.

If you plan to skip any of the Arpeggios, don't make the Dominant Sevenths one of them. It is among the more important elements in music of all types and will get used a great deal when the time comes for the practical application of these basic components.

Recap

Arpeggios are the most technically challenging of the basic tone groupings and often require the strength and reach of the hardest chords combined with the accuracy and agility of the most difficult scales.

Arpeggios rely heavily upon position changes and draw from both chord and scale forms as patterns. The fluid execution of the Arpeggios often necessitates articulation techniques such as hammer-ons, pull-offs, and slides while, for pick-style players, the right hand travels in one direction in what is known as sweeping the strings.

In general, Arpeggios place heavier demands upon both the right and left hand than either the chord forms, scale forms or lead patterns, however their intrinsic musical value should considered equivalent to chords and scales.

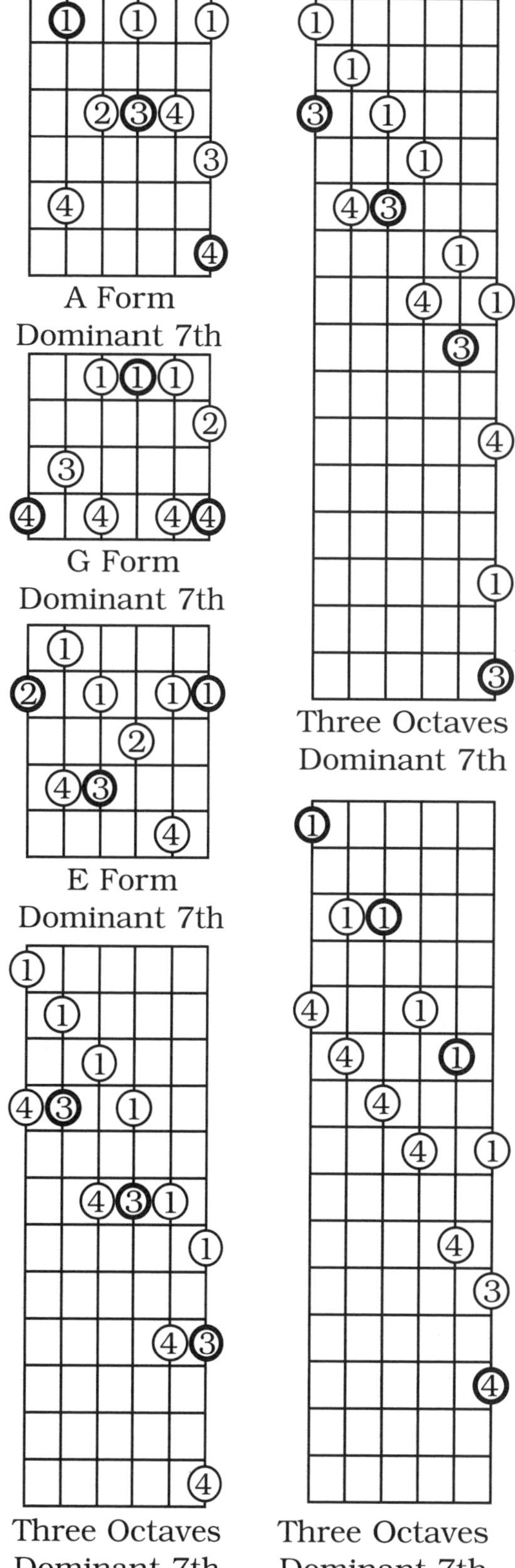

A Form Dominant 7th

G Form Dominant 7th

E Form Dominant 7th

Three Octaves Dominant 7th

Three Octaves Dominant 7th

Three Octaves Dominant 7th

Loose Ends

The goal of Fretboard Logic has been to teach the way things work in a structured context, and not just to spew information with no foundation or framework. One benefit of learning from a method book as opposed to, say, copying stuff from friends and recordings, is that you are (presumably) getting a structured environment. The arrangement of ideas into an ordered format with certain constraints makes learning easier, faster, and more permanent. Plus you can go back and review as your frame of reference expands and things take hold. But sometimes, because of those constraints, certain things get omitted in order to keep from getting off track.

This section is about things that did not fit within the basic organization of the book, but shouldn't be left out, either. First, there are a few chord types that need to be illustrated simply because they are so common and so useful. They are the Suspensions, Suspended 7ths and Ninth chords. They are presented as open forms only, because by now, you should know how to make and use open forms in other positions. There are two primary types of **Suspension,** or ways to *suspend resolution* of a Major chord. The "pull" to the Major is one of the strongest in harmony. One is commonly known as a "Suspended Second," and the other a "Suspended Fourth." I hope you recall the reasoning behind my objection to this contradiction in terms, but right or wrong, the use of *even* degrees in typing chords is common practice. (No doubt the result of a monophonist's influence.) The formula for "Sus. 2nd" is 1 (2 or 9) 5, and the formula for a "Sus. 4th" is 1 (4 or 11) 5. The interior chord tones are commonly misinterpreted as "2nds" and "4ths" - hence the (Continues next page)

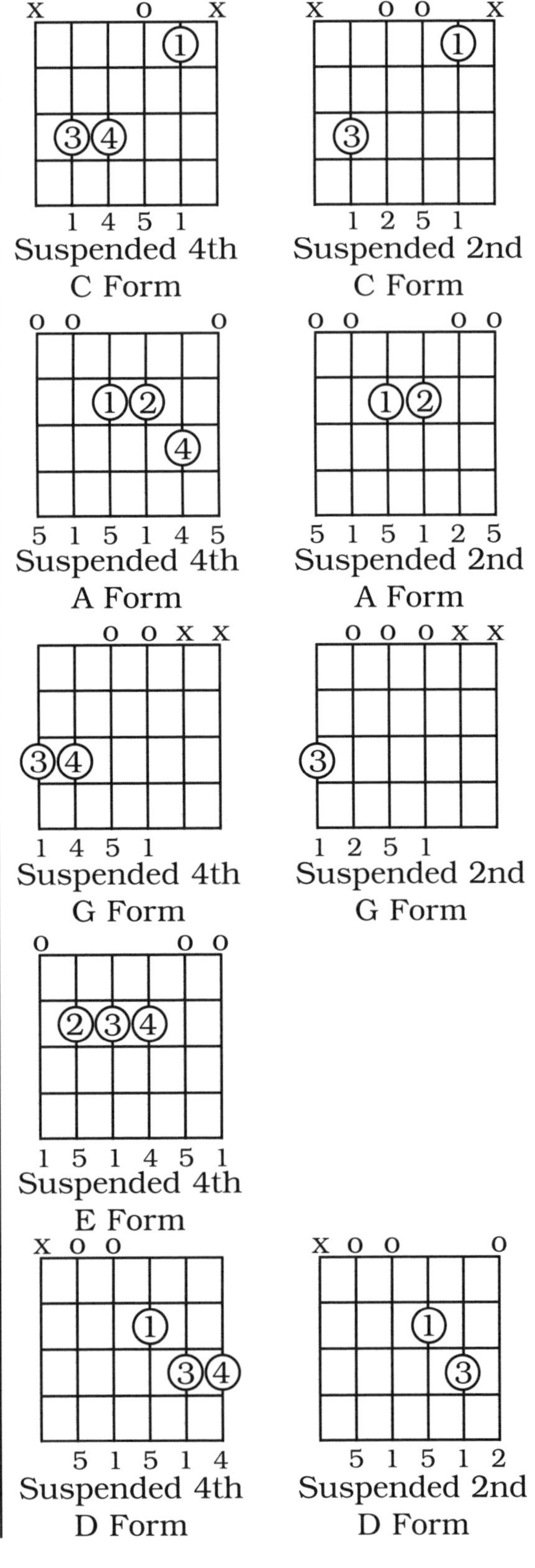

Suspended 4th C Form
Suspended 2nd C Form
Suspended 4th A Form
Suspended 2nd A Form
Suspended 4th G Form
Suspended 2nd G Form
Suspended 4th E Form
Suspended 4th D Form
Suspended 2nd D Form

conflict. Again, all chord tones are derived from an odd-numbered sequence (1 3 5 7 9 11 13). Only key degrees and scale tones are designated with both odd and even numbers. But somewhere along the line, someone mixed things up and the names unfortunately stuck. Both suspensions beg to be resolved to the major triad, and you will recognize this type of harmonic motion in many songs and pieces.

Another common suspension is the Suspended 7th or the Dominant 7th Sus.4. Its formula is 1 (4 or 11) 5 b7. Again what logically is the wrong name is the one commonly used. (You are not "suspending the 7th.") Suspended 7ths are used in much the same way as the other suspensions but are even stronger because of the b7, adding yet another degree of tension to be resolved.

In the right hand column, the next chord type covered is the Ninth chord - essential to blues and many rock songs. The **Ninth** Chord is a Dominant Seventh chord with the ninth degree added. (Notice that no one calls it a "2nd chord.") The formula for Ninth chords is 1 3 5 b7 9.

A familiar usage of this chord is to combine the E7 form in the fifth position with the C form of the 9th chord in the fourth and sixth (index) positions for the three chords of what is known the world over as "12 Bar Blues in A" - the aspiring lead player's playground. (Do you get the feeling the author wants to move on to the Applications part of the method?) The easy way to get the equivalent degree for chord tones such as 9ths 11ths and 13ths, from the scale tone, is to always add 7 to the lower degree. For example, a scale tone that is the 2nd degree is a chord tone of a 9th (2 + 7 = 9). A 4th degree scale tone is an 11th chord tone (4 + 7 = 11), and so on.

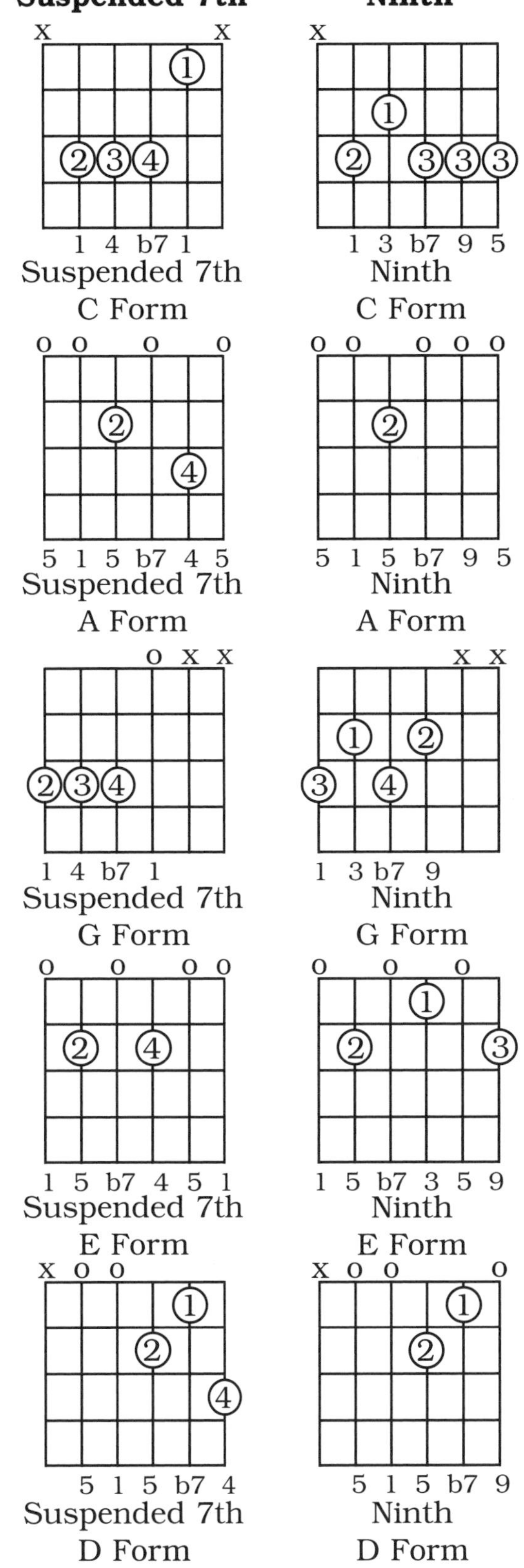

Loose Ends - Scales

The next add-ons are some fairly significant scales. They are the "Blues," Chromatic, Whole Tone, and Diminished scales.

The first scales presented are among the most widely used in popular music. For lack of a better name, they are generally referred to as Blues Scales. The problem with the term "Blues" is that they are used in a variety of styles other than just Blues. They come in two basic flavors: Major and Minor. The term Blues Minor is relatively common although you don't hear "Blues Major" used very often.

Adding the same tone from different starting points creates different scale degrees. The major version adds a flatted third degree (b3) to the pentatonic and the minor version adds a flatted fifth (b5). The illustrations on this page are oriented toward fingering conventions. Target notes for tonality are on the following page.

The right column shows the three octave lead patterns for these scale types. The G Group includes an early crossover.

> When I wrote that I was conscious of being inspired by God Almighty. Do you think I can consider your puny little fiddle when He speaks to me?
>
> Ludwig Van Beethoven
> - said when a violinist complained that a passage was unplayable.

Scale Forms

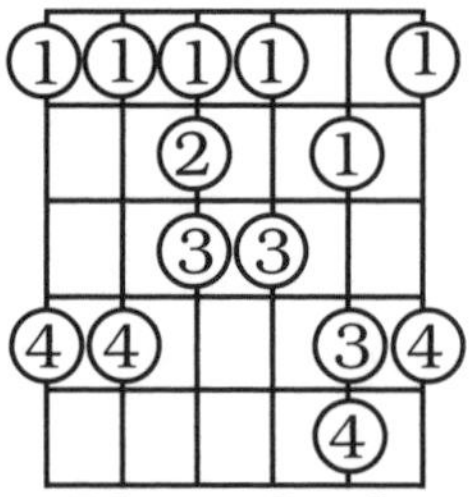

Blues Scale C Form

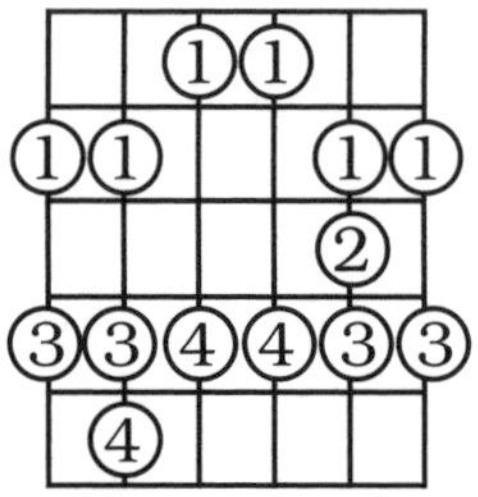

Blues Scale A Form

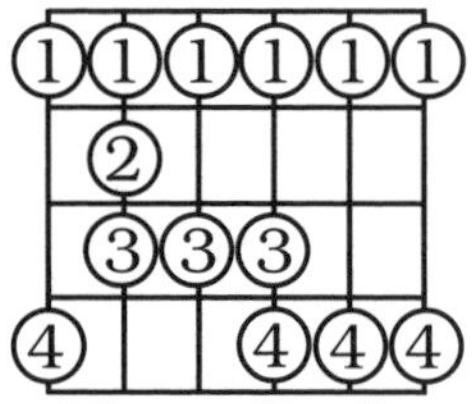

Blues Scale G Form

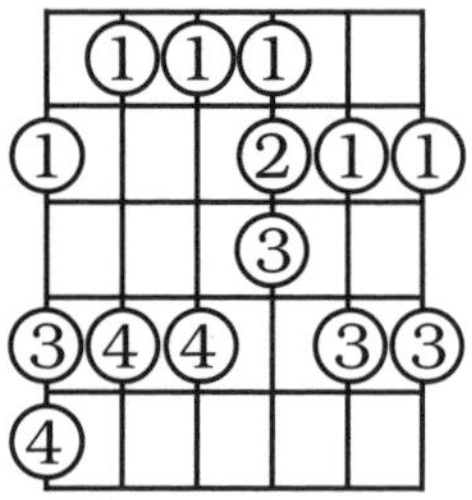

Blues Scale E Form

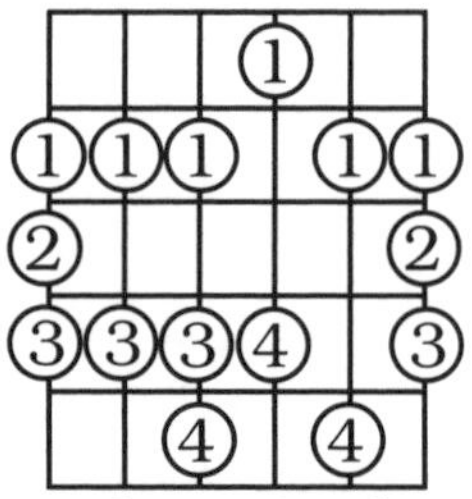

Blues Scale D Form

Lead Patterns

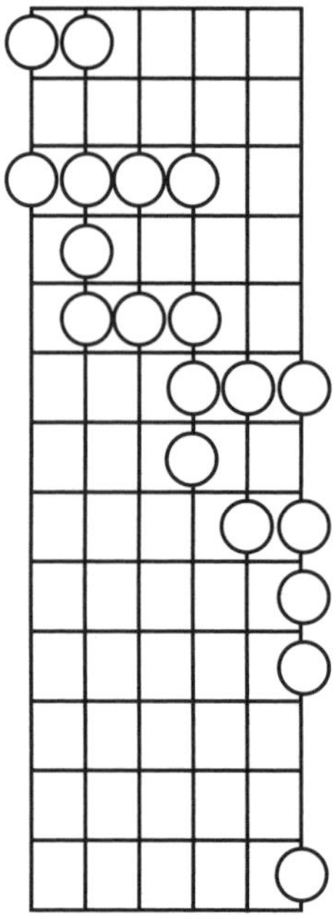

Three Octaves C Group

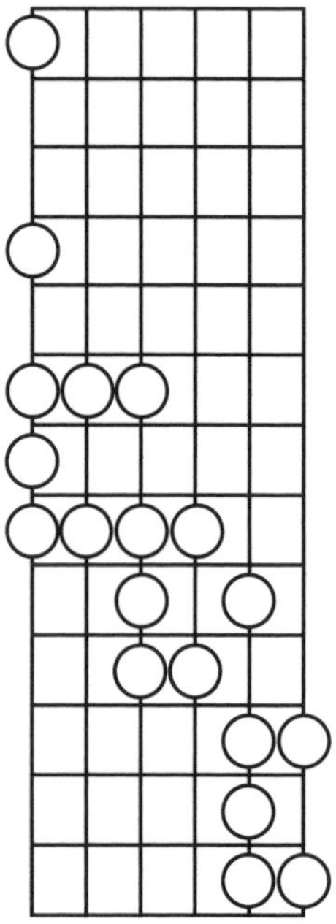

Three Octaves G Group

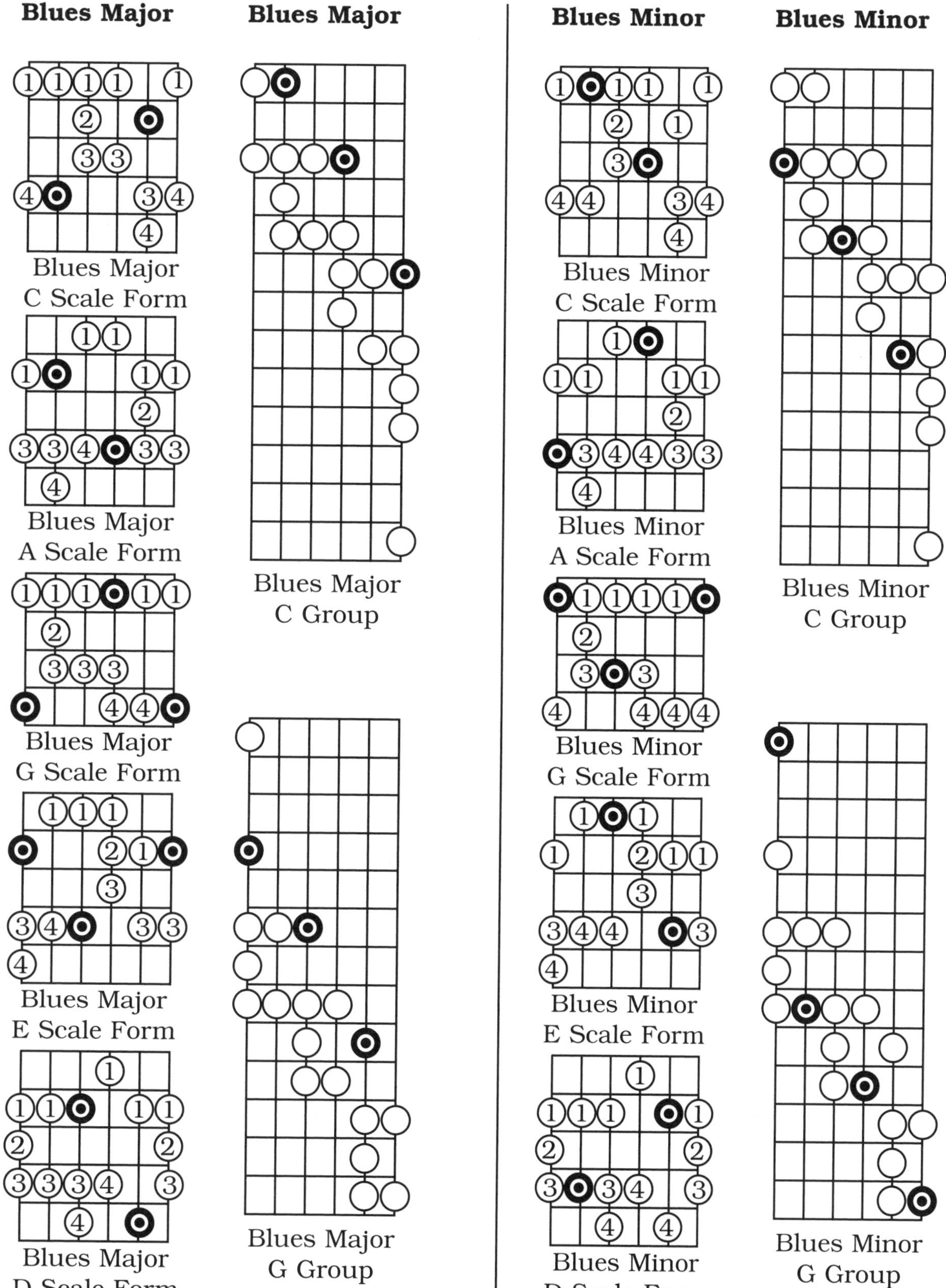
Blues Major
Blues Major
Blues Minor
Blues Minor
Blues Major
C Scale Form
Blues Major
A Scale Form
Blues Major
G Scale Form
Blues Major
E Scale Form
Blues Major
D Scale Form
Blues Major
C Group
Blues Major
G Group
Blues Minor
C Scale Form
Blues Minor
A Scale Form
Blues Minor
G Scale Form
Blues Minor
E Scale Form
Blues Minor
D Scale Form
Blues Minor
C Group
Blues Minor
G Group

The **Chromatic** scale is a half-step scale, and as you know, each fret on the guitar is a half step, musically. There are many ways for traversing the fretboard in half-steps. In the interest of brevity, only a few are provided here. The ones shown represent economy of motion and consistency of form which, on the fretboard, usually translates to accessibility and ease of use.

The Chromatic scale is illustrated for two octaves on the left side. In the first graph, if the last note is played with the pinky finger, then you can start right there and play the descending pattern illustrated in the second graph, from that fret on. As usual, there are a variety of a fingering schemes that are available given the arrangement of notes in the pattern, and you can choose whatever suits you best.

The graph on the right is an extended Chromatic lead pattern that spans four octaves if your guitar has enough frets.

In the presentations where the Chromatic scale spans more than two octaves, the use of the cross-over technique is necessary on practically every string. This causes the longer lead patterns to be somewhat more difficult to pull off smoothly than the shorter ones.

If you are interested in some simple dexterity exercises for promoting technical facility, the Chromatics, Diminished and Whole Tone scales provide excellent material to focus on just right and left hand coordination. The issue of left and right hand synchronization and overall technical dexterity is not to be taken lightly, and comprises an entire section in Vol. III.

Scale Forms

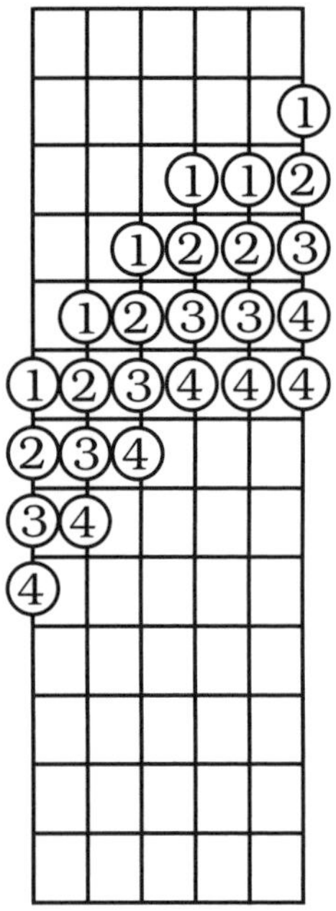

Chromatic Scale
Two Octaves
Ascending

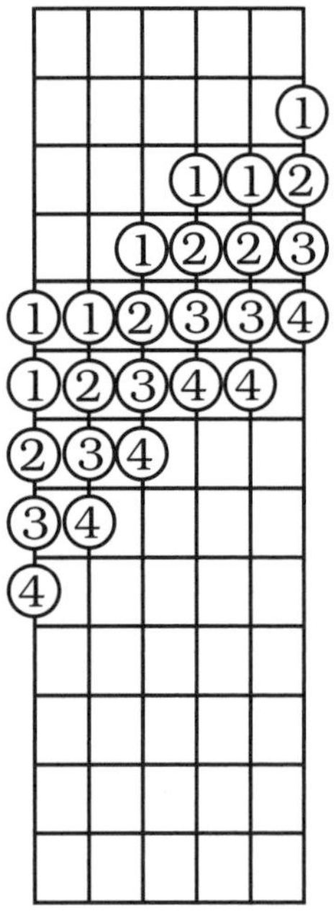

Chromatic Scale
Two Octaves
Descending

Lead Pattern

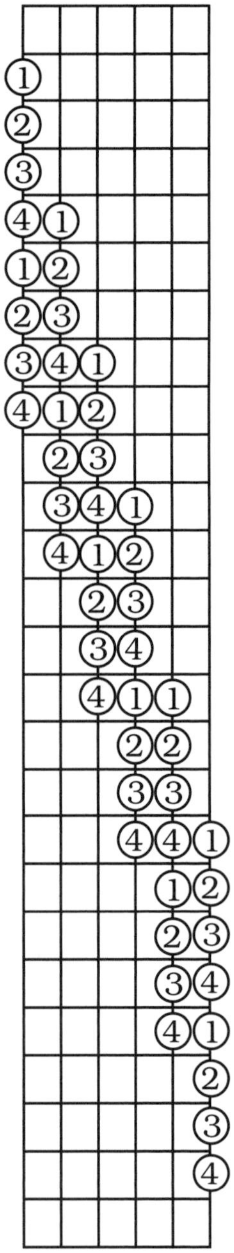

Chromatic
Lead Pattern
Four Octaves

Loose Ends - Scales

This time there are two different types of scales presented on one page: The Whole Tone scale, and the Diminished scale.

The Whole Tone scale is exactly what its name implies and is another very regular pattern on the fretboard. Like the Chromatic, it lacks a specific tone center until you start and/or end it.

The stretching required near the lower fretboard positions makes this scale form a challenge for people with smaller hands.

The Diminished Scales (not to be confused with Diminished Arpeggios) are a hybrid of the Chromatic and Whole Tone scales. A Diminished scale has alternating intervals of - you guessed it - whole and half steps. The two forms presented start and end with the different intervals. The above right graph starts and ends with a whole step, and the lower right hand pattern starts and ends with a half step.

One more digression on usage. As audiences, we have been conditioned to expect either a Major or a Minor tonescape. The Chromatic, Whole Tone, and Diminished scales are not tonally oriented toward either of these, and can spice up an otherwise monotonous (mono-toned) situation.

Without actually changing key areas, you can throw in some weird tonal material and make the listener do an auditory double take. As always, parental discretion is advised.

Whole Tone

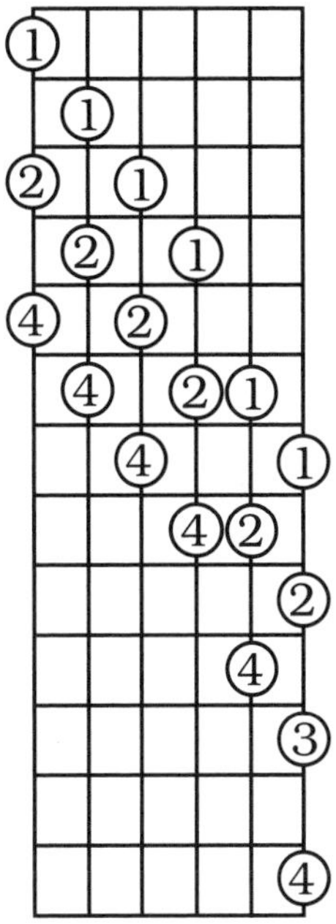

Whole Tone Scale

Diminished

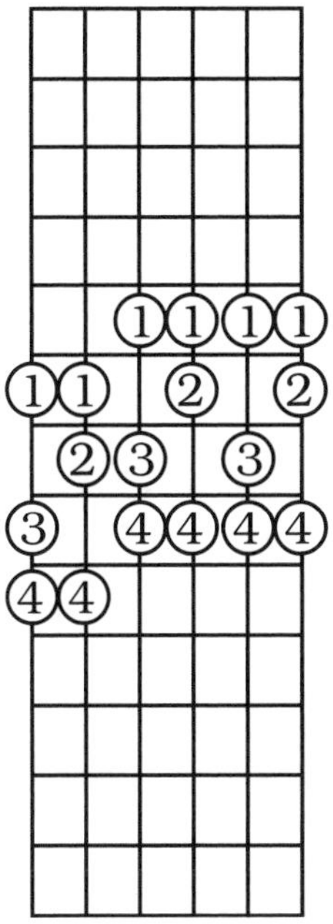

Diminished Scale

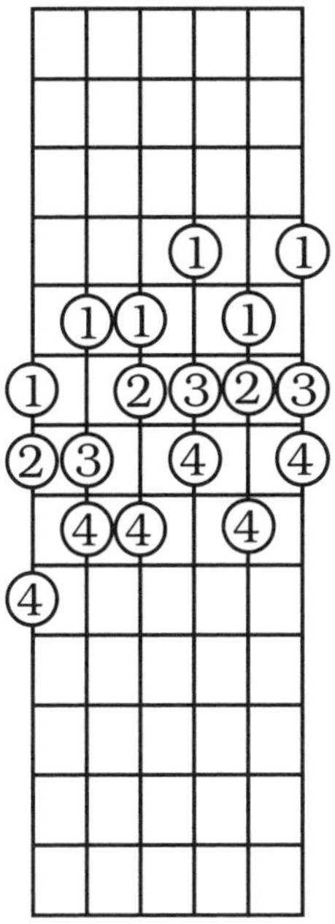

Diminished Scale

Next we'll tackle some diatonic scale forms which are designed to provide the right hand with consistent three-note per string action. Granted, this may seem like the tail wagging the dog, but the one thing we can all agree on is that not every guitarist thinks the same. So keep an open mind about them.

These forms could be considered a cross between the Lead Patterns and the Scale Forms. They combine position changes with pattern irregularity. For that reason they may seem to be the worst of both worlds, but a lot of very strong players use them, so give them a try and keep an open mind. It may help to think of them as variations of the diatonic patterns with which you are already familiar. (Hence, the naming conventions.)

On the practical side, I admit that sometimes if I'm trying to figure out a part by ear and nothing else seems to fall into place, I'll find that these are the best patterns for the job. Once you get used to them, you may wonder how you ever got along without them.

The fingering shown is the one that makes the most sense to me, but may not work best for everyone. As always, feel free to use the finger choices which work best for you.

They are continued on the next page.

Three-Note Diatonic Forms

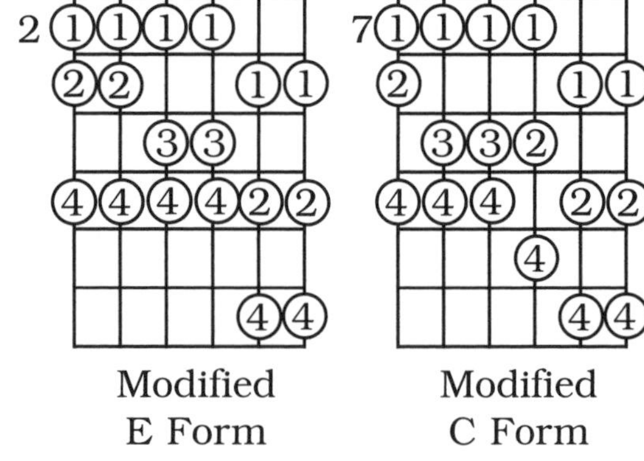

Modified E Form   Modified C Form

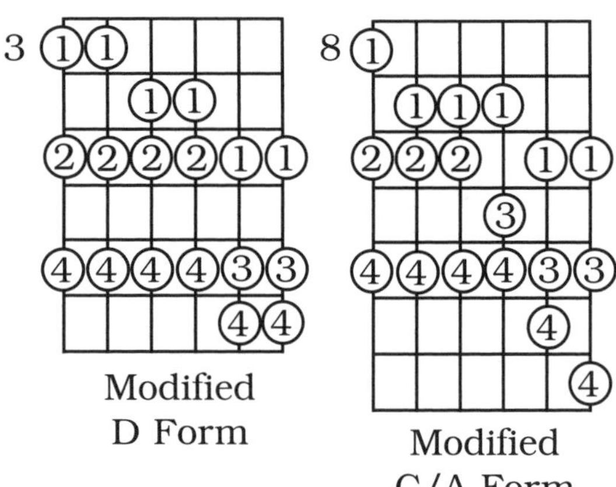

Modified D Form   Modified C/A Form

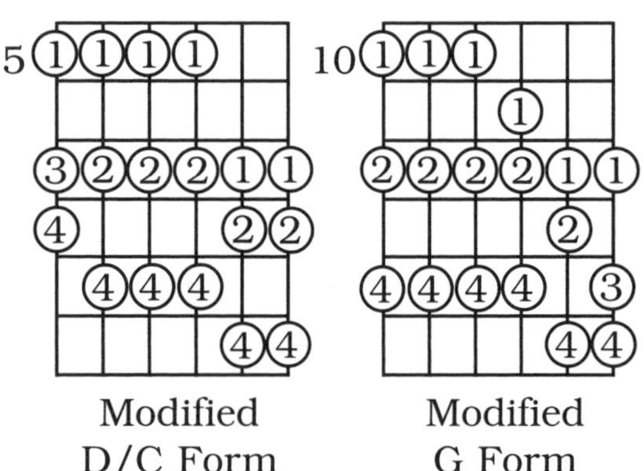

Modified D/C Form   Modified G Form

Loose Ends - Scales

This page completes the three-note per string diatonic scale forms. Since they are diatonic, there are, of course, seven different forms. The last form illustrated is the same as the first, and was included as a tonal reference for those of us who have the fretboard real estate.

Because they are so irregular, you'll probably hit a number of wrong notes trying to learn these so it may help to end up where you started.

It is important to play these in several different keys as soon as you learn them.

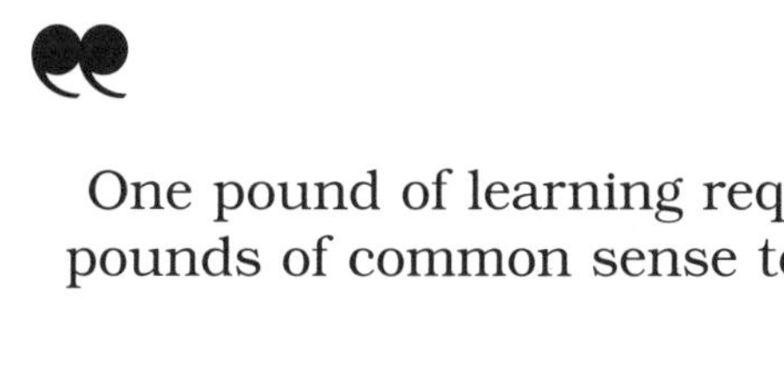

One pound of learning requires ten pounds of common sense to apply it.

Benjamin Franklin

Three-Note Diatonic Forms

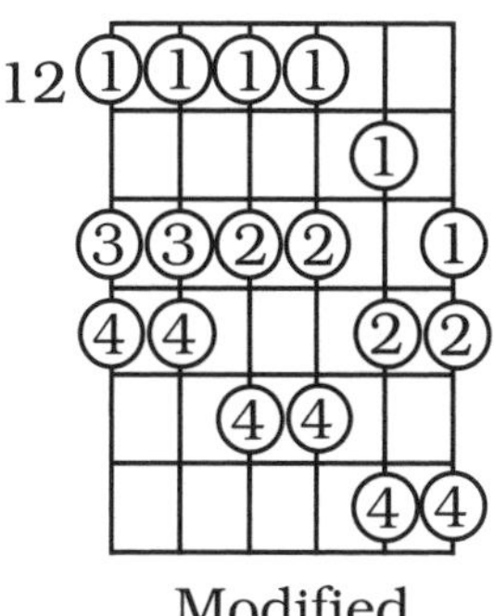

Modified
G/E Form

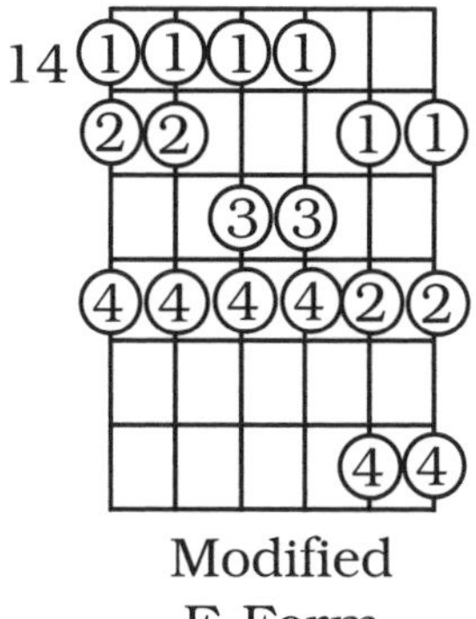

Modified
E Form

Loose Ends - Scales

The last scale type is the **Hexatonic** or six-toned scale. It can be viewed as either a Pentatonic with the addition of a 4th degree or a Diatonic without the 7th - take your pick.

This scale type is a half way house between the tonal security (or boredom) of "Pentatonia" and the somewhat riskier "Diatonia" with its 4th and 7th "avoid" notes.

The Major orientation is given since that is the only way the author has heard it used, but you might want to experiment with that.

As illustrated, with the two Lead Patterns, there is no specific (only relative) position reference given, so don't expect them to match up to a key unless you intentionally use the same target or keynote. E.G., to play them in the key of C Major, locate HLP 1's lowest target note on the 5th string, 3rd fret and HLP 2's lowest target note on the 6th string, 8th fret.

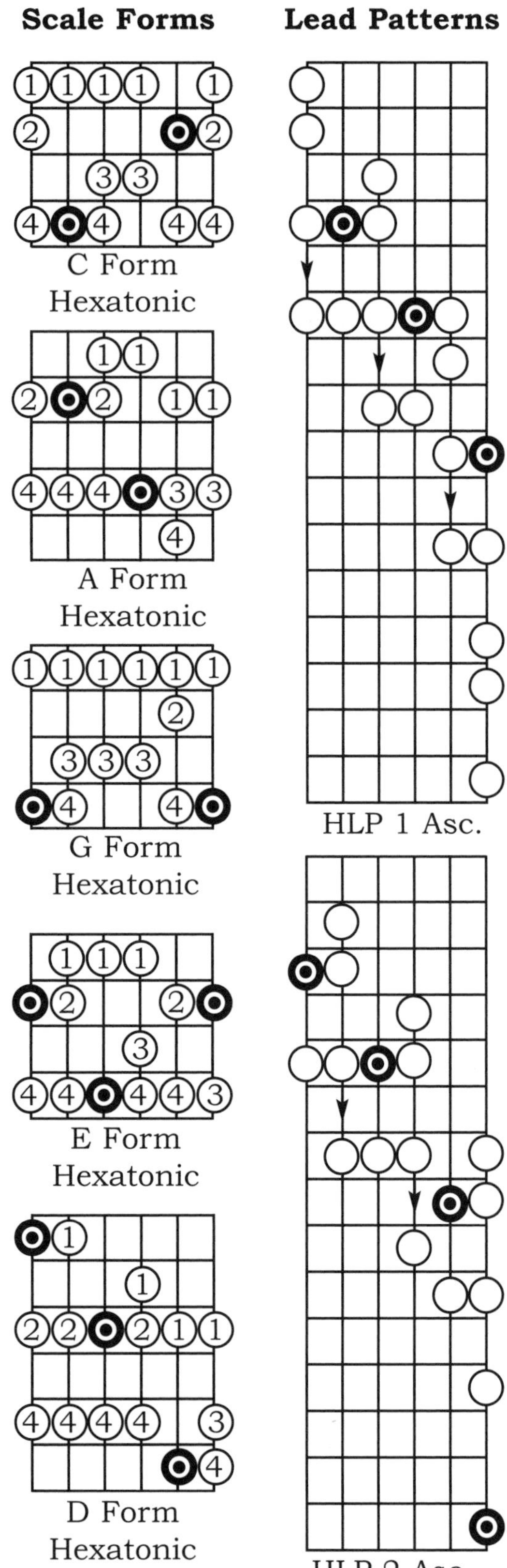

Loose Ends - Arpeggios

The next loose end is the Suspended Fourth arpeggio. It is a very melodious and not yet overused musical figure.

In the left side column it is shown in a three octave ascending pattern. On the right are a couple of two octave descending forms.

The last loose end is the subject of song form. Most guitar players in groups are playing music that comes in the form of a song, but I've noticed that few stop to think what elements make up a song, or what separates a song from other forms of music. A **Song** is comprised of three basic elements: lyrics, melody and harmony. The **lyrics** are the words that are sung. The **melody** is the tune or the musical way the words are sung. The **harmony** in this case is the accompaniment or the instrumental support for the lyrics and melody. Think of melody as the horizontal relationship of the notes in time whereas harmony can be considered the vertical relationship of the notes in time. Songs come in many forms, but if you are involved in writing songs of your own, keep in mind the three basic elements that make it what it is.

Recap

The benefit of approaching any subject in a methodical manner is that the learning process is more efficient. But sometimes the very structure of a method requires that certain issues be side-stepped at least temporarily. In the first three sections of Part II we approached the basic tonal materials of music in such a way that most of the guesswork and memorization could be avoided. The last section was devoted to including a few interesting and useful tone groupings which didn't fall into the core categories of the first three sections.

Suspended

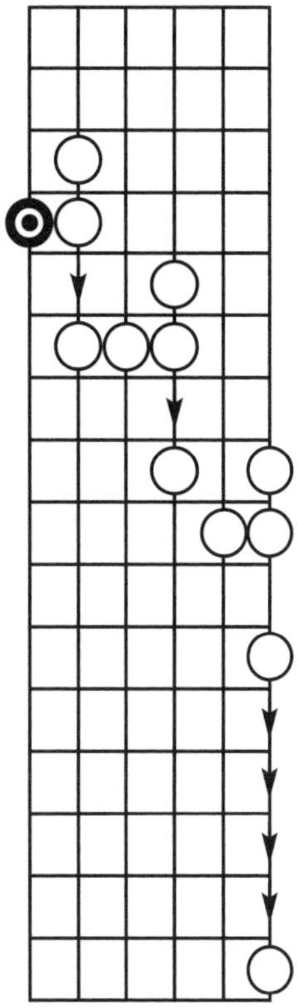

Three Octave Ascending Suspension

Suspended

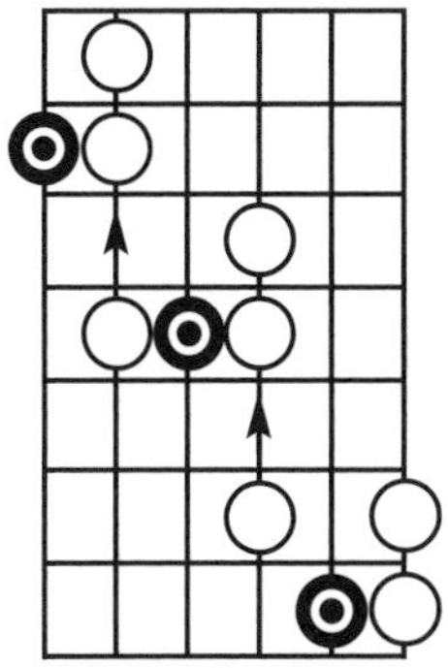

Two Octave Descending Suspension

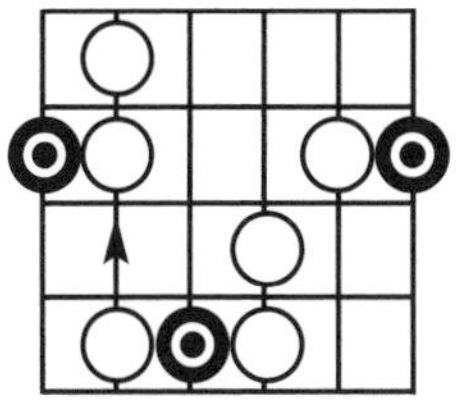

Two Octave Descending Suspension

The Components of Music

The next section is devoted to exploring related areas of music study which are not guitar specific. Almost everything presented up to this point has been discussed in terms of how it directly pertains to the fretboard and its unique properties, as a foundation of the guitar player's learning experience.

The subjects chosen were determined by the consistently high level of interest shown by my own students over a period of more than 15 years. They are: Theory, Technique, Lead and Rhythm Playing, and Styles of music.

The purpose of these introductories is to acquaint those of you having different goals and aptitudes, with a variety of useful information which will help to decide what path might be most appropriate to take next. My mental image of this learning process paints the components that make up guitar music as a kind of wagon wheel with the tuning system at the hub, the different kinds of success on the outside rim, and the various components as the spokes that hold it all together.

Unfortunately, since each area is large enough to merit a book or more of its own, the effort has been in the direction of only attempting to approach each one in the most general terms. The information given is only meant to be a brief exposure to the requirements each will make on you as a student, and the abilities they will confer as a player. I wouldn't presume to decide which of the areas is more important for you as a person. I would hope that your curiosity is piqued in each of these areas and many others, of course. Because I still teach, I get to meet a lot of people who are not sure which direction will get them where they want to go musically. Whenever students ask me which direction should take priority, I will usually try to find out where they would like to see themselves within the next six months, the next year, and the next five years.

Eventually a serious guitarist has to decide whether he intends to earn a living with his instrument, and just exactly how, or would rather keep it as a hobby. This is a traumatic decision for many outstanding players, and one that is likely to be put off for as long as possible. The hard choices are the important ones, though, and this one has a lot to do with which direction to proceed in. I'm personally of a belief that we each invent our own success, and that begins with visualizing our ideas about what we consider success. As we approach it, the image becomes clearer, and vice versa.

Theory and technique are the two areas that every musician on every instrument eventually has to come to grips with. The first is useless without the second for a performer, and the second is useless without the first for a composer, and most professional musical endeavors will fall more into one category than the other. Everyone who plays guitar in a group plays both rhythm and lead at some point, and you will probably find that it is impossible to be involved with the guitar without also being associated with a particular style or styles of music.

I believe that you will eventually come around to finding something useful in each area covered and many more to come.

Introduction to Music Theory

I believe the term *theory,* in the field of music is often misinterpreted. Like many people, I started out equating notational reading and writing skills with theory. Instead, I now perceive **standard notation**, the standard method of notating music, primarily as a way to preserve a composer's music in detail for other musicians and audiences to enjoy. It could accurately be considered the earliest form of *recorded* music. One of the benefits behind this method of recording music was, that by developing a specialized form of notation that was not particularly language-sensitive, people in different parts of the world would be able to share one another's musical creations. Perhaps at least partly because of this, music has become known as the "universal language." Now when we think of *recorded* music, we usually visualize a digitally mastered CD, a computerized multi-track studio, or some other twentieth century technological marvel. In contrast, the best explanation of **music theory** I have come across is viewing it as the study of pitch and time relationships. But in order to look at these relationships in a meaningful way, we need certain tools, and among them is an understanding of the language and symbols used to specify pitches and time, ie., reading and writing skills.

A distinction might be in order at this point. It is one thing to master the skills necessary to perform all the mental and physical requirements to actually learn to play written music. It is another to fully understand the thinking that went into the music you are playing or to actually compose an original work - and there is definitely some overlap here. In order to perform a piece of music correctly, it is useful to understand the thinking behind it. Likewise, to compose a worthwhile piece of music, it obviously helps to be able to work out ideas on an instrument. Even so, there are thousands of musicians and songwriters who haven't the slightest idea whether their creations conform to "proper" theoretical principles or not, and many actually believe they originate their own "theory." This is not unlike reinventing the wheel or rediscovering fire. If what they are composing actually sounds pretty good, then they are no doubt following some established musical guidelines. It is a humbling experience to realize that musically, most "new" ideas can be found to have originated in some very old compositions. Just one prolific genius can be a hard act for others to follow, and there have been many in the history of music. Fortunately, most audiences don't spend their time searching for musical derivations, and newness is relative (or else you wouldn't see so many cover hits). Think of **music** as organized sound, because there are countless ways to organize sound. The bottom line is that if it sounds ok, it is ok, theoretically. Besides, throughout history, the laws of science and rules of conduct have changed to accommodate great minds. So it is no small irony that knowing a lot of theory may not help you as much as you might think. What is also important is to know how to apply what you have learned. Many successful artists can neither read nor write standard notation but it doesn't stop them from making great music. Hard work, creativity and persistence are the stock in trade here as elsewhere. Now when music is *recorded,* it is committed to a tape or disc in a studio.

Introduction to Theory

Many aspiring guitarists reading this want to belong to groups that record and tour. They presume learning theory is going to help them get famous. As a practical matter, I don't necessarily agree. Surprised? Don't be. If your goal is to be a "Big Star," your attitude, acumen and looks will probably have a more direct impact on your success than your knowledge of, say, the use of dissonance in Stravinsky's "Rites of Spring." On the other hand, if you want to do a job, you've got to have the tools to do it with, and one well worn path to failure is to stop striving to learn because you think you already know everything you need to know. I'm pretty sure the majority of guitarists interested in theory don't necessarily have visions of groupies dancing in their heads (ok - I'm an exception). Their primary goal is to expand their capabilities. They want to know how music works. If this is true for you then what follows will be useful. The first thing to deal with is how pitches are written and how time is specified. It is not difficult if you take it one step at a time.

The Basic Elements of Notation

Music is notated against a background of five parallel lines called a staff (pl. staves). Between the lines are spaces that also specify pitches.

Notes are positioned on either a line or a space, and as they are placed higher on the staff, they are played higher in pitch. The order is alphabetical, ascending. The letters A through G comprise the music alphabet, and beyond G, the letters repeat starting with (a higher) A again. At the very beginning of a piece of written music, you will find what is known as a *clef* sign. There are several clef signs but two are used the most: G clef (or treble clef), and F clef (or bass clef). The terms treble and bass roughly mean higher and lower. The G clef derives its name from the fancy letter "G" that circles the second line from the bottom of the staff (which always looked more like an "S" to me). Likewise, the F clef derives its name from the old fashioned script "F" and smaller dots that indicate the second line from the top of its staff. Again, these are just markers that give you a reference point for instruments of different ranges, and there are others.

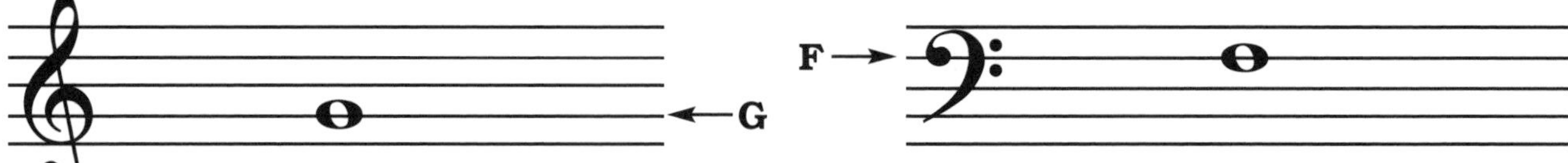

The notes adjacent to the reference "G" and "F" are in alphabetical order in the direction of the top of the page. We aren't normally used to saying the alphabet backwards, so it takes practice to be able to name the notes at random.

Introduction to Technique

I feel the area of technique, or the physical aspects of playing, should be approached with some degree of caution. As both a student and fan of guitar music, I recall numerous instances when one teacher or another would pronounce certain techniques incorrect only to later find some other guitarist using the very same "incorrect" approach with astonishing success. Eventually I got the idea that since there were so many different types of hand physiques, music styles, and thinking patterns, that everyone's approach to technique would be somewhat different. So I'll only try to make recommendations or suggestions for certain circumstances instead of broad generalizations about right and wrong technique. With that said, I will go so far as to make one generalization based upon my experience as a private instructor. I can safely say that I can't remember having any students who *would not* attempt to play too fast when they were learning a new piece. I found myself saying over and over, "You're trying to play it too fast and that is what's causing the mistakes. Slow down and let your fingers learn their sequences." Muscles have a kind of memory and you have to give them a chance to learn their parts. But once a student would make a mistake in a part one or two times, they would continue to repeat it over and over in context. It was always easier if he or she played it dead slow and just right the very first time. I have come to believe that when our fingers are being taught routines, the first impressions are the strongest ones. In other words, it is just as easy to learn a part wrong as it is to learn it right as far as your fingers are concerned. What is hard is unlearning it and forcing yourself to relearn it over again once they get used to a certain feel. This boils down to disciplining ourselves to play very slowly during the learning phase.

As a performer, almost everyone strives for virtuosity. In the absence of this, we'll settle for speed. *Control* over speed (not speed per se) will be a lifelong issue for many of us so try to keep it in the front of your mind as you practice and play. Distinguish between when you are learning a piece and when you are rehearsing or performing what you already know. These are different states of mind and require different approaches. When learning a piece, only play it as fast as you can play it with absolutely no errors. When rehearsing or performing, only play it as fast as you can play it with absolutely no errors (sic). They seem the same but the difference in focus is enormous. In the first case you must resist the urge to let your adrenaline take over and satisfy your desire to hear the part in order to give your muscles, etc. a chance to learn new moves. In a rehearsal or performance, you should be concentrating on the sound of the music and letting the feeling it gives you guide everything. You might say this is more of a mental thing than a physical thing. But which comes first? It seems obvious but I'm not always so sure. Edison, I think, was once quoted as saying that his ideas seemed to grow out of his muscles. Most guitarists are not satisfied with their technique, and face it, this usually means they can't play fast enough to suit themselves. If you can't play fast enough and are looking for ways to increase your speed, maybe it's time to

rethink your methods. We generally associate speed with bursts of great physical exertion. In the fingers, hands and arms, as you probably already know, this can quickly lead to muscle meltdown - cramping. If you want to play fast, learn to practice a task for longer periods of time without stopping instead of for short bursts of speed. It works. Think about it. Playing something over and over again hundreds and even thousands of times makes your fingers strong and efficient. They'll learn to move with a minimum of wasted motion. After enough repetition, speed comes naturally without even trying. Like magic. Playing for duration, or longer uninterrupted periods, is the key. Get a metronome and see for yourself.
If there is a common denominator to the subject of good overall technique it has to be relaxation. In order to play effectively you must learn to play without tension. Because of the demands on each hand system (fingers, hands, wrists, arms, shoulders, back, etc.) this is more easily said than done. Physically, the guitar is a lot more difficult to play than it looks, and acquiring the stamina to play for longer periods requires that you play efficiently, relaxing whenever you can. If you are a beginner don't try to overexert your hands. It makes no sense to attempt to play physically difficult chords like the F (E form first position) before your hand is ready for it. I've met people who actually dropped the guitar altogether because they couldn't make that chord when all they needed to do was move the form up the neck further away from the nut, adjust the guitar or else just leave it till later on. Make it easy on yourself. Do what can be done without unnecessary frustration or overexertion. If you are an advanced player, one of the problems you are going to face from time to time is that sense of having reached a plateau or a leveling off in your (perceived) technical ability. You are no longer doubling your abilities every day or week as you did when you were a beginner, and you'll go for longer periods feeling like you're getting nowhere. One of the best ways to rekindle the interest is to try some different techniques or styles. When guitar technique is examined, it is usually divided into left hand (fretting hand) and right hand demands. The left hand requirements are fairly similar for electric, classic, and acoustic guitars, but the right hand approaches vary greatly. A big split occurs between the people who play with a pick, and those who use just their fingers and/or nails, and most methods will only teach one way or the other. Finger style and pick style techniques are equally beautiful and I can't see any reason why both cannot be learned as equals. Although the right hand is primarily responsible for making the strings vibrate, the left hand is capable of a wide variety of plucking alternatives, termed **articulation techniques.** Slides, bends, vibratos, hammer-ons and pull-offs, and harmonics are but a few of the ways that you can create interest in a non-standard way. By directly accessing the strings themselves, the guitar player can draw from a huge stockpile of technical resources. A piano, by contrast, has only one access to the strings, so the player is limited to playing each key softer or louder (hence the name piano-forte). Guitar players can evoke technical expression that a keyboard player can only long for.

Introduction to Rhythm Playing

Although many people consider rhythm guitar playing a subordinate role to lead, this is a common misconception that requires a slight attitude adjustment. For starters, just remember how much time in a song is spent playing lead and how much is devoted to rhythm. Or take the rhythm guitar part out of the song and have the rest of the band play without it. Many songs would hold up without the lead, but would it survive without the rhythm? I doubt it. The songwriters - the guys who get the royalties - are not composing the song around the lead part either. Besides, the first time we usually hear ourselves sound good as players is when we get the hang of a rhythm part. Rhythm and lead guitar parts are a cake and icing relationship and you should consider both important. Rhythm parts tend to put fewer demands on the left hand than lead, as a rule. The left's biggest problem is making the changes from one chord to another. The first step in making chord changes, is knowing the chord well enough so you can go for it without hesitating. If you are working on learning chord changes, here is a way to get your hands familiar with the forms quickly and minimize the hesitation that breaks down the flow. First, make a new chord, say an open E form. Next, instead of taking your fingers completely off the fretboard, and losing the form, keep them in place and just barely lift them off the strings, and then make the chord again. Repeat this procedure again moving your fingers just a little farther from the fretboard but retaining the chord form. Then repeat again, moving the held form a little farther from the fretboard each time. The idea behind this approach is to train your muscles to begin to make the chord shape before your fingers reach the strings. This will help you to avoid the one-finger-at-a-time approach that drastically slows down chord making. If you are using a pick, the right hand will be learning to keep time without hesitation and without sounding sing-song. Since the right hand is doing considerably less precision work than the left at first, it will sometimes attempt to bully the left into making rash moves by strumming a chord before the form has been made. The coordination between the two hands is best arrived at by mutual consent, and each one has to be allowed to do his job in precise order. Below is the easiest strumming pattern I know, that doesn't sound sing-song. It is based on a four-beat measure. The right hand rhythm is as follows:

1	2	3	4
Down	Down Up		Up Down Up

The hard part at first is to get the pattern to flow from one beat to the next and then one measure to the next. Counting out loud or tapping your foot will help, but a metronome is the best guide. A good exercise to combine basic right and left hand rhythm techniques, is to play this rhythm pattern changing the chord at the end of each four beat measure. Start with basic forms and then add different chord types. Rhythm playing is generally a matter of combining right hand rhythms with left hand chord changes. This beginner's exercise will help you to focus on some of the demands that playing rhythm will place on you.

Introduction to Lead Playing

When we communicate, we are using a highly developed system of symbols, sounds and nuances that have been agreed upon as having common meanings. In the sciences, these symbols, etc. are rigorously defined and adhered to, in order to promote among other things, specificity. For example, 2 + 2 has to equal exactly 4 for everyone or else things wouldn't work. When people communicate with music, however, not everyone who listens to it "gets it" the same way they understand two plus two. Music is not as specific and it doesn't have to be. Moreover, as musicians, we shouldn't strive to make two plus two equal four all the time. As a lead player, you should try to make two plus two equal more than four. Just playing scales against chords is not really playing lead. In a sense, just playing the right notes in the right key is similar to getting four out of two plus two. So what distinguishes lead playing from scale playing? In a word: *phrasing.* Phrasing is the best all around term to describe the difference between someone who communicates with his guitar, and someone who just rambles up and down the fretboard hoping he or she doesn't hit a wrong note. When we talk to one another, we collect our ideas into packages and utter them in units known as sentences. These groupings help to make what we say more easily understood. They also allow us to draw breaths and to formulate our next thoughts into sentences. If you want to play lead, learn to phrase your musical ideas into statements and "breathe" between phrases. Another level of lead playing is the ability to improvise. Take a simple melody and change it around a little. Not so much that you can't recognize it, but enough so that it comes out a little differently each time you repeat it. When improvising, you are free to alter both pitch and time, separately or together. By experimenting with playing and improvising simple melodies, you can do a great deal for your personal understanding of what goes into phrasing groups of notes into musical statements. One of the most common stumbling blocks to the process of improvisation is when a player doesn't know the scale forms and lead patterns that make up the layout of the fretboard. By now you should also be familiar with several different types of scales and arpeggios, and be able to work them into your lead playing. Each element's form and type will bring forth new possibilities. Another common problem is just a basic lack of technical facility. Acquiring strength and coordination in the hands and fingers is an ongoing struggle that never abates. This very struggle causes many players to focus their energy on technique to the exclusion of almost everything else. They become digital over-achievers - absorbed with maintaining their chops often to the detriment of their understanding of music itself. In a sense, they speak eloquently but say nothing memorable. By far the most widely used method of learning how to play lead has been simply playing a recording repeatedly and copying the riffs one by one. This may seem like the hard way of doing things, but it works. Granted, it can lead to artistic inbreeding, but we all learn from one another. Copying is just a first step. Understanding what made it a lead you wanted to copy is the next step. The last step is creating something that others will want to copy.

Introduction to Styles

At the outset I want to make a distinction between music styles, such as rock, country etc., and guitar styles, such as finger-picking, flat-picking, etc. because the term styles is used correctly in both contexts. The guitar styles seem to fall somewhere in between the music styles and technique per se because they sometimes convey a music style in a technical way, but not always. Lines get blurred. Take finger-picking style, aka Travis picking, for example. Elizabeth Cotton and Merle Travis were early proponents of this type of guitar approach, and their musical style was considered mainly folk or country. But when Paul Simon incorporated it into many of his hits, the musical style was considered pop. Same with Kansas with their hit song "Dust In The Wind." But most people still associate the fingerpicking style with folk or country music. So the guitar style and how it is used can contribute to determining the music style but it doesn't necessarily define it.

As you probably know, Fretboard Logic has made efforts to avoid promoting a specific style of music and for two reasons. First, it gets in the way of some primary guitar and music relationships that are independent of the different styles of music. Second, nothing will scatter your students faster than talking about a kind of music they aren't (currently) interested in. But it is pretty hard to fully understand what you're playing without analyzing what makes it the style that it is. What's more, if we are ever to have a meaningful discussion about what makes a style that style, then we'll have to draw comparisons. To keep the focus of Vol. II specific, the study and comparison of different styles of music has deferred until later. Then the idea is to take songs of different styles apart and look at what makes them work, and what makes them so distinctly stylistic. The point is that it is not enough to just copy something from a tape or sheet in order to really understand it. You need to be able to grasp it in the context of the guitar, in the context of music and, if you're a professional, in the context of the market. You might think of the difference in terms of learning the music as opposed to learning from the music.

The Rolling Stone "History of Rock and Roll" is a collection of articles on a wide variety of music subjects from the early blues and gospel singers to pop and rock stars of the late seventies. (Highly recommended.) When the progress of the evolution of popular music is covered in chronological order, you are able to see how the styles of music overlap from artist to artist, and from period to period. One of Fretboard Logic III's intentions is to take a look at some of those obvious stylistic departures and focus on the aspects of the guitar and the music that made them separate and unique.

Ask yourself what the difference between country and blues and rock is, when they all use the same raw materials. There are many artists who broke new ground in popular music, and many songs that, by working so well, created a model for other songwriters and guitarists for years to come. These groundbreaking artists and their music will become the focus in the study of style.

Finale Part II

Okay. That's about it for Fretboard Logic SE Part II. As your attorney I advise you to take the test. Another way to tell if you have learned the material is to do a self-test by going through the book and playing the material from memory. Whoa. Does that mean...rote memorization?? No Beavis. Just build the chords, scales and arpeggios yourself. You have a program now. If you can remember the process, you won't have to memorize each and every one. Furthermore, if you build them often enough, you'll recall them with no trouble anyway. In fact, the goal here is that you be able to build any chord, scale or arpeggio possible by simply combining music formulas and fretboard forms.

Fretboard Logic can be divided into two halves: the constants and the variables. By learning the things that don't change about the instrument and music, you have just passed the halfway point in the course. Where do we go from here? My accountants, Fleecem and Finagle, highly recommend Volume III Applications - Creative and Analytical. But those weasels are only in it for the money. Do they care that five years went into trying to develop a logical conclusion for the series? I think not. They're greedheads, hosers and philistines. Besides, Vol. III's a lot more involved than the first two, and who needs that? And anyway, sooner or later you're going to have to cut the cord and just get out there in front of an audience. When you do, you aren't gonna be thinking about what you learned in some book - I'll guarantee you that.

On the other hand, Fretboard Logic has another part. Now is the time to consider those things that will vary depending on the choices you make - choices that will define you as a guitarist. These variables are discussed in detail in Vol. III and also demonstrated in many different playing situations in the Videos. In order to see the elephant that is Fretboard Logic, you will need to come to grips with several other areas of interest. Depending on where you are heading, some will be more immediately relevant, others maybe less so. One good thing about it is that it's divided up into a lot of different sections so you can tackle things that are of interest, in whatever order you like.

All right, that's it for now. Oh, one last thing. There is an old saying that goes something to the effect that you should be careful about what you wish for, because you might very well get your wish. I would like to paraphrase that a little. Think carefully about what you spend your valuable time doing. Whatever it is, even if it is something as difficult as playing the guitar, you will probably get good at it.

Twenty Questions

1. What is the difference between scale forms and lead patterns?

2. Which two chord forms are used to identify the lead patterns?

3. Name a distinction between playing lead and just playing scales.

4 Which of the basic chord forms has no uninverted or nucleus form?

5. In order to build chords on guitar, what two basic tools do you need?

6. What is an arpeggio?

7. What is a chord formula?

8. What is the difference between a scale and a mode?

9. Write the formulas for the triads and sevenths from memory.

10. What is a reliable method for obtaining greater velocity?

11. What three components define the song form?

12. Which two types of chords are considered symmetrical?

13. What's the difference between the electric, acoustic and classical guitars?

14. What is the term for a musical sequence of chords?

15. What are the tonalities? What is a mode?

16. What are the three common types of minor scales?

17. The guitar's tuning provides two fundamentally different approaches to playing in the different modes. What are they?

18. What does the term quatrads refer to?

19. What is the term for two notes played together specified by the distance between them?

20. Name the three types of forms or patterns that occur on the guitar fretboard as a direct result of its tuning.

Twenty Answers

1) The scale forms are irregular finger patterns that stay in one position and the lead patterns are regular finger patterns that move from position to position.

2) The C form and the G form.

3) Phrasing.

4) The D form.

5) The chord's formula and the order of the degrees of the CAGED chords.

6) A chord that is played like a scale - one note after another.

7) Odd number note groups with the various alterations that identify each chord type.

8) A scale is a succession of notes of a Key, as opposed to a Chord which is the simultaneous sounding of the notes. A Mode differs from a Scale in that a tonal orientation is specified instead of assumed.

9)

Major:	1 3 5
Minor:	1 b3 5
Augmented:	1 3 #5
Diminished:	1 b3 b5
Major seventh:	1 3 5 7
Minor seventh:	1 b3 5 b7
Augmented seventh:	1 3 #5 b7
Diminished seventh:	1 b3 b5 bb7
Dominant seventh:	1 3 5 b7
Minor seventh b5:	1 b3 b5 b7

10) Play for longer uninterrupted periods of time instead of short quick bursts.

11. Lyrics, melody and harmony.

12. Augmented and diminished.

13. The electric burns longer. (Whooee... I'm on a roll.)

14. Chord progression.

15. Major and minor. A group of notes with a specific tone orientation.

16. Natural, harmonic, and melodic.

17. Scale Forms and Lead Patterns.

18. Four note chords, usually called sevenths.

19. Intervals.

20. Chord forms, scale forms and lead patterns.

"Thank you for all your help in the study and the interpretation of the guitar and how to approach it musically and with heart. It's good to have someone treat you with respect and not go thru so much to bull---- you through their own denial & ignorance.

Thank you Jesus for hearing my prayer for Bill who was instrumental in removing all the guff I've payed for in so many other so-called guitar method books."
Vaughn Shepherd
Nova Scotia Canada

"These Volumes are very simple, powerful, incredible & excellent for beginners as well as advanced guitar players of [the] world."
Yogender K. Verma New Delhi India

"I also wanted to let you
know that your revealing of the logic in guitar playing is just what I've been looking for, for 21 years.
I now know I will learn."
E. Jones Greensboro NC

"I Love Fretboard Logic!"
Stewart Heatter Los Angeles CA

"Vol. I was excellent. By the time you receive this letter, my money order for Vol. II should have already crossed your desk. Keep up the great work."
Tim Lipscomb Washington PA

"This is the best book. Really. Fabulous."
Carole Harrison Austin TX

"Thanks for an absolutely wonderful series of books."
Dave Tomanovich Middletown OH

"You've changed my world and your going to change other's worlds and the way they look at the instrument over the long haul. I don't know how anyone who looks at your system and teaches is ever going to go back to Mel Bay, Alfred's or any of that stuff."
John Gilmore Osawatomise KS

"I have read all three of your Fretboard Logic books many times and am amazed at how using that system has increased my musical know how. It is so much clearer working towards the musical ideas from a working knowledge of an instrument rather than the reverse. I supplemented your curriculum with two semesters of guitar lessons, but the lessons would never have shown me anything useful if I didn't know which questions to ask, those questions came from your books. Now I am even impressed at how far I have come."
Brian Owens Kansas City MO

"You're going to change the way the guitar is taught forever..."
Rich DiBiase Bristol CT

"I have, and frequently use, the first two volumes in this series. I have studied music at the university level and have played professionally for nearly twenty years and have never felt as clear about or confident with the guitar as I now do having applied your method. Many thanks."
Mark Lee Amherst NY

"Brilliant."
John Holly Denver CO

"I see the greatness of these books and I understand what you are doing. And I thank you. It's a good thing you're doing."
Bob Savage Friendsville MD

"I've been playing about 28 years believe it or not, and I'm a guitar teacher. I found some of those patterns in Book One but not like you have. You've really done a good job here."
Don LaDolce Cassadaga NY

"I just received your books, and I want you to know they are intensely appreciated. I've been playing almost 30 years, and I've got all kinds of books and videos, but these books mean more to me than all that other [expletive deleted]. I've had teachers but I learn best on my own. Have you studied systems analysis? I'm a scientist and these books are presented in a way that I would have if I knew the material. I wish I'd had these 15 years ago when my fingers weren't so stiff. Why aren't these books in every music store in America?"
Michael Fitzgerald Waukeegan IL

"I would like to say that I've spent more money on guitar lesson books than I have on all my guitar equipment put together. If FRETBOARD LOGIC and FRETBOARD LOGIC II were available when I first started playing guitar I would have saved a lot of money. FRETBOARD LOGIC and FRETBOARD LOGIC II are the best instruction books I own, they are very easy to understand and very well put together. I would recommend these books to everybody from beginner to advanced players.
Scott Spaulding Virginia Beach VA

"I thought Volume I was excellent. It fills in gaps in my fretboard knowledge. I wish I'd had this 25 years ago."
David Tyra Terre Haute IN

"The claims were outrageous, the quotes unbelievable and I thought it just can't be that simple. Now I am feeling sorry for anyone who hasn't gotten your books. They honestly advanced me years beyond where I'm at. Thank you. P.S. *Why doesn't everyone know about this?"*
Rev. Garth Heckman Madison WI

"Bells rang. Lights flashed. A little siren went off - your system is so tight - it makes honest to God sense."
Jeffrey Ford Pendleton IN

"Fretboard Logic is 'The Best'!!"
C. J. Hamwyk Delft Netherlands

"I own all three Fretboard Logic books and both videos. They have enabled me to tie together so many things that I've been exposed to over the years in various guitar method books. I especially like the applications shown on the video tapes. Looking forward to your new projects."
Robert Smigel Glastonbury CT

"Thanks for your help and your wonderful guitar course. Not to litter your in-basket with one more testimonial, but this really is the best instructional material I have ever had the pleasure of using."
John Reid Sammamish WA

"I just bought Fretboard Logic I on 9/7/02 and absolutely love it. Thank you so much for your insight and clear instruction technique. Wow!"
Aaron Rice Moscow ID

"I recently purchased a copy of your book from Amazon.com. It has opened all of the doors. I have played for 25 years. I have studied classical, flamenco, jazz, blues and rock. I always felt that there was something missing, some secret formula that pulled it all together. Alas, there is! It is in your book. God Bless."
Jim Dwyer Washington DC

"I RECENTLY PURCHASED YOUR FRETBOARD LOGIC SE BOOK AND VIDEO, NOW I CAN UNDERSTAND WHY SO MANY PEOPLE HAVE RAVED ABOUT IT. GREAT BOOK BILL!!!"
JERRY GLADE REDDING CA

"When I bought the Fretboard Logic SE over the internet I had a bit of doubt and felt the heartache at having spent such a fortune. It was expensive for overseas shipping, and then we don't really have quality guitar instruction books/schools here in Singapore. But when I received this book I was really glad at how everything which once seemed so confusing has been simplified so much. My doubt and heartache were gone at once. I guess, even if my fingers can't fly like many of my guitar friends at least I would beat them in Fretboard theory. When I've saved up enough I'll get Fretboard Logic III. Really love this book, man!"
Ray Seki, Ai Singapore

"Hello there! I'd just like to say a couple of words in appreciation for your book(s) Fretboard Logic series. I have been devouring book 1 and 2 and already It's making a difference in my playing and my knowledge of the guitar. I finally feel like a musician and I finally know where I'm going on the fretboard. I have been playing for 14 years off and on and have bought dozens of books on the guitar and took three months of guitar when I was in my teens. I learned a little from each book and always felt lost a lot of the time especially when it came to cutting loose and playing solos, riffs etc. My biggest hurdle was 'Where do I go next?' I used to think it was because I didn't take more lessons. I was lost in a sea of dots in guitar books with scale patterns which I tried and tried to memorize. I haven't been playing guitar for a few years and I sold my guitars off because I was frustrated and I always felt that I'd never master the fretboard. Last summer I decided that I would buy a guitar and give it another try. I decided that I had to focus on learning the fretboard once and for all. I actually got word of your book on the internet by searching any site which featured anything to do with the fretboard. I have to say that I was a little doubtful of your book since I did not see it in my local music store. I asked about it of the book dept salesman and he never heard of it. He actually ordered it in and I looked through it from time to time but I wasn't sure if I wanted to buy the book. I thought I'd give it a chance since I spent a fortune in guitar books already and another book wouldn't hurt my library of guitar books. After the first few pages I had two reactions. One was 'It can't be this simple?' the second was how ripped off I felt after spending a fortune on those other books I bought instead of yours. Man I could kick myself (actually I have) for not buying your book sooner. Mr. Bill Edwards thank you for writing a very, very good book. I just got your third book in the mail. I was so impressed with the first two (I bought the SE Edition) that I had to have the third. You've heard the saying that 'Knowledge is Power' well Fretboard Logic is power packed with knowledge that will open your eyes and anyone who has a guitar should have this set of books in their library. I can't thank you enough for the books. Thank You!"
Wayne Boutilier Halifax, Nova Scotia

" I bought Fretboard Logic SE several months ago, and I just wanted to say how pleased I am with it. It has rejuvenated my guitar playing; I had been playing on and off for ten years, but the framework it provides has gotten me 100% into it. In fact, I no longer even have time to practice nightly, because my "practices" end up being 2-3 hour long sessions! Anyway, it's rare something lives up to the kinds of recommendations I saw on your website, but this one really does."
Matt Christensen via the internet

"I have benefited tremendously from your first book and video. Thank you for your highly organized and clearly explained approach."
Rebbie Straubing Mineola NY

"I've just started reading the Fretboard Logic SE and it's amazing. This is the book I have been searching for since I started guitar around 6 years ago. No other book I have read has made more sense and no other book has captured my attention like Fretboard Logic."
Barry Hulse, Aberdeen Scotland

"Thank you. Your books are unbelievable. You're saving me a bundle because my guitar teacher wasn't getting me anywhere very quickly. Perhaps he even had a financial incentive to take his time. I learned more from your books in one weekend than several months of lessons. I've been playing guitar 20 years now and recently signed up for lessons in an attempt to finally "get it". I think the guitar teacher was just moving way too slow for me. Your books allowed me to skip what I already knew and get right to the stuff I didn't. The teacher insisted on following a particular path through many things I didn't care about."
RG Howell Plano TX

"I've been trying to play guitar for years; I can now say two words about guitar playing that I could never say before, 'I understand.' "
Scott Gosling via the internet

"First of all I'd like to say Thanks! You've opened the door for me. Your first book lives up to the hype, so please send me book II. Also, it arrived very quickly!"
Charles M Deighan Ft. Pierce FL

"First I'd like to thank you. Thank you. My brain had been taxed for to many years trying to grasp a concept that I'd thought would transfer easily from the piano to guitar. I was afraid I'd never understand."
Chris Danielson via the internet

"I must say that your Fretboard Logic series is one of the easiest set of books that I've used.It has changed my whole outlook and approach to the guitar and I've been playing for about 20 years."
Jeff Mills Frankfort IN

"All I have to say - wow - WOW... and you're honest when over the phone you people (great) told me it (the method series) would indeed work very well with other method(s)."
Jimmy Sullivan Worcester MA

"I'd like to thank you for developing this material, which as far as I can tell is unique in the world of guitar instructional media, and answers a lot of longstanding issues I've had which had detered me from studying guitar."
Adam Lubkin Frederick MD

"After reading Fretboard Logic and viewing Video I it reminded of the line when you spot your soulmate that you will share the rest of your life with: "Where have You been all my life?"
Dan Cunningham Falkville AL